No Fluff Just Stuff Anthology, Volume 2

The 2007 Edition

No Fluff Just Stuff Anthology, Volume 2

The 2007 Edition

Neal Ford, Editor

The Pragmatic Bookshelf

Raleigh, North Carolina   Dallas, Texas

Many of the designations used by manufacturers and sellers to distinguish their products are claimed as trademarks. Where those designations appear in this book, and The Pragmatic Programmers, LLC was aware of a trademark claim, the designations have been printed in initial capital letters or in all capitals. The Pragmatic Starter Kit, The Pragmatic Programmer, Pragmatic Programming, Pragmatic Bookshelf and the linking *g* device are trademarks of The Pragmatic Programmers, LLC.

Every precaution was taken in the preparation of this book. However, the publisher assumes no responsibility for errors or omissions, or for damages that may result from the use of information (including program listings) contained herein.

Our Pragmatic courses, workshops, and other products can help you and your team create better software and have more fun. For more information, as well as the latest Pragmatic titles, please visit us at

> http://www.pragmaticprogrammer.com

Printed in the United States of America.

ISBN-10: 0-9787392-8-0

ISBN-13: 978-097873928-7

Printed on acid-free paper with 85% recycled, 30% post-consumer content.

First printing, April 2007

Version: 2007-3-19

Contents

Chapter 1

Preface

Where has the time gone? It has been five years since the No Fluff Just Stuff (NFJS) Software Symposium Series started in Denver, Colorado. We will pass two significant milestones in 2007: 100-plus shows with more than 20,000 attendees. Why has NFJS been so successful? you ask. It is all about the personal experience attendees have at each and every show we do. The NFJS series was founded on two basic principles—keep attendance limited (no more than 250 attendees at each show), and make sure all the speakers are really good at delivering their respective content. Because of these principles, we have been able to create an environment where attendees feel connected to the speakers and a great deal of interaction occurs. As a result, attendees come away with a greater understanding of the subject material and also gain some unique insights because of their offline discussions with the speakers. We have developed the NFJS Anthology series as a way to begin a dialogue with the reader on various topics of interest that the NFJS speakers think developers/architects/project managers should consider. This book is not meant as a replacement for attending an NFJS symposium but as a glimpse of what you can expect if you did in fact attend one of the many NFJS tour stops. My sincere hope is that you will join us (or have already) for an NFJS symposium event and find out what sets it apart from all the other conference offerings out there.

Enjoy this great read!

—Jay Zimmerman, creator and director of the No Fluff Just Stuff Java Software Symposium Series

## Chapter 2

Introduction

Editor's Note: This is the second anthology of essays by speakers from the No Fluff Just Stuff conference series. Individually, these are some of the most thoughtful and passionate developers who you'd ever want to meet. In these chapters, each was asked to write on some topic that they plan to present in the coming year. You'll find chapters on languages, the Web, tools, infrastructure, and persistence.

The weekend No Fluff Just Stuff shows run from Friday afternoon through Sunday evening, and the speakers are kept busy. Yet when they aren't speaking, they don't just hole up in their rooms. You'll often find them attending each other's talks (and sometimes heckling from the back of the room) or sitting in the halls with a small group of attendees who have specific questions. There is a spirit of community that pervades this group of regular speakers. As an example, as I was sitting down to write this, I received the following unsolicited, fully written introduction from Ted Neward. Cool!

—Neal Ford, editor
  January 2007

I'm going to let you in on a little secret.

For about thirty weekends or so, a collection of about a dozen or so luminaries within the programming industry descend upon some poor unsuspecting North American city with technology on their minds and a passion to disburse this wisdom in their hearts. (Whether said city is actually ready for this experience has yet to be determined.) For nearly three days, conventional wisdom is upended, myths are debunked, nooks and crannies of technical topics are explored, and tools of the trade are made to perform tasks the audience didn't think possible.

Then, just when it seems minds are about ready to explode, it's Sunday evening, the show is over, and the attendees are left feeling energized and exhausted all at the same time, just in time for work Monday morning. All is quiet for a week or so, and then this frenzied whirlwind of barely controlled chaos descends elsewhere to repeat the experience.

This phenomenon operates under the guise of a technical conference called the No Fluff Just Stuff Software Symposium Series, but on some days it has the feel of a traveling circus, complete with feats to astound and amaze, demonstrations so terrifying the audience can't bear to look away, and of course clowns (cleverly masquerading as a speaker panel) to entertain in between the main acts. But like so many traveling shows of that nature, there is an almost irrepressible desire to know what's going on offstage—what the actors and entertainers are saying and doing while the rest of the show is taking place.

In our case, that backstage event is neatly contained in a single evening, the "speakers' dinner," which occurs on Saturday nights. Shortly after the show is over for the day, the speakers, organizers, and invited guests head out to some popular place of fine cuisine (typically a steakhouse, much to our vegetarian speakers' delight). When in Denver, Colorado, for example, we'll head over to the downtown Dave & Buster's for dinner and pool and video games. Or sometimes, when we're in somebody's home turf (the Redmond Town Center in Seattle, Washington, is mine), we head out to their place for dinner. Or, sometimes, we take over the hotel bar and order in pizza and Chinese food and whatever else sounds good. We do dinner; games ranging from Mafia to Magic to Settlers of Catan to Axis & Allies to Texas hold 'em; or when there's something interesting out, a movie. (Ask Jay about our visit to see *Once Upon a Time in Mexico* sometime.) All in all, it's an evening of wine, women, and song. . . or in this case, Scotch, other techno-geeks, and technical arguments.

Yes, there are arguments—screaming matches the likes of which you've never seen. There is name-calling that would put any *Jerry Springer* show to shame. There are impassioned intellectual discussions that reach far beyond the mundane debates over where the curly braces should go (everybody already knows they go on the next line) or over how to deal with your idiot management (everybody already knows you just ignore them). There are debates over the role of REST in SOAP-based web services; debates over the usefulness of dynamic languages and their relationship to conventional statically typed languages; and even in some cases simpler debates over the future of the industry given the rise of Google, the open sourcing of Java, or the recent release of Microsoft Windows Vista. There is much laughing, much discussion, and much Scotch. No matter the environment, there's always those debates.

Here's the secret: most of us would do these conferences just for those Saturday night get-togethers.

Oh, granted, we enjoy bringing intellectual enlightenment to those who aren't fortunate enough to be in positions where they can research technology the way we can, but the truth is we enjoy finding interesting new tidbits of technology and bringing that information—and the discussion that inevitably follows—to those Saturday-night rituals. It's our equivalent of "hanging with the crew" down at the bar on a Friday night. We show off our new toys (such as the new MacBooks or the Sony e-readers), our new discoveries (such as new programming languages like Scala or Jaskell), our new thoughts on old subjects (such as the scope of unit testing), and so on.

This book, in many ways, is an extension of that. We each picked a topic that was near and dear to our own hearts, slammed out some words, and released a chapter into the mix. There was no theme, no overriding editorial hand, no attempt to try to blend our voices into one bland one so that you can't tell which author wrote which chapters. In fact, one could almost argue that there was no organization to it whatsoever. . . but that would be another story for another introduction. We couldn't invite all of you to join us on those nights (and it would ruin the atmosphere even if we could), so this is the next best thing.

As you flip through these pages, I urge you to grab your own glass of Scotch (or wine, or beer, or Diet Coke. . . but *not* Diet Pepsi) and have a seat in a comfy chair, be it in your own living room, your office, or your favorite restaurant. As you read this, if you listen hard enough, you can probably hear the echoes of the arguments/laughter/friendship in hotel bars and restaurants and speakers' homes, resonating through time and through these pages to reach you in that comfy chair.

Enjoy.

—Ted Neward, speaker, mentor, consultant, author and instructor of
  Java and .NET
  January 2007

New and stirring things are belittled because if they are not
belittled, the humiliating question arises, "Why then are
you not taking part in them?"
  ► H. G. Wells

Chapter 3

Learning to Love JavaScript

by Glenn Vanderburg

Glenn Vanderburg is a programmer, speaker, trainer, and consultant who is shocked to realize that he has more than twenty years of professional software development experience. Mostly what that experience has taught him is that the entire field of software development still has a lot to learn. In trying to fill that void, he has studied far too many programming languages, and JavaScript is one of his current favorites.

Glenn's primary focus is on Ruby and Java development, solid system architecture and design, and agile practices. He was one of the first few people outside Sun to ever write a Java program and is the author of the first advanced Java book—distinctions that have long since ceased to be relevant but that seem appropriate to mention in relation to this chapter.

Glenn lives in Plano, Texas, with his wife and two sons.

3.1 Introduction

We Java programmers were dead wrong about JavaScript. We scorned it, recommended against it, and tried our best to avoid working with it (or learning any more about it than we had to, in many cases). Now it's changing how everyone writes web applications, extending and deepening what a web app can do, and thus changing how people view applications of all kinds.

Recently I've started to think more and more about why we got it so wrong. Sure, there were legitimate reasons to beware of JavaScript in the early days—it was slow and buggy, and the browser support was uneven. If most of us had said "It's not ready for prime time, but just wait," it would be more understandable. But we dismissed JavaScript much more decisively than that.

I, for one, don't want to make the same mistake again. In a field as fast-moving as ours, it doesn't pay to turn up your nose at what is going to be the next major, transformative technology. Why did we misjudge JavaScript so completely? If we understand the answer to that question, we might not make the same mistake again.

In this chapter, I'll look back at those early days of JavaScript and draw a few conclusions about why JavaScript got its worse-than-deserved reputation. I'll conclude with an example that highlights some of JavaScript's deep differences from other mainstream programming languages and that shows how JavaScript's strength can be found largely in those differences. This is primarily my own personal story of coming full circle with JavaScript, but in spite of that narrow focus, I think it will sound familiar to many and be instructive to others.

3.2 Comfortable Confusion

In some ways, JavaScript is Java's evil twin. They're the same age: both were announced and first appeared in beta form in 1995 and reached 1.0 in 1996. They're syntactically similar, and of course the names clearly signal a family relationship.

The first any of us outside Netscape heard about JavaScript was in October of 1995. That's when Netscape released the first beta of Navigator 2.0. JavaScript wasn't included in that release, although it was the first release that included support for Java applets. But at the same time, Netscape announced it was working on an in-page scripting language called LiveScript.[1]

That announcement didn't get much notice. Java applets were the hot web technology of the day, and it was unclear why Netscape needed two in-browser programming languages or what LiveScript could do that Java couldn't.

Two months later, LiveScript saw the light of day for the first time, in Navigator 2.0B3. It had been renamed to JavaScript. A lot of eye rolling accompanied that announcement. "Oh, the thing can't make it on its own merits," we said. "Why is Sun letting this toy ride Java's coattails?" I still think that naming decision was a bad idea. It caused no end of confusion. Many nonprogrammers never figured out that Java and JavaScript were two different things.

One consequence of renaming LiveScript was somewhat subtle, and I suspect it had a huge impact on the language's acceptance. The association with Java made it seem as though JavaScript wasn't entirely a new thing. It's true that Java itself still had not reached version 1.0, but for various reasons Java was perceived as far more mature than it really was—for example, another event of December 1995 was that *Time* magazine named Java one of the top-ten new products of the year. (And they called it a *miniaturized programming language*. Heh.) There were already books available about Java, with many others (including mine) in the works. So when Netscape unveiled its own new technology called JavaScript, it seemed obvious that the small but already vocal group of Java programmers were the best people to understand and evaluate JavaScript.

And in spite of our skepticism, JavaScript did seem like it might have some uses. For one thing, JavaScript was designed to make it possible to control and communicate between Java applets. So those of us who were interested in Java at the time thought it was worth learning about JavaScript. I remember going to the fourth meeting of JavaMUG (the Dallas/Fort Worth–area Java Users' Group) in March 1996 to hear Greg Graham, a local developer, talk about JavaScript. Greg is a good speaker, and I enjoyed the talk. But I came away distinctly unimpressed by JavaScript.

---

1. At the time, many of Netscape's brand names included the word *live*. If you've ever wondered why Microsoft developed a mania for calling things *active*—ActiveX, Active Desktop, Active Directory, and so on—it was in reaction to Netscape's LiveThis, LiveThat, and LiveTheOther.

It seemed like a toy. It was object-oriented, except in the ways that counted. Everything was public, for one thing. No encapsulation. And then there was the fact that you couldn't really create subclasses. There was no distinction between instance variables and methods, which seemed like a disaster. You could change a variable to a method on the fly! And that broken, overloaded plus operator. How could they have made a mistake like that when there was Java demonstrating how to do it right?

I wasn't alone. The particular details of our objections differed from person to person, but for the most part Java programmers were in agreement about JavaScript: we didn't take it seriously as a programming language. We wanted nothing to do with it.

3.3 Collateral Damage

Of course, JavaScript did have real technical problems in the early days. It was buggy and slow, and it worked only in Netscape. Then, when it was supported by Internet Explorer, it wasn't entirely compatible. Also, it was touted as a way to script applets on a page, but it didn't take long for Java applets to fail. They were never widely used. So, the usage of JavaScript quickly settled into a sort of lowest common denominator: people used it for what would work reliably and avoided it for other things.

What worked reliably with JavaScript? Flashy, image-based visual effects, mostly. And people came up with some doozies. Netscape itself led the way with annoying layers that obscured the useful parts of the page (the predecessors of today's "pop-over" ads). There were flashing rollover effects that made us yearn for the days when the <blink> tag was the worst of the web sins. There were scrolling, flickering banners in the status bar at the bottom of the browser . . . and semirandom alert dialog boxes . . . and the abuses went on and on. Microsoft began talking about Dynamic HTML, but it didn't take long for DHTML to become nearly synonymous with buggy, slow, unmaintainable websites that worked only with Internet Explorer.

Oh, and don't forget the security problems. Naturally, when you build a Turing-complete programming language into a document format that gets regularly downloaded to client machines, you have to pay careful attention to security, and Netscape didn't get it quite right. There were security holes in early versions of JavaScript, and it took a while for that to shake out.

The result? Many technically savvy people turned off the JavaScript support in their browsers. Remember, the percentage of Internet users that could be called "technically savvy" was pretty large in 1996, so that was a big blow. That, in itself, created another reason not to depend on JavaScript: a significant percentage of users wouldn't be able to use your page.

Those who *were* using JavaScript weren't doing it well. The serious programmers had rejected it, so the gap was filled by page and graphic designers, and it showed. Most JavaScript books and tutorials of the era provided horrible examples of JavaScript style, and rather than explaining the language in any kind of systematic way, they mostly provided canned examples. (The one exception I'm aware of was David Flanagan's *JavaScript: The Definitive Guide*, which continues to be a terrific resource.)

To make matters worse, many people (perhaps most) didn't learn Java-Script from a book at all. Instead, they would copy snippets of Java-Script from existing web pages, tweaking them to make them work. (For the past two years, I've been giving a fairly in-depth, technical talk about JavaScript at NFJS shows, and I always ask the audience a lot of questions about their prior experience with JavaScript. The large majority learned JavaScript by copying code from other web pages, and most will admit that in many cases they never completely understood the JavaScript code they put into production.)

So, most people learned JavaScript by example. That's a pretty good strategy as long as a couple of conditions hold. The first condition is that people learn from good examples, but that certainly wasn't the case with JavaScript. The second condition is that the new language should be substantially similar, conceptually, to a language that the student already knows. Many people naturally assumed this was the case with JavaScript because of the name and the syntactic similarity with Java.

In fact, though, JavaScript bears only the most superficial resemblance to Java. It actually comes from a completely different part of the programming language family tree. JavaScript is a direct linear descendant of NewtonScript, Self, Smalltalk . . . and Lisp. Waldemar Horwat, a seminal figure in the early history of JavaScript, has said that he considers JavaScript to be just another dialect of Common Lisp. There's a bit of hyperbole in that statement, but if you know both languages, it's easy to see that there's a lot of truth in it as well.

So, there's the situation in a nutshell. A language that was very different from any that had previously seen widespread use, JavaScript was being explored by inexperienced programmers, with other programmers learning by following the examples of those first, inexperienced pioneers. Many web users kept it turned off because of security worries, and most experienced programmers were recommending that it should be avoided.

As if all that weren't enough, the browser wars soon reached a peak, and JavaScript was a weapon. Both sides evolved it rapidly, sometimes deliberately introducing incompatibilities. So, JavaScript became more *capable* but at the same time even more troublesome.

No wonder we all hated it.

3.4 Reconstruction

All during that time, however, I kept hearing hints that there was more to JavaScript than I had realized. Learning that it was a prototype-based object-oriented language descended from Self really intrigued me. (None of the tutorials I had seen really made that point, presumably because the authors didn't have the programming language background necessary to make the connection and understand those features of the language.[2]) Also, people began to point out how many of JavaScript's problems were due to the browsers they were embedded in, rather than the language itself.

Not that that helped any when you had to get real work done. But then Internet Explorer won, Netscape capitulated, and the browser wars were over. Microsoft shifted its magic bug generator ray[3] over toward its CSS implementation (where it has stayed pointed until very recently), and the Mozilla team got serious about compatibility. There were some deep incompatibilities that they couldn't fix without breaking a lot of existing code written explicitly for Navigator, but for the most part the gap has been narrowed, and the differences between the Internet Explorer and Mozilla/Firefox JavaScript implementations are now quite manageable. And of course, the other browser implementors have tried to follow suit.

---

2. That's not a harsh criticism; JavaScript has a fairly obscure heritage. It's like one of a clan of long-lost cousins, if you will.
3. Come on, you know Microsoft must have one.

JavaScript and its support in browsers began a period of steady improvement. But it's a mark of how thoroughly we had written JavaScript off that almost nobody noticed this happening. One event that has almost become legend is the introduction of XMLHttpRequest. The most important new DHTML feature, the big missing piece of Ajax, came into Internet Explorer through the side door. The Microsoft Outlook team added the feature as an ActiveX control to enable Outlook Web Access. In their keynotes at the Ajax Experience in 2006, Dion Almaer and Ben Galbraith got a lot of mileage out of the fact that XMLHttpRequest isn't even mentioned in the press release for the first version of Mozilla that included support for it.

There was a lot of JavaScript activity at this time; it's just that not much of it was happening in web browsers. Macromedia had built its Flash scripting language, ActionScript, on the foundation provided by JavaScript. Adobe was making most of its applications scriptable and extensible using JavaScript. Apple built JavaScript support into its Sherlock application. And of course, the Mozilla project made the decision that large portions of its browser would actually be written in JavaScript. Clearly, JavaScript wasn't just a web page language anymore. In fact, during this period JavaScript became the default choice for applications that needed a dynamic, runtime extension and scripting language. This probably happened because nearly every programmer these days knows at least a little JavaScript, plus the fact that there were two high-quality embeddable implementations available (SpiderMonkey, written in C, and Rhino, written in Java).

In about 2000, a few people (notably Brent Ashley, Alex Russell, and Douglas Crockford) began noticing what was really possible with JavaScript. Brent began exploring ways for JavaScript to communicate with the server and work in what we would now recognize as an Ajax style, and in those days when support for XMLHttpRequest was spotty, he devised and/or formalized several other clever ways of doing the trick. He built a website called Remote Scripting Resources and wrote the JavaScript Remote Scripting (JSRS) library to encapsulate the various techniques in an API that was compatible across different browsers.

Alex Russell started the netWindows project, an attempt to build a rich, programmable, graphical environment within web pages, complete with draggable windows and other widgets. netWindows became nWidgets and eventually gave rise to the Dojo project, today one of the premier Ajax toolkits.

Finally, Douglas Crockford began exploring the richness of the language. He built a set of instructional web pages appropriately titled JavaScript: The World's Most Misunderstood Programming Language, in which he documented many little-known techniques for using JavaScript well and for working around some of its flaws.

Brent, Alex, and Doug (and a few others) were voices crying in the wilderness for a while, but when the rest of the web development community was finally ready to pay attention, their efforts were there making the way easier for us.

What I know of JavaScript during this period, from roughly 2000 to mid-2003, I've pieced together after the fact. I certainly wasn't paying attention at the time. I was asleep in Java land, like so many others. But I was also, while I could find the time, becoming an expert in Ruby, and that experience helped prepare me for my second look at JavaScript.

Then, in June of 2003, my friend David Raphael showed me netWindows. After I picked my jaw up off the floor and David assured me that Alex wasn't completely insane, I woke up and began looking closely at JavaScript again. And although I didn't know it at the time, it's clear now that some folks at Google were doing the same thing.

3.5 Revolution

Everybody reading this surely knows the story of the period when Ajax exploded onto the scene. But I'll cover it briefly for completeness.

The first Ajax application I was aware of was Gmail. It was clear what was going on—that it was downloading a big gob of JavaScript and then doing further server communication behind the scenes, avoiding page refreshes. It was truly impressive, but partly for that reason it seemed a bit out of reach for most project teams. I remember thinking that Google must have built a sophisticated custom tool to make such a complex mix of server- and client-side logic manageable.

The Google application that really opened my eyes was Google Suggest. You might not have seen it (although if you're using Firefox 2.0 you've surely used its latest incarnation, which is baked into the Google search field in the navigation toolbar). As you type your search terms, Google Suggest queries the server for popular searches that match what you've typed so far, showing the results to you in a drop-down completion list, ready for you to select.

Google Suggest was more compelling to me than Gmail in two ways. First, it was simple enough in concept that any reasonably good web development team could aspire to include such rich functionality in their applications. Second, it was communicating with the server each time the user pressed a key, which helped me see just how much server interaction was possible in a web app. I was sold.

It didn't take long after that for Google Maps to hit the street, and at about the same time, Jesse James Garrett coined the term Ajax, sparking an enormous amount of discussion about these techniques by... well, just by making it easier to discuss, because we had a concise, recognizable name for what was previously just a way of using some browser features.

Since then, of course, Ajax has become just the way web applications are built. Along with the explosion in applications, there is now a wide selection of libraries, toolkits, frameworks, and development tools to make JavaScript development easier. I would go so far as to say that's JavaScript's new problem: too many choices.

3.6 Stop Worrying, and Love the DOM

I've mentioned a lot of reasons why JavaScript had such a bad reputation for so long. Some of them are good reasons, and some of them aren't. But I want to revisit one that I think is crucial. It's crucial because it's the one that most clearly illustrates the way programmers sometimes are blinded by their experiences, failing to notice or understand new things that they should be using.

You've probably realized what I'm talking about. A big reason we Java programmers failed to understand JavaScript is that it was just too different, in too many ways, from the things we did understand.

Remembering the list of things I didn't like about JavaScript at first, it's amazing how many of the items are simply *missing constraints*. Things are open and dynamic in JavaScript to a degree that they simply aren't in Java. Java is much more static and restricted. That's not necessarily a bad thing—at least, it's not bad in all contexts. But Java programmers understand the language (and their programs written in it) largely in terms of those constraints. We don't have to worry about what happens when an object changes its class, either when we're designing a new system or when trying to understand an existing one, because in Java that can't happen.

	2007	2008	2009	2010	2011	Total
Computers	500	450	425	425	375	2,175
Networking	300	300	275	200	250	1,325
Hardware	**800**	**750**	**700**	**625**	**625**	**3,500**
Dev Tools	400	500	550	200	250	1,900
Platforms	2400	2200	2100	1850	1100	9,650
Monitoring	200	250	300	200	200	1,150
Software	**3,000**	**2,950**	**2,950**	**2,250**	**1,550**	**12,700**
Grand Total	**3,800**	**3,700**	**3,650**	**2,875**	**2,175**	**16,200**

Figure 3.1: AN EXAMPLE FORECAST TABLE

So when we encounter a language that has no such restriction, it seems a bit frightening. How do you avoid chaos in such a situation?

I don't mean to make us sound like a bunch of frightened children. It's the responsibility of a software developer to avoid chaotic, confusing systems, and we all have a bag of tricks—in the form of concepts, rules, and principles—that we use to fulfill that responsibility. When we're working in a language that has built-in restrictions, it makes sense to lean on those language features to help. It's disorienting to move away from that, toward a language that allows much more freedom.

To illustrate, I'm going to tell the story of the first time I ever wrote JavaScript like a native speaker. Up to that point, all of the JavaScript code I had written resembled Java or C, depending on whether I was trying to do things in an object-oriented style. But one day I decided I needed to learn how to play to JavaScript's strengths. It took a conscious effort to make the change, but I've been really glad I did, and I've been a happy JavaScript programmer ever since.

I was working on an application that included support for long-range departmental forecasting and planning. The requirements specified a page with a table something like that shown in Figure 3.1. (Of course, the categories were variable, as was the number of years.)

The detail cells were editable, and the bold cells represented totals across each row or subtotals and grand totals down the columns.

Where JavaScript came in was that, of course, the totals were supposed to update dynamically as detail values were filled in or changed.[4]

I'm embarrassed to admit that I began with the most complicated case, editing a forecast, because it was the most interesting. I wanted to try to write idiomatic object-oriented JavaScript, so I created a new "class" with a name that only a word geek could love: Totalizator.[5] The table needed to be marked up in a particular way, but I tried to keep that as simple as possible. A unique id attribute identified the table tag, and class attributes were used to mark subtotal and grand total rows (the final column was assumed to be the total column).

The only thing the new Totalizator instance needed to know was the ID of the table. The object would scan the table for the appropriate class attributes, find all the cells that it needed to deal with in various roles, build a couple of indexes that would help later with quickly recomputing totals, and install a bunch of event handlers so that it could know when field values had changed. My code would have been cleaner if the Prototype library had been around back then, but it was pretty neatly factored into eleven small methods. So far, so good. (And so far, I haven't told you anything about the idiomatic use of JavaScript. For that matter, at this point in the story I hadn't learned much about it either. I have to confess I was a bit disappointed.)

Then it came time to write the "View Forecast" page. On that page, naturally, the table was not editable. First I thought "I'll just write the same logic on the server side for computing the totals," but fortunately that thought lasted only a fraction of a second. I would use Totalizator for the read-only case, too. What must I change to make that work?

It turned out that almost no changes were necessary. All the cells were still there, in the same roles. There wouldn't be any input fields, so the part of the code that installed event handlers just wouldn't install any. The only thing that needed rethinking was getNumberFromCell(cell). That method expected to find an <input> element in the table cell, and in this case there wouldn't be one . . . just text. How to rework that?

---

4. Such behavior is crucial for an app like this. Some quixotic individuals no doubt think that such plans are produced by carefully estimating the fine-grained figures and using the totals that result. Of course, in reality the totals are decided first, and the details are made to fit. Instant feedback about the effect of changes on the totals is very helpful to this process.

5. A *totalizator* is "a machine for computing and showing totals, especially a pari-mutuel machine showing the total number and amount of bets at a racetrack," according to American Heritage's dictionary. There's definitely some gambling going on when people do five-year forecasts.

I considered several options. The first was to add an if statement to the method, but that seemed clumsy and arbitrary. Then I thought about writing a subclass (perhaps called ReadOnlyTotalizator), but I didn't like that idea for several reasons. Then I briefly considered applying the Strategy pattern, but that seemed like killing flies with a bazooka.

You can probably see what I was doing wrong. I was thinking in Java, not JavaScript. I caught myself and began consciously thinking of the ways JavaScript was different, and mostly those ways consisted of being more dynamic, allowing things in times and places where they would be prohibited by Java. One thing I remembered was that individual objects could have their own methods, not associated with any class.

Immediately I saw the easy solution. I changed Totalizator to expect the implementation of getNumberFromCell(cell) to be passed into the constructor:

```
function Totalizator(table_id, gnfc_function) {
    this.table_id = table_id;
    this.getNumberFromCell = gnfc_function;
    // ... code to process table and find cells ...
}
```

```
// and then, to create an instance for the read-only case:
new Totalizator('forecast_table', function(cell) {
    return Number(cell.innerHTML);
});
```

You might not agree with me when I call that the easy solution. Easy to implement, perhaps, but easy to use? It seems crazy to make someone supply a missing method every time they create an instance.

But that was just the first draft. There are a couple of ways to make it better. I supplied useful implementations as properties of the Totalizator function itself (not as instance methods). And then I made one of those the default and made the second constructor parameter optional by testing it against undefined before using it. Finally, I documented things really well:

```
function Totalizator(table_id, gnfc_function) {
    this.table_id = table_id;
    if (gnfc_function) {
        this.getNumberFromCell = gnfc_function;
    }
    // ... code to process table and find cells ...
}
```

```
Totalizator.getNumberFromSimpleCell = function(cell) {
    return Number(cell.innerHTML);
}

Totalizator.getNumberFromTextInputCell = function(cell) {
    var children = cell.children || cell.childNodes;
    return Number(children[0].value);
}

Totalizator.prototype.getNumberFromCell = Totalizator.getNumberFromSimpleCell;
```

With that work done, there's some flexibility in how you create an instance:

```
new Totalizator('forecast_table');
new Totalizator('editable_forecast', Totalizator.getNumberFromTextInputCell);
new Totalizator('some_new_forecast_type', function(cell) {
    // ... a custom getNumberFromCell method
});
```

Now let's reflect on all of that for a bit. Does that design seem sloppy to you? Maybe it does, if you're still thinking in Java terms. But Java-Script is dynamic, loose, and open for good reasons. If anything, I think my design is wildly overengineered for the situation. But I don't feel bad about it (except maybe for the class name). It was a great learning exercise, very easy to document, and kept the code nice and DRY. Plus, now that I've learned to think in JavaScript's terms, this solution would occur to me almost instantly and take almost no time to implement. Frankly, looking at the code now, I'm embarrassed by most of it; however, it was a milestone in my understanding of JavaScript.

But the important lesson is this: before I could conceive of that design, *I had to really know the language!* Just look at all the peculiarities of JavaScript that you have to understand before you could arrive at such a design:

- Functions are first-class objects.
- Methods are just functions attached to objects.
- You can add methods to classes at any time (even after instances have been created).
- Individual objects can have their own methods.
- "Class constructors" are just functions.
- Functions, being objects, can have their own properties.
- You can call functions with fewer (or more) arguments than the function is declared to take.

- If no value is passed for a function argument, it gets the value undefined.

3.7 Conclusion

Here is the big mistake I made back in 1996: I dismissed JavaScript without really trying to understand it. I took a quick glance, and it didn't match what I thought a good language should be, so I turned away. Of course, there isn't time to do a deep dive on every new language that comes along, but the next time a language appears that offers compelling new capabilities (as JavaScript did) or that smart, experienced, respected developers are recommending, I'm going to make sure I spend some quality time with it, learning to use it as it was intended, before I make up my mind either way.

My friend Stuart Halloway has said that the really important thing about Ajax is that it has tricked us into adopting a more powerful language than we would have chosen on our own. I think that's true, and I'm glad I've learned how to deal responsibly with all the freedom that JavaScript gives me.

But Stu has another version of that quote that I like better: "Ajax is a gateway drug for JavaScript." I'm glad I'm hooked.

3.8 Web Resources

Time magazine's ten-best products of 1995...
... http://www.time.com/time/magazine/article/0,9171,983903,00.html
Looking back on this eleven years later, it's clear that everything _Time_ said about Java was actually true of JavaScript instead.

Douglas Crockford's JavaScript pages...
... http://www.crockford.com/javascript/
A collection of writings about the world's most misunderstood programming language.

Ajaxian.com .... http://www.ajaxian.com/
News and commentary about all things Ajax, including cool applications, development tools, and JavaScript tips.

Firebug .... http://www.getfirebug.com/
As of early 2007, the gold standard for JavaScript/Ajax development tools.

## Chapter 4

The Joys of Continuations and Asynchronous Architectures

by Rebecca J. Parsons

Rebecca is the chief technology officer for ThoughtWorks, Inc., a global company with a mission to transform the way software is developed. She has a checkered past in the computer industry, having programmed in many languages and worked in many different sectors, including manufacturing, high-tech, government research, and academia. She is a self-proclaimed language geek and systems person. She gave up trying to make her mother understand what she does for a living.

4.1 Introduction

Event-driven architecture (EDA) and service-oriented architecture (SOA) are, for various reasons, gaining prominence as approaches to the development of enterprise applications. One feature common to both these approaches is the reliance on different application components interacting asynchronously. This asynchrony provides many benefits, including testing, scalability, and resilience. However, the patterns used in constructing asynchronous applications are quite different and not as familiar to many developers.

Continuations, long a part of the functional language community, are currently regaining popularity, primarily in web programming, although there is still a fair amount of controversy as to whether this is a good thing.

This essay first introduces the idea of continuations and demonstrates their usefulness in various contexts. I'll then demonstrate the role continuations can play in EDA and SOA systems.

4.2 Neat and Nifty Tricks with Continuations

The easiest way to think about a continuation is that it represents the rest of the computation at any given point in time. If you think about any program and some random point in the execution of that program for some input set, there are two clear sets—those instructions that have already happened and those instructions that are left to execute. That second set is the continuation.

One of the important aspects of this notion of a continuation is that, as pointed out in the Wikipedia definition, the continuation contains the context of the execution to that point. For example, consider the following code fragment in no particular language:

```
x = 42;
y = 6;
z = x + y;
```

After the assignment statement x = 42;, the continuation includes an assignment y = 6; and the assignment z = x + y; in a context where the variable x has the value 42;. Effectively, the continuation is a closure that has a binding for the variable x. Another continuation exists after the assignment to y that has the context of variable bindings for both x and y.

Admittedly, this isn't a terribly interesting continuation. Consider the following code for a recursive function, this time written in Scheme:

```
(define times (lambda (l)
    (if (empty? l)
            1
            (* (times (rest l)) (head l)))))
```

This presents a recursive function that returns the product of a list of numbers.

To clarify the syntax, lambda expressions define functions. In this case, I am naming the function times. The if has three subexpressions: the predicate, the true clause, and the false clause. The function returns the value 1 when the list is empty; otherwise, the return value is the product of the recursive call on the rest of the list and the first element in the list.

Now compiler writers will cringe and want to convert this recursive function into a loop to make it more efficient. There is a standard translation to a form called *continuation passing style* that can in general be used to translate a recursive function into an iterative loop. The core of this translation is to establish what needs to happen after each of the recursive return statements. In tail recursive form, no computation is required on the return values; the final, innermost return value bubbles up to be the return value from the entire call stack. Clearly, the earlier fragment is not tail recursive since, after each return, you have to take into account the value at that level (the previousReturnValue * head(l)). You could achieve a simple transformation as follows:

```
(define times (lambda (l)
        (cpsTimes l 1)))

(define cpsTimes (lambda (l v)
        (cond (empty? l)
                v
                (cpsTimes (rest l) (* v (head l))))))
```

This results in a tail recursive implementation. In this case, the analog to the continuation is the built-up, temporary result that is returned at the end.

Those with experience in compiler optimization will note that there is a flaw here for floating-point arithmetic: the order of the multiplications is reversed.

One quick way to fix that is to simply change the first function to the following:

```
(define times (lambda (l)
        (cpsTimes (reverse l) 1)))
```

This results in the same order of multiplication. Another approach, which demonstrates a more sophisticated continuation, is as follows:

```
(define times (lambda (l)
        (cpsTimes l (lambda (x) x))))

(define cpsTimes (lambda (l c)
        (if (empty? l)
                (c 1)
                (cpsTimes (rest l) (lambda (v) (c (* v (head l)))))))))
```

Here, the continuation created at each recursive call captures the computation that would have occurred in the original recursive function. At each level of the recursive call, you create a new continuation that captures the input continuation contained in the parameter and the value from the first element in the list at that level. When the recursion bottoms out, the continuation is applied to the value 1, and the values cascade through the continuations, eventually reaching the identify function that was specified as the initial continuation.

This example demonstrates a crucial aspect of continuations. Continuations are simply functions that take some value as input, incorporate that input into the context, and continue with whatever rest of computation they represent. Now, you might be wondering why I chose this particular example. Consider the following optimization:

```
(define times (lambda (l).
        (cpsTimes l (lambda (x) x))))

(define cpsTimes (lambda (l c).
        (if (empty? l)
                (if (zero? (head l))
                        0
                        (cpsTimes (rest l) (lambda (v) (c (* v (head l)))))))))
```

Although this admittedly relies on the mathematical properties of multiplication, it shows both the power of continuations and one reason why they should be used carefully. In this example, as soon as a zero is encountered in the list, all the rest of the computation, which is captured in the continuation parameter c, is discarded. Continuations are capable of behaving like the dreaded goto of years past.

Continuations represented by closures break the tyranny of the call stack and provide clear mechanisms to combine inputs or to break out of a sequence that is no longer relevant.

4.3 Why Continuations Are Useful in Designing Asynchronous Systems

About now you're probably saying "That's terribly interesting, but what in the world does this have to do with EDA or SOA or..." since there doesn't seem to be much that is earth shattering here. Let's consider, though, the following code fragment:

```
creditStatus = receiveCreditHistory(customer);
tradingStatus = receiveTradingHistory(customer);
decision = determineMarginAccountLimits(customer, creditStatus, tradingStatus);
```

The names in this fragment are intended to reflect that there are external interfaces involved in obtaining some information about a customer. In a synchronous application, the execution of such code would proceed by making the first request, waiting for the response, making the second request, waiting for the second response, and then combining those two responses into a decision, which is presumably sent someplace useful. Generally speaking, such external systems are independent of each other, so the wait times can, in theory, be overlapped. However, the synchronous implementation ensures that the systems never attempt to make a decision without both pieces of information. We really don't know how much time it will take to get an answer back from independent external systems either, but the previous synchronous implementation can be cheerfully oblivious to that complication as well. This implementation, though, suffers from all sorts of problems with resource utilization and resilience to failure of the external systems for starters. A well-designed asynchronous system would fire off the two requests for external information at the same time and then make the decision once all the information was received. However, we don't know which response will return first.

For simplicity, I will assume we have a database that stores the current state of each customer, and I will assume that results from the external system are processed by some message receiver that queries the database for the current state of the customer. I will also leave out a fair amount of error handling.

The state for a customer will be a continuation representing what computation is left and what context already exists. When the requests go out to the two external providers, the current state of customer Jay looks something like this:

```
func (status)
    if status.type("Credit")
            new custState = func(status1)
                    decision = determineMarginAccountLimits("Jay",
                            status, status1)
        else if status.type("Trading")
            new custState = func(status1)
                    decision = determineMarginAccountLimits("Jay",
                            status1, status2)
```

In this example, continuations are unnamed functions of one input parameter, the message status returned from an external system. The continuation for customer Jay, after the initial request, is a computation that expects some status, figures out which it is, and then creates a new continuation, another unnamed function of one input parameter, that waits for the other kind of status. Once the other status arrives, the continuation still has the previous context and can make the decision.

Collecting multiple independent inputs and combining them in a computation occurs frequently in business systems, particularly those modeled by workflows. These systems often have complex logic to try to either accept inputs in any order or introduce artificial sequencing to simplify the process. This continuation model provides a simple but powerful mechanism to collect disparate inputs in whatever order and defer all other processing until the inputs have arrived.

Now, some of you out there are probably saying that you could just record the intermediate results directly in the database. I don't need these continuations. There are several problems with the database approach at an implementation level. The database constraints must be weakened to allow for incomplete records. This isn't necessary in the continuation approach, because the information from the individual statuses is not truly incorporated into the customer's status until all has been received. The database design and the message formats can also be more readily decoupled using the continuation approach. The continuation representation makes it obvious what is still to come and what will be done with that information once it arrives. Such information could be difficult to uncover if, for example, the same type of data was returned from two sources and had to be somehow reconciled.

There are many other common patterns occurring in service-oriented applications that can be cleanly modeled with the concept of a continuation. Customized exception handling is easy to implement in a continuation-based system. The caller supplies the exception handler in the form of a continuation that is invoked only if that particular exception is thrown. The caller controls the context (including whatever portions of the call stack are relevant) that is used if that exception is encountered. Different continuations can be supplied for different exceptions. The notion of a success continuation is useful in a situation where the application is waiting for a signal to finish but might have to process some unknown inputs before then. The standard continuation simply continues to collect inputs until the completion signal is received. The collected results are then given as input to the previously supplied success continuation, and the computation completes. Many other patterns are possible as well.

4.4   What's the Catch?

So, there has to be some downsides to this way of thinking. The biggest downside to continuations is actually considered a general downside to asynchronous systems. Understanding a continuation-based application is challenging because it is not always easy to know the order in which things happen. However, unlike the spaghetti code that resulted in the old days from nonstructured control flow, continuations include their context, and hence there is far less ambiguity about what might happen when the continuation executes. More simply, although the order in which things happen may not be clear, what happens at any given continuation execution is clear.

Another issue with continuations is the implementation-level support for them. Different language environments have varying levels of support for continuations. Effectively, the creation of a continuation is run-time code generation. Many systems, particularly those that are compiled, have limited support for full continuations. However, although continuations are easily created using closures, more declarative representations of continuations are possible. Care must be taken in such circumstances, though, to not introduce too much complexity.

Another caution regarding the creation of continuations: these constructs embed in code some logic that could potentially be more readily captured declaratively.

Continuations can certainly implement work flows, for example. Sometimes, however, utilizing a workflow framework may make more sense.

4.5 What Does It Mean, and Why Should I Care?

The increasing popularity of service-oriented and event-driven architectures is increasing the need for patterns and implementations to simplify asynchronous computation. Continuations, by capturing both data and control contextual information, provide a clean way to think about asynchronous computation. Although continuations are often associated with "those weird functional languages," the notion is a powerful one that should not be dismissed.

4.6 Web Resources

Programming languages group................http://www.plt-scheme.org/
Home page for a group of programming languages folks, including various implementations of Scheme

Scheme implementation .... http://www-swiss.ai.mit.edu/projects/scheme/
A popular implementation of Scheme

Scheme resources...............................http://www.schemers.org/
A good collection of Scheme resources

Continuations resources http://library.readscheme.org/page6.html
Online citations to many papers on continuations and continuation passing style

Continuations in web applications...
...... http://www-128.ibm.com/developerworks/library/j-contin.html
Article on using continuations in web applications

...We have this horrible balancing act. On the one hand we really need simplicity, and on the other hand we really need power. And those are evil twin brothers of each other. Building systems that have a lot of power just sort of attracts complexity.

▶ James Gosling (speaking about Java vs. scripting languages)

Chapter 5

The Case for Groovy

by Scott Davis

Scott Davis is the editor in chief of aboutGroovy.com. He is also an author and independent consultant. He is passionate about open source solutions and agile development. He has worked on a variety of Java platforms, from J2EE to J2SE to J2ME (sometimes all on the same project).

He is the coauthor of JBoss at Work [MD05],[1] quite possibly the world's first agile J2EE book. He is also responsible for several mapping books, including the Google Maps API[2] and GIS for Web Developers: Adding Where to Your Web Applications [Dav06].[3]

Scott is a frequent presenter at international conferences and local user groups. He was the president of the Denver Java Users' Group in 2003 when it was voted one of the top-ten JUGs in North America. After a quick move north, he is currently active in the leadership of the Boulder Java Users' Group. Keep up with him at http://www.davisworld.org.

---

1. http://www.jbossatwork.com
2. http://www.pragmaticprogrammer.com/titles/sdgmapi
3. http://www.pragmaticprogrammer.com/titles/sdgis

5.1 Introduction

We live in complicated times. Politics are complicated. Society is complicated. And, yes, our industry is getting more complicated by the year.

Do you remember your first program? Mine was written in BASIC. I remember it verbatim:

```
10 PRINT "Scott is cool."
20 GOTO 10
```

I was quite pleased with it at the time. After all, it ran flawlessly, and its logic was irreproachable. (Notice it didn't assert "Other people think Scott is cool" or "Junior-high girls think that BASIC programmers are cool....") That was the last time my life as a programmer was so simple.

Looking at that program with modern eyes, I think to myself, "Did he use IntelliJ or Eclipse to write that? Ant or Maven to build it? Where is he going to deploy it—JBoss? Tomcat? Should it be fronted by Apache? Where are the unit tests? If he just would've created a WishfulThinking interface, he could've used Spring to polymorphically swap out the implementation at runtime." Even the Java port seems to lose some of the previous example's expressiveness:

```
public class MyFirstJavaClass{
    public static void main(String[] args){
        while(true){
            System.out.println("Scott is cool.");
        }
    }
}
```

5.2 News Flash: Java Is Complex

No one should be surprised by the assertion that Java is—umm—less basic than BASIC. So, why did you choose Java? What made the step up in complexity worth it? Many would suggest *power*. James Gosling (the father of Java) makes that point in the quote at the beginning of this chapter. Rather than seeking to be complex, he says that Java seeks to be powerful, and complexity is just an unfortunate byproduct.

At the risk of sounding contrarian, I argue that the beauty of Java is its simplicity *and* its power—not the simplicity of writing applications in it but the simplicity of *deploying* applications written in it. "Write once, run anywhere" (WORA) is no empty promise. I can drop a JAR onto my classpath, and it just works. I can write a web application on my Mac with full confidence that I can deploy it to a Linux or Windows server with zero chance of failure.

I think the assumption that the spectrum runs from easy to powerful is flawed: the units of measure are mixed. The spectrum should run from easy to complex. WORA gives us at least two aspects of the development process to measure: how easy is the application to write, and how easy is the application to run? Your definition of power then rests on how you weight the criteria. I'd argue that something "powerful" skews to the easy side of the scale on as many axes as possible.

5.3 assertEquals(Power,Simplicity)

At the risk of adding complexity to the discussion, let's add a few more criteria to the mix. How easy is it to add new functionality to the system? Will it be easy to maintain over the life of the product? Can it be unit tested easily? Can it easily be integrated with my existing systems? Can it easily be integrated with my existing development staff? Is the code easy to read?

I could go on and on with this exercise. Maybe you have your own criteria to add. Maybe some of the criteria that I suggested aren't important to you. Regardless of what is included in the final evaluation, the power of the system is measured (paradoxically) by how many of the decision criteria end up being easy.

For the argument's sake, Figure 5.1, on the next page, shows my subjective rating of the power of Java.[4] It's difficult to generalize about Java when so many different factors affect the "easy" scale. Few factors in Java hinder you from unit testing, but few factors actively encourage you to create unit tests; consequently, I give "Easy to test" a neutral rating. "Easy to persist objects" (not shown here) might depend on whether you use entity beans or Hibernate, a traditional relational database or an object database, annotations, XDoclet, IDE tooling, and so on. The bottom line is that I've long since moved past asking "Can I do it in Java?" I now ask, "Can I do it *easily* in Java?"

---

4. Thanks to Kathy Sierra and her wonderful blog "Creating Passionate Users" for the slider metaphor. For additional information, see the website at http://headrush.typepad.com/creating_passionate_users/2005/11/how_to_come_up_.html.

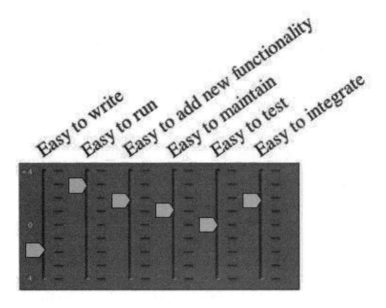

Figure 5.1: JAVA POWER RATINGS

5.4 Beyond Java

Few people argue that Java isn't a capable programming language. But sometimes it feels like a $20 solution to a $0.05 problem. Let's say I want to open a text file, walk through it line by line, and print each line out to the screen. In idiomatic Java, it takes me nearly 35 lines:

```java
import java.io.BufferedReader;
import java.io.FileNotFoundException;
import java.io.FileReader;
import java.io.IOException;

public class WalkFile {
    public static void main(String[] args) {
        BufferedReader br = null;
        try {
            br = new BufferedReader(new FileReader("../simpleFile.txt"));
            String line = null;
            while((line = br.readLine()) != null) {
                System.out.println(line);
            }
        }
        catch(FileNotFoundException fnfe) {
            fnfe.printStackTrace();
```

```
        }
        catch(IOException ioe) {
            ioe.printStackTrace();
        }
        finally {
            if(br != null) {
                try {
                    br.close();
                }
                catch(IOException ioe) {
                    ioe.printStackTrace();
                }
            }
        }
    }
}
```

Of course, I could shorten this example by a few lines here and there. I could import java.io.*. I could catch(Exception e). I could bend stylistic conventions by moving single-line blocks up and consolidate multiple closing curly braces onto a single line. But reducing lines of code isn't the same as reducing complexity.

This verbosity is what makes me give Java low marks on the "Easy to write" scale. It just comes in at the wrong level of abstraction for many common aspects.

Since we're programmers, "Easy to write" is a tough metric to overlook. It has led many bright developers to other programming languages such as Perl or Ruby that make "easy things easy and hard things possible."

The problem with choosing a different language is that usually as the "Easy to write" slider moves up, the "Easy to integrate" slider moves down. If you are doing greenfield development with no existing database schema, no existing system to integrate with, and no legacy code to mesh with, then switching languages is a viable option. If, however, you are in an established Java shop, these issues can be showstoppers. Another factor that can't be ignored is developer velocity: even if the new language offers you syntactic niceties, how long is it going to take you to ramp up your skills in the new language to the level you were at in Java? Does that mean your options are either "Java" or "Not Java"?

5.5 Java Is Dead. Long Live Java!

After ten years of treating Java as a language, we are moving into a new era where Java is now a *platform* where you can use the language of your choice. JSR 223 (Scripting for the Java Platform) is implemented in Java 6 today. JSR 292 (Supporting Dynamically Typed Languages on the Java Platform) shows you where the platform is going in the future.[5] But even today on Java 1.4 or Java 5, more than 200 languages are supported on the JVM.[6] If you are a Python fan, there is Jython.[7] If you prefer Ruby, there is JRuby.[8]

But caveat emptor. Just because these languages run on the JVM, don't assume that you can freely mix them with your Java code. Can you call your Java code from the new language? Can you call the new language from your Java code? Can the new language be compiled into bytecode and stored in a JAR? And perhaps most important, how complementary is the new language to eyes used to looking at Java?

Complexity, it seems, is in the eye of the beholder. If you already know the intricacies of Ruby, then JRuby is a step toward simplicity: use Java for its strengths, and leverage JRuby where it helps. If you don't already know Ruby, then you are faced with the task of learning a new syntax. Granted, this is not an insurmountable task, but it does add complexity in the short term. You end up betting that the long-term gains will be worth the short-term costs.

But what if there was a simpler, more expressive language that was targeted at Java developers? Something that looks mostly like Java with just a touch of syntactic sugar, rather than something completely foreign? More a new dialect of Java than a new language?

5.6 Enter Groovy

Groovy[9] is a dynamic language that runs on the JVM. But before I get into the nitty-gritty details of the language, I should allow it to introduce itself. How does Groovy solve the previous Java problem of opening a file, walking through it line by line, and printing out the results?

```
new File("simpleFile.txt").each{ line ->
    println(line)
}
```

---

5. See http://www.artima.com/lejava/articles/dynamic_languages.html.
6. See http://www.robert-tolksdorf.de/vmlanguages.
7. See http://www.jython.org/.
8. See http://jruby.codehaus.org/.
9. See http://groovy.codehaus.org.

These three lines of code in Groovy (which could technically be one) solve what it took Java more than thirty to do. new File() opens the file. each is a closure[10] that iterates through *each* line of the file. And println(), as the name implies, prints out the result.

To create the script, type it in the text editor of your choice. Name it anything you'd like—WalkFile.groovy. To run it, type groovy WalkFile at a prompt. No compiling. No classpath. No worries. This, my friends, moves the "Easy to write" slider back into positive territory without affecting the others, including "Easy to integrate."

But what about integration? If you prefer, you can compile this code. You can type groovyc WalkFile.groovy at a command prompt, or you can use the Ant task of the same name. The resulting class is bytecode that is 100% callable from Java. Maybe you'd like to wrap it in a class and a method so that you can easily call it from a Java class:

```
class FileHelper{
        void printLines(fileName){
                new File(fileName).each{ line ->
                        println(line)
                }
        }
}
```

The syntax should look shorter than Java but still familiar. The public qualifiers are dropped (public is assumed in Groovy in the places you'd expect it to be), but they can be added back in if it helps clarity. Of course, if you'd like things to be private or protected, you can explicitly qualify them as well:

```
public class FileHelper{
        public void printLines(fileName){
                new File(fileName).each{ line ->
                        println(line)
                }
        }
}
```

Variables are duck typed[11]—no type declaration is required. Semicolons are optional. Even the familiar System.out.println is shortened. But you can put all this back in if you'd like:

```
public class FileHelper{
```

---

10. Closures are available in many languages. In Groovy, they are often used as concise replacements for Java iterators.
11. See http://en.wikipedia.org/wiki/Duck_typing.

```
public void printLines(String fileName){
        new File(fileName).each{ line ->
                System.out.println(line);
        }
    }
}
```

You're not catching any exceptions here, but you could wrap the code in a try/catch if you'd like. The same IOException you'd expect to be thrown is thrown here. As a matter of fact, the File that we are dealing with is, in reality, a java.io.File. Groovy decorates it with some additional methods (such as each), but it is a pure Java File through and through.

I could take this example all the way back up to the Java example with which I started. Groovy would compile it without complaints (although it *would* gossip about you behind your back). The point here is that the "Easy to write" slider becomes subjective in an interesting way. If the Groovy syntax looks strange and increases complexity, dial it back to something more Java-like. If the Java syntax looks too verbose and cumbersome, mix in Groovy.

5.7 Inviting Groovy to the Party

Installing Groovy is as easy as installing Ant, Tomcat, or even Java itself:

1. Download[12] the latest version of Groovy, and unzip it to the directory of your choice.

2. Create a GROOVY_HOME environment variable.

3. Add GROOVY_HOME/bin to your path.

Type groovy --version to verify that everything is OK, and you are off to the races.

Embedding Groovy in your Java application is as easy as embedding JDOM or Log4J. Look for groovy-all-(version).jar in GROOVY_HOME/embedded. Copy it to your lib directory, and you are set.

Most modern IDEs and text editors have Groovy plug-ins.[13] IntelliJ IDEA, Eclipse, NetBeans, and JEdit all support Groovy. Plug-ins for

---

12. See http://dist.codehaus.org/groovy/distributions/.
13. See http://groovy.codehaus.org/IDE+Support.

text editors such as TextPad, TextMate, and even Emacs are available as well.

Groovy even ships with a couple of command-line tools to help. Type groovysh to play around with the Groovy shell. (groovyConsole opens a nice Swing-based GUI.)

```
$ groovysh
Lets get Groovy!
================
Version: 1.0 JVM: 1.5.0_06-64
Type 'exit' to terminate the shell
Type 'help' for command help
Type 'go' to execute the statements

groovy> foo = "World"
groovy> "Hello ${foo}"
groovy> go

===> Hello World

groovy> foo.class
groovy> go

===> class java.lang.String

groovy> foo.class.methods.each{println it}
groovy> go
public int java.lang.String.hashCode()
public volatile int java.lang.String.compareTo(java.lang.Object)
public int java.lang.String.compareTo(java.lang.String)
public boolean java.lang.String.equals(java.lang.Object)
public int java.lang.String.length()
public char java.lang.String.charAt(int)
public java.lang.String java.lang.String.toString()
...
```

Our visit to the shell shows off some additional language features. Groovy Strings—called (ahem) GStrings by the brave creators of the language—allow parameter substitution using the familiar ${} notation found in other libraries like Ant and JSTL. You can, of course, always use the more Java-like "this " + that + " the other" version of string concatenation as well.

Groovy also has strong metaprogramming support. The last command demonstrates getting a list of all the methods of the class and using the each closure to print them out. In the earlier file example, I named the closure parameter line for clarity. This time, I use the native it variable that gets assigned to non-named parameters.

5.8 How Did He Know How to Do That?

Groovy operates on the principle of least surprise; once you know how to iterate through a file using each, you come to expect it on all collection-like objects. Thankfully, you can use closures to iterate through Lists, Arrays, and even JDBC ResultSets in the same way:

```
//Arrays and Lists are syntactically identical in Groovy
nephews = ["Huey", "Dewey", "Louie"]
nephews.each{ println it }

//conn, user, password, driver
sql = groovy.sql.Sql.newInstance(
    "jdbc:derby://localhost:1527/MyDbTest;create=true",
    "test",
    "test",
    "org.apache.derby.jdbc.ClientDriver")

sql.eachRow("select name from APPS"){ row ->
    println("${row.name}")
}
```

The Groovy website is a great source of code snippets and samples. For example, let's see what other cool things Groovy allows you to do with Strings:[14]

```
sentence = "It's cool that I don't have to escape internal quotes."
person = 'Arthur "The Fonz" Fonzarelli'
paragraph = """ My favorite episode of
Happy Days was the one where
${person} said, "${sentence}" """
```

All three of the previous examples are valid String variables. Groovy allows you to mix single and double quotes like you can in JavaScript. This can potentially save you from having to escape quotes in the middle, although the "usual \"Java\" way" is still supported. Groovy also allows you to use triple quotes to create multilined strings like you can in Python. Everything between the starting and ending triple quotes is stored in the paragraph variable.

The triple quote feature becomes especially interesting when it comes to testing. Being able to capture snippets of XML easily in your Groovy-TestCase (JUnit is included with Groovy) makes writing unit tests remarkably easy:[15]

```
import groovy.util.GroovyTestCase
```

---

14. See http://groovy.codehaus.org/Strings.
15. See http://groovy.codehaus.org/Unit+Testing.

```
class XmlTest extends GroovyTestCase{
  void testWebServiceCall(){
    expectedXml = """
        <book publisher="O'Reilly" pages="287">
            JBoss At Work
        </book>
    """
    assertEquals( expectedXml, MyService.getBookByIsbn("0-596-00734-5") )
  }
}
```

Groovy is unabashedly a mongrel when it comes to language features. (Perhaps *best of breed* is a more flattering term?) The first thing you see on the Groovy home page is, "Groovy is an agile development language for the Java Platform with many features that are inspired by languages like Python, Ruby, and Smalltalk, making them available to Java developers using a Java-like syntax." This takes a page from Perl's mantra, TMTOWTDI ("There's More Than One Way To Do It"). Thankfully, there is plenty of documentation to show you the various ways to do it.

For more information about how Groovy decorates native Java objects, the Groovy GDK[16] is a good place to start. For more information about native Groovy classes, the Groovy API docs[17] are a valuable resource. For the definitive language reference, pick up a copy of *Groovy in Action*,[18] written by the leaders of the Groovy project.

To keep up with the latest Groovy news, swing by aboutGroovy.com[19] from time to time. There you'll find links to news stories and interesting blogs, upcoming Groovy-related events, and rich content such as tutorials, podcasts, screencasts, and videos.

5.9 Rapid Web Development with Grails

No discussion of Groovy would be complete without mentioning Grails.[20] Inspired by Ruby's profoundly influential rapid web development framework Rails, Grails brings the speed and elegance of Rails to the Groovy platform. Not just a simple port of Rails, Grails uses Rails for inspiration ("Convention over configuration," scaffolding, and so on)

---

16. See http://groovy.codehaus.org/groovy-jdk.html.
17. See http://groovy.codehaus.org/apidocs.
18. See http://www.manning.com/koenig/.
19. See http://aboutgroovy.com.
20. See http://grails.codehaus.org/.

but is grounded in proven Java technologies such as Ant, Hibernate, and Spring. This whirlwind tour of Grails will give you a taste of how quickly you can have a website up and running.

Grails is as easy as Groovy to install. Download it, create GRAILS_HOME, and add GRAILS_HOME/bin to your path. Since Grails includes an embedded version of Groovy, you could even skip installing Groovy if you'd like. Grails includes an embedded web server/servlet container (Jetty). It includes an embedded database (HSQLDB). It includes Hibernate. It includes Spring. It includes Sitemesh. It includes Quartz (for scheduling). It includes the Ajax libraries Prototype, Script.aculo.us, and Yahoo UI. (There's an included task to install the Dojo toolkit if you'd prefer to use it instead.) Grails even includes its own copy of Ant. Literally everything you need to get started is included in the download.

To verify your installation, type grails at a command prompt:

```
$ grails
Buildfile: /Library/grails/src/grails/build.xml

init-props:
  [echo]
  [echo]                  Welcome to Grails 0.3.1 - http://grails.org/
  [echo]                  Licensed under Apache Standard License 2.0
  [echo]
  [echo]                  Grails home is set to: /Library/grails
  [echo]

help:
  [echo] Usage: grails [target]
  [echo]
  [echo] Targets:
  [echo] "create-app"          - Create a new grails app
  [echo] "create-controller"   - Create a new controller
  [echo] "create-service"      - Create a new service
  [echo] "create-domain-class" - Create a new domain class
  [echo] "create-taglib"       - Create a new tag library class
  [echo] "create-test-suite"   - Create a new test suite
  [echo] "create-job"          - Create a quartz scheduled job
  [echo] "generate-controller" - Generates a controller from a domain class
  [echo] "generate-views"      - Generates the views from a domain class
  [echo] "generate-all"        - Generates the all artifacts from a domain class
  [echo] "install-dojo"        - Installs the Dojo toolkit into the current project
  [echo] "test-app"            - Run current app's unit tests
  [echo] "run-app"             - Run the application locally and wait
  [echo] "create-webtest"      - Create the functional test layout
  [echo] "generate-webtest"    - Generates a WebTest from a domain class
  [echo] "run-webtest"         - Run the functional tests for a running app
  [echo] "war"                 - Creates a deployable Web Application Archive (WAR)
```

```
[echo] "shell"          - Opens the Grails interactive command line shell
[echo] "console"        - Opens the Grails interactive swing console
[echo]
```

```
BUILD SUCCESSFUL
Total time: 4 seconds
```

To set up your initial application, type grails create-app. I'll show how to create a simple bookstore, so type bookstore when it prompts you for the name of your application. You'll see a flurry of activity as Grails creates directories and copies files to their proper locations.

Change to the newly created bookstore directory and look around:

```
$ ls -1
total 8
-rw-r--r--  1 sdavis  sdavis  1748 Dec 15 14:29 bookstore.launch
drwxr-xr-x  9 sdavis  sdavis   306 Dec 15 14:29 grails-app
drwxr-xr-x  2 sdavis  sdavis    68 Dec 15 14:29 grails-tests
drwxr-xr-x  2 sdavis  sdavis    68 Dec 15 14:29 hibernate
drwxr-xr-x  2 sdavis  sdavis    68 Dec 15 14:29 lib
drwxr-xr-x  3 sdavis  sdavis   102 Dec 15 14:29 spring
drwxr-xr-x  4 sdavis  sdavis   136 Dec 15 14:29 src
drwxr-xr-x  8 sdavis  sdavis   272 Dec 15 14:29 web-app
```

The grails-app directory is where your Model-View-Controller code will ultimately live. Unit and functional tests live in grails-tests. Hibernate and Spring configuration files live in the eponymous directories. You can drop additional JARs into the lib directory. You can find all static HTML, CSS, and JavaScript files in web-app.

Honestly, for this breakneck tour, I'm not going to spend time in any of these directories other than hand-editing one file in grails-app. You can customize your application to your heart's content, but I'll show how to leverage Grails' out-of-the-box capabilities to their fullest.

Type grails create-domain-class to create your first class. Type book when prompted for the name of the class.

```
$ grails create-domain-class

create-domain-class:
    [input] Enter domain class name:
book
     [copy] Copying 1 file to /Users/sdavis/tmp/nfjs/bookstore/grails-app/domain
     [echo] Domain class created: grails-app/domain/Book.groovy

internal-create-test-suite:
     [copy] Copying 1 file to /Users/sdavis/tmp/nfjs/bookstore/grails-tests
     [echo] Created test suite: grails-tests/BookTests.groovy
```

Grails creates an empty plain old Groovy object (POGO) in grails-app/ domain/. Pull it up in the text editor of your choice, and add a few fields. This is the only change you need to make to the application before you have a fully functional website that offers complete create, retrieve, update, and delete (CRUD) capabilities.

```
class Book {
        String title
        String author
        Integer pages
}
```

Notice that there is no need to hand-code getters and setters. Grails ensures that the fields are private and through metaprogramming dynamically creates the expected methods: String getTitle(), void setTitle(String title), and so on. Grails also uses Groovy object/ relational model (GORM) to silently provide persistence via Hibernate.

To complete the application, type grails generate-all to set up a controller and put the boilerplate view code in place. Again, be sure to type book when prompted.

That is it. You have a rudimentary bookstore in place. Type grails run-app to start the web server. By default, Jetty starts on port 8080. (If that port is already in use, type grails -Dserver.port=9999 run-app to fire it up on an alternate port.) Visit http://localhost:8080/bookstore in your browser. Click around to prove to yourself that full CRUD is available on your newly created POGO. (See Figure 5.2, on the facing page.)

There is so much more you could do with this application. You could create authors and publishers and allow GORM to manage the relationships for you. (Of course, the autogenerated views would make the relationships seamless in the browser as well.) You could tweak the data sources in grails-app/conf to point to external databases, even different ones for development, testing, and production. You could type grails war to generate a WAR file, ready to be dropped in Tomcat, JBoss, or Apache Geronimo. You could type grails console to poke around your live website from a command prompt.

The Definitive Guide to Grails[21] was written by Graeme Rocher, the Grails team lead. He takes you through every aspect of creating a full-featured Grails application. And like Groovy, there is always more than

---

21. See http://www.apress.com/book/bookDisplay.html?bID=10205.

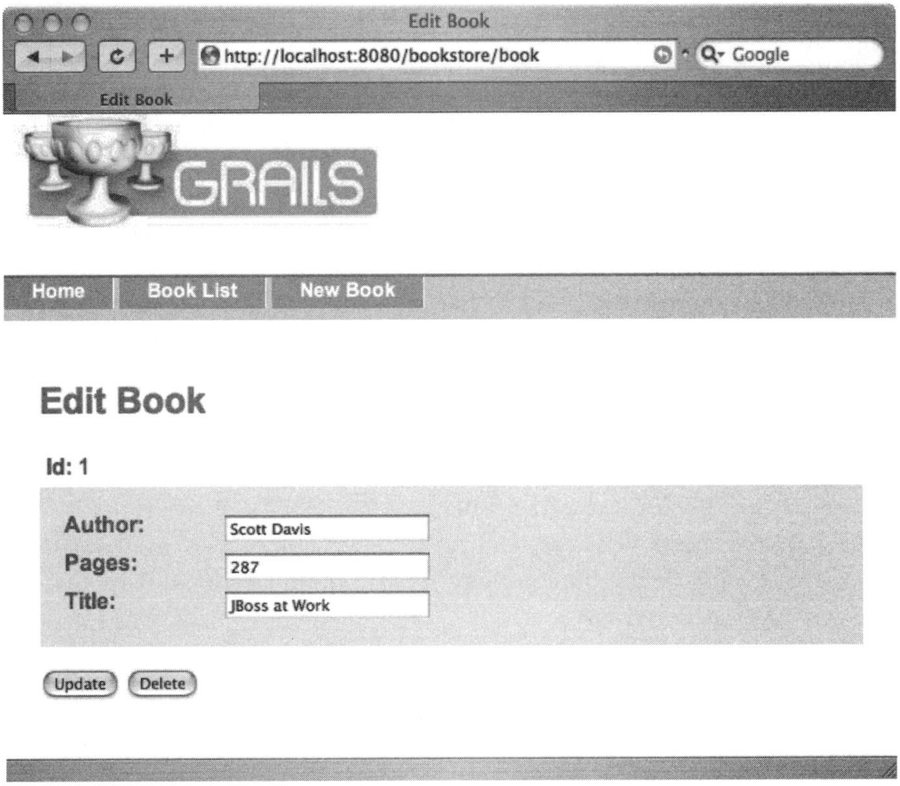

Figure 5.2: GRAILS UP AND RUNNING

one way to do things. If you don't like the default data bindings provided by GORM, Graeme shows you how to back into the Hibernate mapping files yourself. The beauty of Grails (and Groovy as well) is that you are almost never painted into a corner. Use your syntax slider to adjust things to the optimal level.

5.10 Wrapping Up

I hate having to quit here. I feel like we were just getting into the groove of Groovy. But this won't be the last time you hear about Groovy in 2007. Groovy is a first-class citizen in Spring 2.0. You can implement your rules in Groovy in JBoss Rules (a.k.a. Drools). In the SOA/RESTful space, NetKernel supports Groovy. In the blogging space, Blojsom supports it. JSPWiki has a Groovy plug-in. You're going to see Groovy sneak into more and more mainstream applications all over the place. Because Groovy and Java are so similar, adding support for Groovy is a usually a minor task at best.

Groovy will almost certainly be coming to a technical conference near you. The No Fluff Just Stuff tour has featured it prominently in the past (whether it was me, Venkat Subramaniam, Andy Glover, or one of my other fellow speakers), and this year will be no different. JavaOne has had Groovy talks ranked in the top ten for the past several years running. The Spring Experience offers several presentations showcasing Groovy. Grails eXchange 2007 is scheduled for late May in London. Groovy is increasingly showing up on the schedules of Java Users' Groups across North America and Europe.

Three Groovy books went to print in early 2007, and more are in the pipeline. Dedicated websites such as http://aboutgroovy.com are springing up. Visibility in the blogosphere has risen as Groovy moved toward a 1.0 release in late 2006.

In conclusion, don't be afraid to take the easy way out. Easy isn't the antonym of powerful. There is no glory in complexity. Power and complexity have been conflated for too long. Choose the solution that is both easy and powerful.

Most important, define *easy* on your terms. I'm attracted to Groovy because of its spirit of inclusiveness. It extends my platform of choice; it doesn't replace it. It offers full bidirectional integration with Java. It offers a nearly flat learning curve for experienced Java developers. But those are my sliders, not yours. Label your sliders accordingly, and pick the best solution that most fully defines *powerful* for you.

5.11   Web Resources

BASIC..http://en.wikipedia.org/wiki/BASIC
You never forget your first love...

Kathy Sierra: Creating passionate users....http://headrush.typepad.com/
A blog well worth reading for big thoughts instead of little semicolons

Languages for the JVM .... http://www.robert-tolksdorf.de/vmlanguages
A list of nearly 200 languages other than Java that run on the JVM

Jython.................................http://www.jython.org/Project/index.html
Python on the JVM

JRuby . . . . http://jruby.codehaus.org/
Ruby on the JVM

Groovy . . . . .http://groovy.codehaus.org/
A dynamic language for Java developers

Grails . . . . http://grails.codehaus.org/
A Groovy-based web framework that includes Spring, Hibernate, and Ant

aboutGroovy . . . . http://aboutGroovy.com
An information portal for all things Groovy and Grails

Groovy GDK . . . . http://groovy.codehaus.org/groovy-jdk.html
A listing of additional Groovy methods that have been added to standard Java classes

Groovy API Docs . . . . http://groovy.codehaus.org/apidocs
Javadocs for Groovy classes included with the Groovy runtime

Dynamic Languages in Java6 . . .
. . . http://www.artima.com/lejava/articles/dynamic_languages.html
An interview with Danny Coward on JSRs 223 and 292

## Chapter 6

Give It a REST

by Brian Sletten

Brian Sletten is a liberal arts–educated software engineer with a focus on forward-leaning technologies. He has a background as a system architect, a developer, a mentor, and a trainer. His experience has spanned defense, finance, and commercial domains with security consulting, network matrix switch controls, 3D simulation/visualization, grid computing, P2P, and Semantic Web–based systems. He has a bachelor's of science degree in computer science from the College of William and Mary and currently lives in Fairfax, Virginia, where he and his wife run Bosatsu Consulting, Inc. (http://www.bosatsu.net).

6.1 Introduction

Every so often our industry goes insane and obsesses on a topic, convinced that it will change our world. Industry leaders, influential companies, marketing folks, and technologists with short-term memory loss (or who are too young to remember the last time something like this was done) pick up the scent of hype and run with it. Right now we're heading down that road with the WS-Inanity complexity we are using to implement web services.

It's like the situation described in Danish writer Hans Christian Andersen's[1] tale, "The Emperor's New Clothes." It is a morality tale that criticizes being out of touch, slavish vanity, and individuals who enable such behavior by being afraid to speak up. It lauds those who refuse to suck up to the authorities in favor of telling it like it is. In the story, a vainglorious emperor is suckered by a couple of thieves who convince him that they can weave such exquisite fabric[2] that it becomes invisible to those who are stupid or in a lower class. The ruler pays these shysters large amounts of money, puts on the imaginary clothes, and then parades around town in his underthings believing he is wearing top fashion.

His subjects are afraid to appear stupid or low class, so they play along with the fantasy. They applaud him and comment on what fine raiments such a fine emperor is wearing. A lone child, lacking an awareness or fear of consequences, asks everyone what they are talking about. He points out the obvious fact that the emperor is not actually wearing anything. As this truth is publicly acknowledged, everyone becomes embarrassed and goes about their business.

As we watch the web services story unfold in trade rags, blogs, books, and conferences, many of us are left wondering about this "invisible fashion" that everyone seems to be accepting as the Next Big Thing. We need to remember the example of the young child and stop to ask questions about what we are all talking about.

I have no real beef with two-thirds of the web services holy trinity. SOAP is a reasonable way to send message-oriented requests when using the Doc/Lit style and the newly added constraints of the 1.2 specification.

---

1. See http://en.wikipedia.org/wiki/Hans_Christian_Andersen.
2. Don't think for a moment that the fact that many people refer to "a fabric of web service" has escaped my attention!

Furthermore, Web Services Description Language (WSDL) is an acceptable mechanism for defining contracts when you need to specify the inputs and outputs of your service. The fact that we have tools to generate code for consuming these services in languages such as Java, C#, and Ruby is often used as an argument in favor of these technologies. Although nice, these tools are hardly a strength of the approach; they are conveniences that route around the approach's complexity. The third part of the trinity, UDDI, is simply a wrong-headed solution to publishing and querying metadata about web services.

Many of the problems that I see with the standard technologies are direct consequences of their design goals. By decontextualizing requests into language- and transport-independent messages, we are required to encumber the messages with unnecessary amounts of state. Once we do that, we then need ways to verify that the state can be trusted in a context-free request (which involves more state). Much of the pain in web services emerges from these early decisions and the accretion of features that grow like a pearl in an oyster. Although this pearl has grown impressively large in the last few years, the quality and luster are lacking.

My real issue with the current stack is that we are ignoring technologies that already exist, creating new ones that do not need to exist, and still not achieving the mythical interoperability we have been promised.[3] I consider myself a member of the *RESTafarian* community, a group of people who have coalesced around a particular architectural style. There is often as much dogma in this camp as others, but it is the pragmatic adherents who make the most sense to me. As such, I believe that in using the REST architectural style, we can achieve the goals of web services in most scenarios more simply, effectively, scalably, and with greater flexibility to support the content of the future.

Many people are confused about REST, its goals, and how it is supported. This chapter is not intended to flame the holy trinity as much as it is intended to try to clear the air around REST. I am not suggesting

---

3. Clay Shirky has deftly dismissed the web services stack as "turtles all the way up." This is a reference to a well-known creation myth made famous in Terry Pratchett's books. (See http://en.wikipedia.org/wiki/Turtles_all_the_way_down.) Shirkey uses the trope to suggest we keep creating new web service technologies on top of other web service technologies in order to achieve interoperability in the next layer (which, when repeated, we will never achieve). See http://webservices.xml.com/pub/a/ws/2001/10/03/webservices.html for his discussion.

that SOAP, WSDL, and its inbred brethren[4] are incapable of producing working systems. And I'm not suggesting that REST is the only way to go. I simply want to encourage architects, development managers, and businesspeople to stop to think about the approach they are taking and to make sure all the cost and complexity are worth it.

6.2 REST Defined

So, what exactly is REST then? The common understanding seems to be that it is a way of exposing services through URLs. Although this is certainly part of the REST experience, it is by no means the full story.

The major ideas grew out of the early web concepts, protocols, and technologies but were notably described in Roy Fielding's thesis, "Architectural Styles and the Design of Network-Based Software Architectures."[5]

The full name for the architectural style is Representational State Transfer (REST). What this refers to is the passing back and forth of a representation of the state associated with a resource. A resource is anything that can be named: a file, a concept, a person, or an organization. We identify resources through resource identifiers, more commonly known as uniform resource identifiers (URIs) or the more specialized uniform resource locators (URLs). Most people are familiar with web pages that they get to through a URL. They are unlikely, however, to stop to think about what is actually happening: they are identifying a resource and transferring a representation of it back for display in the browser. When all we do is a fetch a page, nothing is changed on the server by our request.

If you have ordered anything online, you have probably filled out a form and submitted it to the company's site. You have taken a representation of your order (specified in your browser) and transferred it to the server. If there is no such order yet, the server will create it. If you need to update your payment method, address, or quantity, you will send an update to the existing resource.

---

4. OK, I have a bias!
5. Although it is not generally my practice to recommend PhD theses to nonacademics, this is a very accessible document, and it really laid the foundation of this whole architectural style. You can find it at http://roy.gbiv.com/pubs/dissertation/top.htm.

What is really going on is that the REST style breaks up the service request into three parts:[6]

- Noun space
- Verb space
- Content space

Noun Space

The things to which we can refer are the nouns in the system. We have the freedom to pick whatever meaningful naming schemes are appropriate for our domain or organization. Examples of the nouns in systems like this might be as follows:

- http://localhost/employee/
- http://localhost/employee/012345
- http://localhost/account/
- http://localhost/account/standard/12345

You can think of each of these URIs as an information space to navigate. The first URI might be a reference to all employees, where the second one refers to a specific employee. The third URI might be all accounts, while the fourth URI refers to a specific account of a specific type. Note that at this point we are simply referring to things. The act of referring to something is distinct from the act of dereferencing it (identifying and transferring the content). The mapping of the request for a resource to the representation to be returned is handled by the container.

What constitutes a good URI for a resource is a larger discussion than we have time for right now, but you should take the time to design your noun space references up front. Get buy-in from your user community, and spend some cycles thinking about how resources might be organized in the future, how language choice (for example English or French) affects how resources are named, and so on. Try not to base your resource hierarchies on organizational structures that are likely to change (through company reorgs, new business priorities, and so on). Also, do not confuse the noun space with the verb space. Many people coming to REST from SOAP and other open-ended APIs tend to create URIs that look something like http://localhost/getemployee. The action of

---

6. The first place I saw this discussion made explicit was at RestWiki, the RESTafarian watering hole. See http://rest.blueoxen.net/cgi-bin/wiki.pl?RestTriangle.

getting an employee or a list of employees should be kept separate from how you organize your data. The verbs manipulate the nouns.

Verb Space

A key decision of the REST style is to employ a constrained set of semantically meaningful verbs. Both the RPC and Doc/Lit styles of SOAP messaging use open-ended semantics that require the message handling to understand the particulars. Although this is as you would expect it to be, it renders intermediary processors unable to make decisions without knowing how to process the messages in their entirety. This makes delegating caching and security checks through a network infrastructure an expensive and difficult process.

The REST verbs are usually thought to comprise GET, POST, PUT, and DELETE, but the real guidance is simply to use a small set of semantically meaningful actions upon the nouns (resources); you are free to add verbs if it makes sense to do so. One obvious consequence of minimizing the number of actions in a system is to keep it simple. In normal API development, this is referred to as keeping the surface area of the API small. Doing so makes it much easier for developers to learn, and they become productive more quickly.[7]

The meanings of the common verbs are as follows:

- *GET*: A consequence-free request to transfer the state from server to client. Because a GET cannot[8] have side effects, an intermediary processor that has a cached copy of the resource can make a decision about whether to ask for another copy or return its copy. From a security perspective, an intermediary processor might offer a wider latitude on access to an information resource if it knows you cannot modify it.
- *POST*: A creation or update request to transfer state from the client to the server. POSTs do not require the actual URI of the resource. You can POST to a processing engine like a servlet, which has the option of creating the resource. POSTs can also update a portion of a resource or append it (such as an address or phone number).

---

7. Jeff Bone, a RESTafarian high priest, has an interesting comment on this, relating the REST approach to the Unix approach to achieve simplicity and productivity: http://www.xent.com/pipermail/fork/Week-of-Mon-20040517/030341.html.
8. In reality, this should say *should not*, since you are free to develop pathological software; however, there is probably guidance against doing so somewhere.

- *PUT*: A creation or update request to transfer state from the client to the server. PUTs do require the URI of the resource. PUTs either create or update resources, but unlike POSTs, they represent an overwrite action.
- *DELETE*: A request to remove the resource from a server.

HTTP supports a few other verbs, but they are mostly constrained forms of GET (for example HEAD). Regardless, you are not required to stick to the HTTP verbs in your RESTful environment. They do provide a good starting point for considering the manipulation of arbitrary resources, though.

Content Space

The final separate dimension in REST concerns what is returned when a resource request is made. Interestingly, this is both a constrained interface and an open-ended interface. The data type is limited to a bytestream tagged with metadata, but this is a sufficient format to represent just about everything we do: XML, images, plain text, sound files, movies, and so on. This degree of freedom allows us to change what is returned as the result of a request either over time or in response to different contexts. Contrast this with a WSDL contract that specifies exactly what will come back (some form of XML or Base64-encoded blobs).[9]

My point is not that REST does not also require changes, but just that there are fewer moving parts and more flexibility. This freedom actually causes some people heartburn. For them, it is possible to add infrastructure to constrain a RESTful request to particular input and output schemas. However, if you do not want to return XML, you are free not to do so. It is certainly more pleasant to return PNG files as byte streams than as Base64-encoded blobs in XML.

Stateless Requests

The next major aspect of REST I will discuss is the stateless client-server request style. This might seem like a strange thing to design in, but the intent is to promote horizontal scalability. With all the parameters being passed in as part of the request, it is possible to simply

---

9. Supporting a different result type will usually involve a different WSDL file (which in turn requires code changes to objects generated from the WSDL). If you are careful about your WSDL schema definitions, you can sometimes avoid introducing incompatible changes.

add more web servers or other RESTful containers to respond to the request. Although SOAP does support a conversational style, the basic Doc/Lit exchange mechanism also supports stateless requests that can be handled by a horizontally scalable layer.

The difference is the presence of URIs and URLs in the REST style. When you combine the ability to name the resource, the request (with all of the parameters), and a semantically constrained idempotent (consequence-free) request such as GET, you can begin to see how a processing engine (or intermediary) might cache actual results.

Think about this for a second. When you are exposing arbitrary code (servlets, Spring beans, and so on) through RESTful APIs, it is now theoretically possible to avoid processing requests that have already been handled (for which you have cached results) when nothing else has changed on the back end. You will see how REST environments such as NetKernel support this mechanism in Section 6.7, *REST Environments*, on page 61. A SOAP-based system would have to reprocess the message. It might be able to return a cached result, but it cannot decide that until it has processed the request. This is one of the really exciting aspects of REST.

There is much more to REST that helps systems achieve the goals of scalability, flexibility, and "evolvability," but I hope you are beginning to see what it has to offer. Let's talk about a few more topics dealing with RESTful web services.

6.3 WS-Tenacity

If you ask the average enterprise or SOA architect to define web services, you will get an answer that sounds something like this: "loosely coupled, asynchronous services exposed in language- and platform-independent ways." If you ask them about REST, they will probably say this: "REST? No, we are doing web services here."

By that they probably mean the particular technologies of SOAP, WSDL, and UDDI. These are the industry standards for sending requests and describing services both contractually and through metadata. The fact that these specifications have been crafted and accepted by representatives of the community lends them both a real and a perceived importance.

The real importance has to do with industry momentum, the existence of tools, and the potential for interoperability. Organizations usually do not want to build tools that they can buy or download for free. And they usually do not want to feel like they are innovating in the middleware space. With its more successful PR campaign, SOAP et al have definitely gotten the attention of risk-averse decision makers. The crazy thing is that a lot of people think they are adopting a riskier long-term strategy.

The perceived importance is a more tenuous genuflection at the altar of industry titans; these folks are clearly smarter, wealthier, and have obviously thought about the problems more deeply than us, right? The problem is that this is not always the case (well, OK, they are probably wealthier than us). Additionally, vendors and clients do not always have the same goals. Enabling you to build a web services–based infrastructure using expensive tools, buses, environments, and so on, is part of their goal. Success, cost management, and ease of maintenance are probably what the clients want. Sometimes these goals align; sometimes they don't.

What this ends up meaning to you is that most of your struggles adopting RESTful web services are going to be political, not technical. This should not discourage you from considering them. Your life is the one most likely to improve through REST, not the people whose job it is (apparently) to say "no." Just understand that you should start to socialize these decisions across the organization long before you are planning to roll things out. You do not want to get shut down by some Napoleon in suspenders who has been made to fear "rogue web services." If it looks like choosing REST instead of SOAP is going to be a problem, considering planning to support both. See Section 6.9, *Supporting Both Styles*, on page 64 for why this might be a good idea anyway.

6.4 Complexity

When I consider web services, I do not think about implementation details; I think about architectural styles. I will agree with those random architects and settle on the notions of loose coupling, asynchronous invocations, and language and platform independence. I also think about service discovery, scalable infrastructures, security, data ownership, access policies, flexibility, maintainability, and evolvability. This mind-set suggests that before you even begin to think about the details, you already have some serious issues to consider. This represents the *real complexity* of web services, and there is not a whole lot you can do to simplify the landscape.

The factors you can control are the implementation details of how you build systems that satisfy these requirements. It is with this perspective that I first start to favor the REST style when it is appropriate. I get the feeling that the industry is nervously moving full throttle in the direction of the holy trinity without really stopping to consider the realities of rolling out systems that are this complex. Complexity of this form affects maintenance, security, evolvability, and scalability. I consider this to be a form of *artificial complexity*—complexity that makes a system harder than it needs to be. This complexity comes from the decontextualized requests, the open-ended APIs, the need to distribute complex message-handling processors, the need to specify even simple services with WSDL, and all of the layered cruft that falls out from this strategy. The designers of these technologies did not set out to make these issues unnecessarily complex; they simply tackled a really hard problem with too many degrees of freedom in some dimensions and not enough in others.

I can understand why nervous people find using WSDL to define contracts for large, publicly exposed services so appealing. Contracts set expectations and define what the terms of interaction will be. They take time to create, and they lock you into a single way of doing things for a while. Having to use WSDL for simple services, however, reminds me of Mitch Hedberg's[10] attitude about buying doughnuts.

Artificial Complexity and Doughnuts
by Mitch Hedberg, Comedian (R.I.P.)

I bought a doughnut, and they gave me a receipt for a doughnut. I don't need a receipt for a doughnut. I'll just give you the money; you give me the doughnut. End of transaction. We don't need to bring ink and paper into this. I just cannot imagine a scenario where I will have to prove I bought a doughnut. Some skeptical friend? "Don't even act like I didn't get that doughnut. I've got the documentation...right here. Oh, wait, it's back home in the file, under D...for doughnut."

If you are writing a simple service, there is often no need to involve WSDL, XML schemas, and so on. I will send you some simple arguments; you give me something back. End of transaction. This is heresy to those in the conventional web service camp as well as to the peo-

---

10. See http://www.mitchhedberg.net.

ple who think enforcing static types saves you from runtime errors. Although both WSDL and static typing might catch simple violations of structure and expectation, I think they provide a false sense of security while simultaneously impeding more rapid productivity and flexibility. The good news is that if enforcing this kind of content validation is important to you, you have that option in REST. If not, you are free not to do so.

This represents a facet of REST that is not necessarily obvious. As mentioned previously, one of its guiding principles is the *separation of concerns* in the noun, verb, and content dimensions. Identifying the thing you want to interact with is distinct from your attempts to interact with it. It is also separate from what is returned as a consequence of your interaction. The content that is returned from RESTful invocations is simply a bytestream tagged with metadata including the type of the content and when it was last modified. The client and the server can negotiate the particular forms of the content, or the client can choose how to display it; REST does not dictate what to do in this situation. This seems too loose of an interaction style for many folks, but it is really no different from the metadata-driven dynamic dispatch of languages such as Ruby.

If you do not define contracts in WSDL, how can you possibly explain what your services take or return? The answer to that question depends on the audience of the documentation. If you are talking about teaching developers how to use the software, then HTML and natural language (English, Japanese, French, and so on) seem like a reasonable approach. As you see in Figure 6.1, on the next page, this approach can simply be an explanation of how to use a service. The idea is that if you hit a root HTTP context without additional parameters, you might get a document describing what the service offers and how to invoke it.

The salient point here is that this style of web services does not *require* you to apply contracts to your services, but it does *allow* you to if you want to or you need the extra structure. There is no reason you could not create a query parameter that returns an XSD or RelaxNG schema describing the inputs and outputs of your service. Additionally, you are not stuck in time. The current version of the schema can come back by default, but you can add support for additional query parameters to specify that you want to invoke earlier versions of the same service. (Note: Adding query parameters is unlikely to give you the ability to call future versions of the service.)

Time Service

The *Time Service* illustrates the use of NetKernel scripting to provide a RESTful web service.

The following are supported requests:

Request	Description
.	Returns this page
timezonelist.html	Returns all supported time zone codes
timezonelist.xml	Returns all supported time zone codes
timezone/<time-zone>	Return the current time in the specified time zone.

Examples:

Request	Description
timezone/America/Phoenix	Returns time for Arizona
timezone/EST	Return the time for US Eastern Standard Time
timezone/US/Hawaii	Return the time for US Hawaii Time

If you enter an invalid timezone the service will default to GMT.

Version 1.0.67

Figure 6.1: DESCRIBING WEB SERVICES WITHOUT WSDL

6.5 REST and Security

One of the things that drives me absolutely crazy is when holy trinity purists make the claim that REST is not secure. If someone ever says this to you, you have permission to stop listening to them. In fact, you are encouraged to just walk away.

What I believe these folks mean is that REST does not have the same hefty collection of security APIs, formats, and so on, that the SOAP stack does. Would you believe an incomplete list of those technologies includes XML Encryption, XML Signature, XKMS, SAML, XACML, WS-Security, WS-Trust, and XrML? This position clearly mistakes security features for security. To trust that you have a secure system, you have to understand both the system and how the security features fit into it. In this scenario, complexity is a bane to security.[11]

11. Although it is still in a research stage, the W3C is working on a pretty cool way of establishing policies for specifying access to web resources called the Policy Aware Web. The W3C has working prototypes that could be adapted for use by browsers and various client-side APIs. For more information, check out http://www.policyawareweb.org.

Part of the problem with the SOAP security stack is that you pass a message from one context to another, perhaps through intermediary processing steps. At this point, you have to bend over backward to keep your faith in the integrity of the request. By potentially decontextualizing the message from the request context, the message must have credentials and other security pixie dust sprinkled into it. You need to validate that the message has not been altered and that it originates from the source from which you expect it.

When you keep a REST message in the context of the request, you can rely on the transport to be responsible for authentication and keep the message unencumbered by this cruft. This is a big part of what keeps REST simpler in secure environments. You can leverage existing technologies such as HTTP Basic Auth or bidirectional SSL to authenticate the client. In the event that you need to cross container or process boundaries as part of handling your REST request, you can always pass on the credentials. Many enterprise single sign-on (SSO) systems work this way by associating temporary tokens with authenticated sessions. What works for web applications works for REST-oriented web services. A key distinction here, though, is that you are keeping the message in the context of the request. Once you start crossing boundaries and going beyond point-to-point, REST will have similar complexity issues, and you will have to look beyond SSL as a means of protecting the payload.

6.6 REST and Metadata

Although I do not want to spend much time going into it, I do want to point out that not only do REST web services not need UDDI, but they are quite capable of thriving in its absence. Existing metadata standards such as the Resource Description Framework (RDF) provide exactly the capabilities needed.[12] Although RDF data can be every bit as complicated as UDDI, it offers a richer, more open-ended data model for attaching metadata to services. Even better, RDF is designed to relate objects to URI-addressable resources through whatever predicate you like. As a monotonic,[13] open world system, RDF allows you to create

---

12. See http://www.w3.org/RDF/.
13. This just means that facts about entities can be added over time. It is not a closed world like in a system such as Prolog. See http://en.wikipedia.org/wiki/Monotonicity_of_entailment.

new vocabularies and associate them with your service whenever you like. You could start off indicating the author of a service, her email address, her department, and when it was published. Then, six months from now, you could add version information and your favorite color if you wanted. This would be a silly trait in the business world, yes, but it indicates that you can extend the model basically whenever and however you want.

The question then becomes how to find services with this metadata. Fortunately, we have standard RDF query languages such as SPARQL[14] and efficient means of storing and retrieving RDF such as Mulgara[15] and Sesame.[16] Even Oracle has gotten in the game with 10g Release 2. If you think this is a crazy way to handle metadata for services, you might stop to ponder why WebMethods recently purchased Cerebra, a company known for its ability to do semantically powerful queries over RDF-based metadata.

The following is a sample RDF snippet demonstrating how open-ended the data model is. It shows several statements (serialized here as RDF/XML) describing a service exposed at http://localhost/employee. The first three predicates are from the Dublin Core[17] vocabulary for describing resources. They indicate who created the service, when it was created, and give a simple description of its purpose. The other predicates are from notional vocabularies describing company department metadata and the locations for input and output schemas for the service.

`code/sletten/metadata.rdf`

```
<rdf:RDF xmlns:rdf="http://www.w3.org/1999/02/22-rdf-syntax-ns#"
    xmlns:dc="http://purl.org/dc/elements/1.1#"
    xmlns:dept="http://www.bosatsu.net/vocab/dept#"
    xmlns:contract="http://www.bosatsu.net/vocab/contract#">
 <rdf:Description rdf:about="http://localhost/employee">
    <dc:creator>Brian Sletten</dc:creator>
    <dc:date>2006-12-02T06:42</dc:date>
    <dc:description>An employee navigation service.</dc:description>
    <dept:name>Human Resources</dept:name>
    <contract:inputSchema rdf:resource="http://localhost/schemas/employee-in.rng"/>
    <contract:outputSchema rdf:resource="http://localhost/schemas/employee-out.rng"
 </rdf:Description>
</rdf:RDF>
```

---

14. See http://www.w3.org/TR/rdf-sparql-query/.

15. See http://ww.mulgara.org.

16. See http://www.openrdf.org.

17. See http://www.dublincore.org/.

subject	predicate	object
http://localhost/employee	http://purl.org/dc/elements/1.1#creator	"Brian Sletten"
http://localhost/employee	http://purl.org/dc/elements/1.1#date	"2006-12-02T06:42"
http://localhost/employee	http://purl.org/dc/elements/1.1#description	"An employee navigation service."
http://localhost/employee	http://www.bosatsu.net/vocab/dept#name	"Human Resources"
http://localhost/employee	http://www.bosatsu.net/vocab/contract#inputSchema	"http://localhost/schemas/employee-in.rng"
http://localhost/employee	http://www.bosatsu.net/vocab/contract#outputSchema	"http://localhost/schemas/employee-out.rng"

Figure 6.2: WEB SERVICES METADATA TRIPLES

When explored through something like Mulgara's web viewer (shown in Figure 6.2), it becomes easier to see the particular triples expressed as Subject, Predicate, and Object.

The nice feature of the RDF model is that you can always add new metadata about a service in your RDF database. You do not need to migrate database schemas associated with these services or anything; you simply accumulate extra information. You can create your own vocabularies or adopt some from others. You can imagine querying an RDF source for this metadata to find web services based on particular properties, values, or relationships. Although you would express it in an RDF query language such as SPARQL, in English you would be asking something like "Please give me the URL for any web service written by Brian Sletten for the human resources department in the past six months."

6.7 REST Environments

It should be pretty obvious by now that simply exposing web services calls through REST APIs is not likely to give you the full scalability benefits of REST. Such an approach will facilitate simple, lightweight services in language- and platform-independent ways, but it represents a shallow notion of REST. The URL maps to a servlet that uses some objects that perhaps talk to a database through a connection pool, and so on. The issue is that you are mapping resources to code to code to code to code to data. Nothing is tying things together coherently, and no common shared abstractions exist.

Simpler REST APIs such as Restlet[18] are designed to take you in the direction of a REST-oriented architecture. They allow you to break the direct tie between REST invocations and the servlet API that is bound to a blocking IO model. Newer containers such as Jetty 6[19] and Asyncweb[20] are being built around the Java NIO libraries, which allow for more scalable request handling. Even if you are not ready to switch your container, the Restlet API can be a great playground for prototyping a REST API without the burdens of a container. Once you and your clients agree on a particular API, you can implement the particulars in your regular container. The following example shows a (very) simple REST server developed with Restlet:

`code/sletten/SimpleServer.java`

```java
import org.restlet.*;
import org.restlet.data.*;

public class SimpleServer {
    public static void main( String [] args ) throws Exception {
        Restlet restlet = new Restlet()
        {
            public void handle(Request request, Response response)
            {
                response.setEntity("Hello, REST!", MediaType.TEXT_PLAIN);
            }
        };

        new Server(Protocol.HTTP, 8183, restlet).start();
    }
}
```

This example shows a simple client:

`code/sletten/SimpleClient.java`

```java
import org.restlet.Client;
import org.restlet.data.Protocol;

public class SimpleClient {
  public static void main( String [] args ) throws Exception {
    Client client = new Client(Protocol.HTTP);
    client.get("http://localhost:8183").getEntity().write(System.out);
  }
}
```

---

18. See http://www.restlet.org.
19. See http://jetty.mortbay.org.
20. See http://asyncweb.safehaus.org.

Obviously these are trivial and useless examples, but it gives you a sense of how you can start with an absolutely simple base and then layer on complexity as needed.

Deeper REST architectures depend on infrastructures that are more closely aligned with the principles of REST. NetKernel[21] is an example of this kind of an environment. Here, everything is URI addressable, so you have a common information structure independent of the resource being referenced. The flattened information space allows orchestration between your services, other services (SOAP, RMI, REST, socket), relational database queries, script execution, XML queries...you name it. Additionally, the stateless requests are handled efficiently by a micro-kernel-based architecture. Where possible, results are managed in a cache regardless of whether they are a database call, are a style sheet transformation, or are calculating pi to 10,000 digits. An environment built upon REST can determine whether it needs to execute a request based on the state passed in as part of the request. Some languages support this feature through a technique called *memoization*. The beautiful thing about RESTful software such as NetKernel is that they bake it into the architectural layer for free; there is no need to plan for it. All of these factors add up to a highly productive environment that makes it possible (if not downright easy) to create software systems that scale linearly. A system like this is also first in line for taking advantage of the new multicore CPUs being marketed by the major processor vendors.[22]

6.8 Where REST Does Not Fit As Well

It is always important for a technology advocate to highlight the limitations of the technology he is promoting. Anyone who refuses to do so is probably trying to get you to buy something, even if it is just their opinion.

There are not many places where individual web services cannot be successfully deployed as REST web services. At this level, it becomes a matter of packaging a request via a particular implementation and

---

21. See http://www.1060.org.

22. As we were wrapping up the edits for this book, I read a blog entry that I thought summarizes nicely why deep REST environments such as NetKernel are so interesting. As a web-oriented architecture (WOA), it already solves many of the problems people are identifying as needing to be solved for more conventional SOA web service environments: http://www.1060.org/blogxter/entry?publicid=80D8BDC43441FBA6165F11DE48ADE7C8.

gathering the results. In that context, simpler and more flexible seem like better options. You can reuse existing security tools and keep your complexity levels down.

The place where message-oriented SOAP is probably a more suitable answer is in transactional processes that span multiple execution contexts. Imagine that a request from a customer enters an order-processing system and gets transferred to an inventory system and then an accounting system as part of the same flow. In this case, the request moves from one application to another, accumulating state but maintaining the transactional identity for rollback purposes.

These sorts of systems are not impossible to build using REST web services, but they are a slightly less natural fit. It therefore might justify the added complexity of the secured, decontextualized SOAP message packing up its credentials and hitting the road. Ultimately, deep REST environments mixed with conventional message-oriented middleware (MOM) are likely to be just as successful and probably simpler to maintain. In the current landscape, however, SOAP-based tools and environments have a better story to tell.

6.9 Supporting Both Styles

Although the thought of supporting multiple interfaces to a system probably sends most development managers screaming, it is also not unthinkable to export both styles of web services. The benefit of this approach (besides allowing the developers to pick the interfaces that make sense to them)[23] is that you might push your request-handling code into a more generic mechanism such as the *Command pattern*. This pattern encapsulates a request into an object without any special knowledge of what invokes it. In this scenario, REST vs. SOAP becomes a question of routing requests to a command processor. This opens you up to being able to support the next overhyped distributed technology before it is even conceived.

---

23. Amazon famously rolled out both REST- and SOAP-oriented web service interfaces to its business processes. According to Amazon, the development community spoke loudly and clearly by selecting the REST versions 80%–90% of the time.

6.10 Conclusion

Despite its simplicity, REST has a lot to offer. It is certainly not *the* answer for all web services, but it is an awfully good answer for more situations than you might have initially realized. By taking advantage of the work that has gone into defining the core web standards, you can build simple, flexible, and scalable systems with much less complexity than with SOAP and WSDL.

Through the particular design goals of separating the different spaces (noun, verb, content), promoting stateless interactions, and semantically constraining the actions you use, you create an opportunity to move toward the vision of freedom, interoperability, and reusable services in both today's and tomorrow's network infrastructures. These are the same goals attached to what most architects mean by web services. Perhaps in the not too distant future, asking these folks about REST might get a response of "Yeah, we do web services here."

Here's hoping that REST reaches that kind of acceptance level in the enterprise. Until then, remember Hans Christian Andersen's story, because it has instructive power beyond some of the lunacy with web services. As representatives of our industry, we must have the awareness and confidence to point out when our emperor is wearing clothes and when he is just making us all look foolish. Pick technologies that work for you, and keep it as simple as you can, but no simpler.

6.11 Web Resources

Shirky's discussion. . .
. . . http://webservices.xml.com/pub/a/ws/2001/10/03/webservices.html
Clay Shirky's discussion about web services

Roy Fielding's discussion . . . . http://roy.gbiv.com/pubs/dissertation/top.htm
Roy Fielding's discussion defining REST

The RESTafarian watering hole. . .
. . . http://rest.blueoxen.net/cgi-bin/wiki.pl?RestTriangle
Discussion about the REST style breaking up the service request into three parts

Jeff Bone's discussion. . .

. . . http://www.xent.com/pipermail/fork/Week-of-Mon-20040517/030341.html

RESTafarian high priest Jeff Bone's interesting comment on relating the REST approach to the Unix approach to achieve simplicity and productivity

Artificial complexity and doughnuts. . . . . http://www.mitchhedberg.net

Mitch Hedberg's dead-on comedy routine about artificial complexity and doughnuts

Policy Aware Web . . . . http://www.policyawareweb.org

W3C's description of a way of establishing policies for specifying access to web resources

RDF specification http://www.w3.org/RDF/

Resource Description Framework (RDF) specification

SPARQL http://www.w3.org/TR/rdf-sparql-query/

Standard RDF query language

*I don't think anybody tests enough of anything. But that's
sort of a truism.*
  ▶ James Gosling

Chapter 7

Guerilla Testing with Cobertura, TestNG, and EasyMock

by Howard Lewis Ship

Howard is an independent consultant and trainer, specializing in Apache Tapestry, the open source Java web application framework he created. Howard lives in Portland, Oregon, with his wife, Suzanne, a novelist. Howard hopes that someday, somehow, he can explain to his Mom what he does for a living.

7.1 Introduction

Ask a crowd of developers "Is it good to test your code?" and you'll be hard-pressed to find anyone who'll say no. Follow up with the question "Do you test your code?" and you'll see something startling but not unexpected. Most of those same developers will sheepishly admit that they don't test their code or, at least, don't test it in any meaningful, helpful way.

Why not? Testing is universally accepted as a *best practice*. It's a hallmark of professionalism. You'll be asked in job interviews "Are you test-driven?" and you'll say "Yes!" because answering anything else is foolish. Despite all that, there's still the riddle of the developers who don't, or can't, test their code. Perhaps our industry is filled with adrenaline junkies who relish the uncertainty and challenge of deploying a major application and *not knowing whether it actually works*.

Obviously not. What's really going on is that testing is *too hard*. There are just too many obstacles to doing testing, and it's too easy to come up with excuses such as "I can't test *my* code, because I'm waiting for Fred's code" or "I don't have time to test; I have to make my deadline!"

I've been test-driven for nearly twenty years, first in PL/1, then Objective-C, and now Java. I've been refactoring code long before I knew the term (our team used to call it *Howardizing*). I've long found that reworking code to make it testable results in just plain better code, regardless of the testing angle. I'm not talking about any silver bullets here, just what it takes to tackle ugly, untestable code and turn it into working, tested, reliable code.

This chapter will introduce you to basic Java testing tools that should be in everyone's toolkit. Better yet, they are all open source!

7.2 Testing and Measurement

When the question "What do I test?" arises, the flip response is "Why, everything, of course," but the reality is you will need to prioritize your efforts, and you need a way to check that the tests you write actually test the code you think they do.

Here, a code coverage report is your friend. Code coverage tools will track the execution of your code by your tests and identify exactly which lines of code have been executed and which have not. Unexecuted lines should raise a red flag. If it's just a getter or setter method, you can let

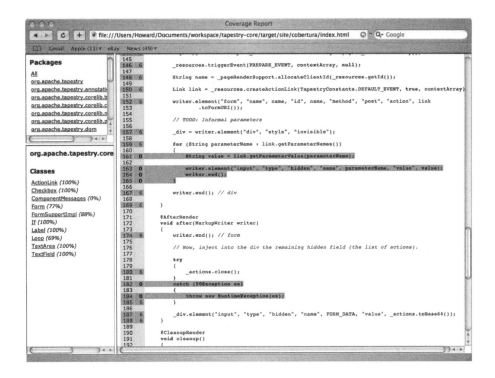

Figure 7.1: COBERTURA CLASS COVERAGE REPORT

it slide. . . but if it's the core pathway through your pricing engine, you want to make sure every line is tested.

If you aren't already using a code coverage tool, a great place to start is Cobertura. Cobertura (Portuguese for "Coverage") is a freely available open source project. It works by instrumenting your production code to record execution data. . . which lines have been executed and how often. You then run your tests using the instrumented code to collect coverage data and generate an HTML coverage report.

Figure 7.1, shows a report for a single class. The source code is reproduced, with lines that have executed appearing with green execution counts (on the left) and unexecuted lines highlighted in red. Cobertura also gives you a broader view of your entire code base. You'll see the code coverage percentages at the package level, with a roll-up of all packages. In addition to line coverage, this report also shows *branch coverage*, which tells you which branches have fully executed. This refers primarily to the if statement, which must evaluate both ways, true and false, to be fully counted.

> ### Using Cobertura with Ant
>
> Of course, you can use Cobertura with Ant as well. It's relatively easy to integrate, though not as easy as with Maven. The full documentation is available at the Cobertura home page at http://cobertura.sourceforge.net/.

If you are using Maven, then it's exceptionally easy to integrate Cobertura directly into your build process. Start by adding (if not already present) a reporting element to your pom.xml, and then add a plugin element to integrate the Cobertura report:

`code/hls/tapestry-ioc-pom.xml`

```
<reporting>
    <plugins>
        <plugin>
            <groupId>org.codehaus.mojo</groupId>
            <artifactId>cobertura-maven-plugin</artifactId>
            <version>2.0</version>
        </plugin>
    </plugins>
</reporting>
```

As of this writing, the 2.1-SNAPSHOT version isn't quite ready for primetime, though it is based on the 1.8 version of Cobertura, which generates a slightly more useful report. The 2.0 version gets the job done.[1]

With all this in place, getting the report is easy. Just execute mvn site. The Cobertura plug-in hooks into the overall build process; your compiled classes will automatically be instrumented (into a new folder under target), and your tests will be rerun against the instrumented classes. The coverage report, showing which lines of your production code have actually executed, are generated and integrated into your Maven project site (under the Project Reports menu).

---

1. However, it's not without its own quirks. By default, the 2.0 version of the plug-in places the cobertura.ser file, the file in which line execution data is collected, right in your project directory (not where it belongs, under target). Not only must you be careful to not accidentally check this file into source code control, but you have to remember to delete it manually before building your site (something mvn clean should do but doesn't).

Joe Asks. . .

Why Isn't This Integrated into the IDE?

It seems like a bit of extra trouble to have to drop down to the command line and use Maven to generate the report and then read it as HTML. Shouldn't a modern IDE just show this to me? Some tools do support this, such as Clover, a proprietary (nonfree) code coverage tool from Cenqua (http://www.cenqua.com/clover/). Clover includes a plug-in for Eclipse that shows code coverage information as annotations. . . green and red flags in the gutter for each line of code.

Whether you use Cobertura or any other code coverage tool, tracking code coverage should be part of your regular development process. You should know the current code coverage numbers when you check out your code, and you should watch out for check-ins that lower the code coverage percentage; code coverage should go in only one direction: up.

Returning to the initial question—"What do I test?"—how do you know when enough is enough? Where's the point of diminishing returns? My *anecdotal* experience is that you need to reach at least 85% overall code coverage. This has always been my transition point; whenever I've raised code coverage to more than 85%, I've found bugs—often, blatantly obvious bugs. Certainly, you need some flexibility here; writing tests that exercise simple accessor methods (with no side effects) is not a very good use of time (even if it keeps you from hitting 85%). On the other hand, stopping at 85% without testing every line and every variation for your most important code does not help you gain confidence that your application works.

Some code just isn't going to be reachable, even inside your unit tests. For example:

`code/hls/runtime-exception.java`

```java
try
{
  stream.close();
}
catch (IOException ex)
{
  throw new RuntimeException(ex);
}
```

If the stream is for a local file, you'll be hard-pressed to get this code to throw IOException from close(), even though that's part of the method signature. Since you should never just swallow an exception, softening it to a RuntimeException is a reasonable default behavior; however, if you never get that line of code to execute, it's nothing to lose sleep over. Be pragmatic.

Cobertura has a lot more to offer; for example, you can set minimum values for line coverage and branch coverage, and it will cause build failures when those goals are not reached (I'd consider that *the stick*). Alternately, Cobertura can generate an XML, not an HTML, report that can be parsed by other tools. This allows you to create your own format reports or have a continuous integration build send praise mail whenever a check-in improves overall code coverage (that would be *the carrot*).

Code coverage tools give you an idea of where you are and where you're headed, but beyond that, they don't contribute to testing. In the next section, I'll start discussing the best tools for getting your code actually tested.

7.3 TestNG: Testing, the Next Generation

For years, *unit testing* was synonymous with a particular framework, JUnit. This was a good thing, because all those articles and example code helped people make the leap into *test-driven development*. On the other hand, JUnit has its share of problems:

- *Test cases*, the Java classes that contain test methods, had to extend from base classes provided by JUnit.

- There was no control over the *order* in which tests were run.

- JUnit gives you no easy way to run just a subset of your tests, say your fast unit tests vs. your long, slow-running integration tests.

A lesser known testing framework is TestNG, created by Cédric Beust and Alexandru Popescu. TestNG is a *complete* testing solution for Java; it isn't limited to very pure unit testing, the way JUnit is. TestNG gives you control over when and if each individual test is executed. It allows you to categorize your tests and run only the ones that are appropriate. It gives you far more hooks and callbacks, allowing you to perform environmental setup and cleanup around groups of tests, rather than around individual tests.

TestNG works with either JDK 1.4 or JDK 1.5 (and newer). Plug-ins for Eclipse, NetBeans, and IntelliJ are available. Easy integration with Ant and Maven is also provided.

TestNG Basics

So, you've written a little bit of code for your new project and you want to test it before continuing (this indicates that you are *test-driven* rather than *test-first*).

A standard practice, one enforced by Maven, is to place all your test-only code in a separate source code directory. So if you are placing your *production code*, the code that will eventually be packaged and deployed as your application, in src/main/java, you will place your test cases and related code into src/test/java.

You should name your test case the same as the Java class it exists to test, with a Test suffix. The test case class should go in the same Java package as the production class it tests, just under the src/test/java source root. These two conventions are useful and important. Using the same package and the same name (with a suffix) makes it easy to locate the test case for a production class. In fact, Eclipse will often display them adjacently when browsing. Further, it is sometimes effective to change certain fields or methods from **private** to package private, just so that they can be accessed by the test methods.[2]

So, how do you build a test case class? Let's start by considering the base class from which to extend. Technically, TestNG does not require you to extend from any particular base class. However, just as with JUnit, you'll be invoking various assertXXX() methods. The path of least resistance is to extend from org.testng.Assert, the class that defines all these static methods. Doing so will save you the trouble of adding a bunch of static imports.

Let's switch to a more concrete example from the Tapestry 5 code base. The internal utility class IntegerRange represents a sequence of integer values (it can be used with Tapestry's Loop component). The key

---

2. There is a point of view that any class that cannot be tested entirely through its public API is broken and should be refactored into two or more classes that would allow such testing. I'm not certain that's either true or pragmatic. I rarely resort to this trick, but I like to keep the option to use it open.

method is Iterator(), which returns an Iterator<Integer> for the sequence of values defined by the range.[3]

`code/hls/IntegerRange.java`

```java
package org.apache.tapestry.internal.util;

import java.util.Iterator;

/**
 * Represents a sequence of integer values, either ascending or descending.
 * The sequence is always inclusive (of the finish value).
 */
public final class IntegerRange implements Iterable<Integer>
{
    private final int _start;
    private final int _finish;

    private class RangeIterator implements Iterator<Integer>
    {
        private final int _increment;
        private int _value = _start;
        private boolean _hasNext = true;

        RangeIterator()
        {
            _increment = _start < _finish ? +1 : -1;
        }

        public boolean hasNext()
        {
            return _hasNext;
        }

        public Integer next()
        {
            if (!_hasNext)
                throw new IllegalStateException();

            int result = _value;

            _hasNext = _value != _finish;

                        _value += _increment;

                        return result;
        }
```

---

3. The code listing here (IntegerRange.java) and below (IntegerRangeTest.java and Type-CoercerImplTest.java) are Copyright 2006, The Apache Software Foundation. A complete copyright notice is included in the downloadable code.

```java
    public void remove()
    {
        throw new UnsupportedOperationException();
    }
}

public IntegerRange(final int start, final int finish)
{
    _start = start;

    _finish = finish;
}

public int getFinish()
{
    return _finish;
}

public int getStart()
{
    return _start;
}

@Override
public String toString()
{
    return String.format("%d..%d", _start, _finish);
}

/**
 * The main puprose of a range object is to produce an Iterator. Since
 * IntegerRange is iterable, it is useful with the Tapestry Loop
 * component, but also with the Java for loop!
 */
public Iterator<Integer> iterator()
{
    return new RangeIterator();
}

@Override
public int hashCode()
{
    final int PRIME = 31;

    int result = PRIME + _finish;

    result = PRIME * result + _start;

    return result;
}
```

```java
/**
 * Returns true if the other object is an IntegerRange with the same
 * start and finish values.
 */
@Override
public boolean equals(Object obj)
{
    if (this == obj)
        return true;
    if (obj == null)
        return false;
    if (getClass() != obj.getClass())
        return false;
    final IntegerRange other = (IntegerRange) obj;
    if (_finish != other._finish)
        return false;
    if (_start != other._start)
        return false;
    return true;
}

}
```

The following code shows the test case for IntegerRange (the listing is abbreviated to just the first test method, start_less_than_finish()). This method is a test method because it is public and is annotated with the @Test annotation. Before you JDK 1.4 users start to panic...JDK 1.4 is supported by using XDoclet-style comments instead of JDK 1.5 annotations. This is all discussed in the TestNG documentation, but for simplicity, I'll stick to JDK 1.5 examples.

code/hls/IntegerRangeTest.java

```java
package org.apache.tapestry.internal.util;

import java.util.Iterator;

import org.testng.Assert;
import org.testng.annotations.Test;

public class IntegerRangeTest extends Assert
{
    @Test
    public void start_less_than_finish()
    {
        IntegerRange r = new IntegerRange(1, 3);

        assertEquals(r.toString(), "1..3");

        assertEquals(r.getStart(), 1);
```

```
        assertEquals(r.getFinish(), 3);

        Iterator<Integer> i = r.iterator();

        assertEquals(i.next().intValue(), 1);
        assertEquals(i.next().intValue(), 2);

        assertTrue(i.hasNext());

        assertEquals(i.next().intValue(), 3);

        assertFalse(i.hasNext());

        try
        {
            i.next();
            unreachable();
        }
        catch (IllegalStateException ex)
        {
        }
    }
    private final void unreachable()
    {
        throw new AssertionError("This code should be unreachable.");
    }
}
```

If you are used to JUnit, this method will look familiar, with a few
oddities. I created a new IntegerRange and put it through its paces,
checking that it returns the correct values. The assertXXX() methods
are similar to those in JUnit *except that the parameters are reversed!*
In JUnit, you will pass the expected value (usually a constant) as the
first parameter and the actual value (usually an expression) as the second parameter. TestNG passes the actual value first, with the expected
value second.[4] This ordering makes a lot of sense because the focus of
the assert call is on the first part, the actual value. Also, code format-
ters do a better job when the long part of a statement is early. Still, this
switch around can be painful, especially when moving back and forth
between TestNG tests and JUnit tests. Nothing mandates that you use
TestNG's Assert; however, you can continue to use TestNG with JUnit's
junit.framework.Assert class instead.

---

4. If you include the message parameter in your assertions, it goes first in JUnit and last
in TestNG. However, I've found that the value of the message parameter is very low in
most circumstances. Generally, a failure identifying the two values and a stack trace is
enough description of what went wrong.

\\// Joe Asks. . .

What's with the Underscores in the Method Names?

The odd Java naming is *not* part of TestNG: it's a suggestion by Neal Ford. Neal realized that these method names often appear in reports generated by TestNG or by Maven and that the underscore style of naming is much more readable in those reports than the camelCase equivalent (take a peek at Figure 7.2, on the facing page, for an example). For whatever reason, I've found that when using underscore-style names for my test methods, I end up writing much longer, more descriptive names than I did in the past.

I now have production code to test and a test case for that code, and it's time to run that test case. Using the Eclipse TestNG plug-in, all that is necessary is to right-click inside the source code and choose the menu item TestNG –> Run As Test. TestNG will run the methods inside the test case and show you the results. The TestNG view appears in Figure 7.2, on the next page.

Getting a single test to execute is useful, but in the next section, I'll cover executing entire suites of tests, both inside Eclipse and from the command line, using Maven.

Integrating TestNG with Maven

Running individual tests inside the IDE is useful enough, but you'll want to easily run *all* your tests inside the IDE and run the *same* set of tests as part of your command-line build.

Using TestNG in your project involves adding more plug-ins to your pom.xml (Figure 7.3, on page 80) and creating a testng.xml control file for TestNG.

The testng.xml file identifies which packages to scan for test case classes. Figure 7.4, on page 81, shows the TestNG control file for the core module of Tapestry 5. A TestNG control file defines a *suite* that might contain one or more *tests*. Each test consists of test case classes identified within specific packages. For the most part, grouping test cases into tests and suites simply affects the generated reports, but as you'll see

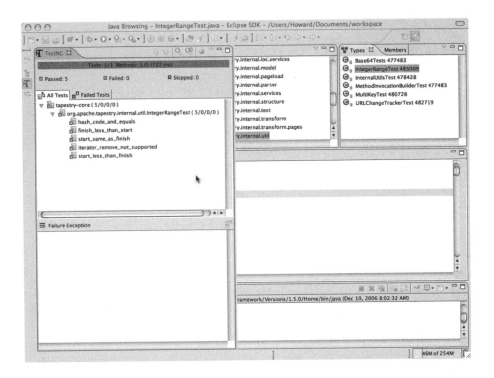

Figure 7.2: TestNG Eclipse view

in a bit, it might also affect the order in which test execution and configuration occurs.

The parallel= attribute allows tests to run in parallel, driven by a pool of worker threads. This can shave quite a bit of time off of tests, especially if you have a multicore processor or tests that will be IO bound (for example, if they access a database). Alas, I've had mixed results with TestNG when parallel execution is enabled; often a small number of tests are mysteriously skipped, so I leave parallel= with its default value *false*.

Strangely, despite that you select the JDK 1.5 version of the TestNG JAR inside the POM (Figure 7.3, on the following page), you must still alert TestNG that you are using JDK 1.5 annotations. Finally, the verbose= attribute controls how much debugging output TestNG generates as it executes (higher values, up to 10, enable more output).

```
code/hls/tapestry-ioc-pom.xml
```

```xml
<dependencies>
    <dependency>
        <groupId>org.testng</groupId>
        <artifactId>testng</artifactId>
        <version>5.1</version>
        <classifier>jdk15</classifier>
        <scope>test</scope>
    </dependency>
</dependencies>
<build>
    <plugins>
        <plugin>
            <groupId>org.apache.maven.plugins</groupId>
            <artifactId>maven-surefire-plugin</artifactId>
            <configuration>
                <suiteXmlFiles>
                    <suiteXmlFile>src/test/conf/testng.xml</suiteXmlFile>
                </suiteXmlFiles>
            </configuration>
        </plugin>
    </plugins>
</build>
```

hls/tapestry-ioc-pom.xml

Figure 7.3: POM ADDITIONS FOR TESTNG

You can use the same TestNG control file to execute tests in Eclipse. Using the Run As menu, you can create a new TestNG run configuration linked to your testng.xml control file.

Test Configuration

TestNG uses the term *configuration* to describe code that is executed before or after tests in order to set them up or tear them down. This is an area where TestNG clearly differentiates itself from JUnit.

JUnit is a world of pure unit tests—tests that truly and completely are independent of each other. True unit tests can be run in any order, or in parallel, with the same outcome, because there are no (and can be no) dependencies of one test on another. In JUnit, individual tests might provide setup or teardown logic by implementing the setUp() or tear-Down() methods. These methods are invoked before *each* test method of a test case is invoked. Further, each test method is invoked on a *new instance* of the test case class.

```
code/hls/testng.xml
```

```xml
<!DOCTYPE suite SYSTEM "http://testng.org/testng-1.0.dtd">
<suite name="Tapestry Core" parallel="false" annotations="1.5" verbose="2">
  <test name="Tapestry Core">
    <packages>
      <package name="org.apache.tapestry.integration"/>
      <package name="org.apache.tapestry"/>
      <package name="org.apache.tapestry.dom"/>
      <package name="org.apache.internal"/>
      <package name="org.apache.tapestry.internal.aspects"/>
      <package name="org.apache.tapestry.internal.services"/>
      <package name="org.apache.tapestry.internal.structure"/>
      <package name="org.apache.tapestry.internal.util"/>
      <package name="org.apache.tapestry.services"/>
      <package name="org.apache.tapestry.util"/>
      <package name="org.apache.tapestry.runtime"/>
      <package name="org.apache.tapestry.internal.bindings"/>
      <package name="org.apache.tapestry.internal.model"/>
    </packages>
  </test>
</suite>
```

hls/testng.xml

Figure 7.4: TestNG control file

In developing real frameworks and applications, this rigidity becomes unbearable. In some cases, external resources (most often, a database) are involved in testing. Deleting and reloading this database for every individual test is simply not practical. What's desired is the ability to perform setup and teardown across a number of related tests and to share some of the external resources (such as the database). TestNG supports this; a test case might contain configuration methods (marked by one of several annotations). These configuration methods exist to perform setup or teardown. Methods annotated with @BeforeMethod or @AfterMethod are roughly analogous to JUnit's methods. More useful and common are @BeforeClass and @AfterClass, which are invoked before or after all test methods of a class. Since test case classes are instantiated just once, these configuration methods can store common resources inside instance variables for use by the individual test methods.

A good example of this appears in the Tapestry code. In addition to unit testing individual classes, Tapestry performs a reasonable amount of integration testing to sanity check that the various classes are being combined properly. To do this, the test suite starts up an instance of Jetty running a sample Tapestry application and uses two parts of the Selenium tool: a Selenium server that runs the Selenium scripts inside an automatically launched browser and a Selenium client that uses the Selenium server to run through the Tapestry application and verify the results.

Fortunately, all these bits and pieces can coexist within the same process. It's all combined inside IntegrationTests, which uses configuration methods to start Jetty and Selenium only once, for all of the individual test methods. The code below shows the setup and cleanup code, along with one test method, app1_basic_output(), and a couple of supporting methods.

code/hls/IntegrationTests.java

```java
package org.apache.tapestry.integration;

import org.openqa.selenium.server.SeleniumServer;
import org.testng.Assert;
import org.testng.annotations.AfterClass;
import org.testng.annotations.BeforeClass;
import org.testng.annotations.Test;

import com.thoughtworks.selenium.DefaultSelenium;
import com.thoughtworks.selenium.Selenium;


@Test(timeOut = 50000, sequential = true, groups =
{ "integration" })
public class IntegrationTests extends Assert
{
    private static final int JETTY_PORT = 9999;

    private static final String BASE_URL =
            String.format("http://localhost:%d/", JETTY_PORT);

    /** 60 seconds */
    public static final String PAGE_LOAD_TIMEOUT = "600000";

    private Selenium _selenium;

    private SeleniumServer _server;

    private JettyRunner _jettyRunner;
```

```java
@BeforeClass
public void startup() throws Exception
{
    _jettyRunner = new JettyRunner("/", JETTY_PORT, "src/test/app1");

    _server = new SeleniumServer();

    _server.start();

    _selenium = new DefaultSelenium("localhost", SeleniumServer.DEFAULT_PORT,
            "*firefox", BASE_URL);

    _selenium.start();
}

@AfterClass
public void cleanup() throws Exception
{
    _selenium.stop();

    _selenium = null;

    _server.stop();
    _server = null;

    _jettyRunner.stop();
    _jettyRunner = null;
}

@Test
public void app1_basic_output() throws Exception
{
    _selenium.open(BASE_URL);

    clickAndWait("link=Start Page");

    // This comes from the Border cmponent's template

    assertTrue(_selenium.getTitle().contains("Tapestry"));

    // Text from Start.html

    assertTextPresent("First Tapestry 5 Page");

    // This is text passed from Start.html to Output as a parameter

    assertTextPresent("we have basic parameters working");
}
```

```
    private void clickAndWait(String link)
    {
        _selenium.click(link);
        _selenium.waitForPageToLoad(PAGE_LOAD_TIMEOUT);
    }

    private void assertTextPresent(String text)
    {
        if (_selenium.isTextPresent(text))
            return;

        System.err.printf("Text pattern '%s' not found in:\n%s\n\n",
                text, _selenium.getHtmlSource());

        throw new AssertionError("Page did not contain '" + text + "'.");
    }
}
```

This listing also demonstrates some other ideas incorporated into TestNG. The @Test annotation is allowed at the class level, as well as at the method level. This allows defaults for the test methods to be set, such as setting the timeout for any individual test to be fifty seconds. Further, you can enforce that the methods in the test case are executed sequentially, even if the rest of the test suite is executed in parallel. This is necessary because of the shared resources, particularly the Selenium instance. Finally, tests can be arbitrarily grouped together; here I've indicated that the tests are part of the "integration" group (TestNG can be configured to run tests within a specific group).

Parameterizing Tests

TestNG is full of more features than I can possibly categorize in this short introduction. However, one I particularly rely upon is *parameterized methods*. These are methods, usually test methods, that take parameters. The values for the parameters are supplied externally: either in the TestNG control file or by another method.

Tapestry uses this TestNG facility in several areas; one example includes tests for the TypeCoercer service. This service is responsible for coercing values from one type (say, String) to another (say, Integer). The implementation of this service is quite complex, because it can "deduce" complex coercions from a base set of simple coercions. For example, starting with coercions for Object to String, String to Long, and Long to Integer, the TypeCoercer can deduce how to coerce from StringBuffer to

Integer. It's a fun algorithm but one worthy of some significant testing and validation.

The test case for this implementation class feeds a large number of inputs and expected outputs through the service to verify that it does the correct thing. The code below shows the test method. The dataProvider attribute identifies the set of data to be passed into the method. The test method will be invoked multiple times, passed a different set of parameters each time.

```
code/hls/TypeCoercerImplTest.java
```

```
@Test(dataProvider = "coercions_inputs")
public void builtin_coercions(Object input, Class targetType, Object expected)
{
    Object actual = _coercer.coerce(input, targetType);

    assertEquals(actual, expected);
}
```

Where do those parameter values come from? They can come from the testng.xml file or from another method within the same test class. In this case, the @DataProvider annotation on the coercion_inputs() method identifies it as the source of parameters for test method builtin_coercions().[5] The method returns Object()(), that is, an array of arrays of objects. Each of the inner arrays represents one set of parameters to be passed to the test method. For this test, each inner array consists of an input value, the desired output type, and an expected output value. Of course, this method could do anything, such as build the array of objects by reading from a file or database.

You could accomplish the same thing as one big method that simply calls builtin_coercions() repeatedly, but that would show up as just a single test in the test listing. Using parameterized tests, each invocation of builtin_coercions() shows up as its own test, and the parameters passed to the test method will show up in the generated test reports.

TestNG gives you the overall structure needed to build your tests. In fact, I've only scratched the surface of what TestNG can accomplish. So far, you've seen how to leverage TestNG to test isolated classes, but real systems involve *interactions* between different classes, and that's where the next section will start.

---

5. I name the data provider method the same as its reference name and wish that TestNG would just connect the dots for me.

```
@DataProvider(name = "coercions_inputs")
public Object[][] coercions_inputs()
{
  String bigDecimalValue =
    "123456567483524358423852345982349582345743585723485.3584353↵
    4285293857298457234587";
  String bigIntegerValue = "12384584574874385743";

  Object object = new Object();

  return new Object[][]
  {
    { this, String.class, toString() },
    { 551, Integer.class, 55 },
    { "", Boolean.class, false },
    { "  ", Boolean.class, false },
    { "x", Boolean.class, true },
    { " z ", Boolean.class, true },
    { "false", Boolean.class, false },
    { "  False ", Boolean.class, false },
    { null, Boolean.class, false },
    { new Double(256), Integer.class, new Integer(256) },
    { new Double(22.7), Integer.class, new Integer(22) },
    { new Integer(0), Boolean.class, false },
    { new Long(32838), Boolean.class, true },
    { new Integer(127), Byte.class, new Byte("127") },
    { new Double(58), Short.class, new Short("58") },
    { new Integer(33), Long.class, new Long(33) },
    { new Integer(22), Float.class, new Float(22) },
    { new Integer(1234), Double.class, new Double(1234) },
    { Collections.EMPTY_LIST, Boolean.class, false },
    { Collections.singleton(this), Boolean.class, true },
    { bigDecimalValue, BigDecimal.class, new BigDecimal(bigDecimalValue) },
    { new BigDecimal(bigDecimalValue), Double.class, 1.2345656748352436E49 },
    { bigIntegerValue, BigInteger.class, new BigInteger(bigIntegerValue) },
    { new BigInteger("12345678"), Long.class, 12345678l },
    { -12345678l, BigInteger.class, new BigInteger("-12345678") },
    { object, List.class, Collections.singletonList(object) },
    { null, String.class, null },
  };
}
```

7.4 EasyMock: Weird, Wonderful, and Invaluable

Of all the testing and build tools I use on a regular basis, EasyMock is the strangest and, ultimately, the most valuable. EasyMock has changed the way I write tests, and that has changed the way I write code. EasyMock is how you unit test the *interactions* between a class and its *collaborators*, the other objects with which a class interacts. The magic of EasyMock is that those collaborators don't have to exist yet as anything more than an interface. EasyMock is a way to create *mock objects* on the fly, objects that can *stand in* for your collaborators. In effect, you write a "script" for what the mock object will do: what methods will be invoked on it, with what parameters, and with what values it will return (or what exceptions it will throw).

Why would you want to use mock objects and not the real instances?

- If you have an *interface*, you can create and control a mock object for that interface. . . even before you've written an implementation for that interface.

- You can train a mock object to behave unreasonably. . . returning values a real implementation wouldn't or throwing an exception where a real implementation wouldn't. This will often let you get code coverage for code that otherwise could not be reached.

- The use of EasyMock limits the scope of your test to just the one class you are testing. If you are testing a OrderProcessor service that works with an InventoryManager service, you don't have to worry about the InventoryManager actually reading or updating your inventory database; you will be scripting its interactions with the InventoryManager without doing any real work.

A Starting Example

code/hls/Order.java

```
package com.howardlewisship.easymockexamples;

public interface Order
{
    void addLineItem(String productId, int quantity, boolean backordered);
}
```

code/hls/InventoryManager.java

```
package com.howardlewisship.easymockexamples;

public interface InventoryManager
{
    int quantityAvailable(String productid);
}
```

`code/hls/OrderProcessor.java`

```java
package com.howardlewisship.easymockexamples;

public interface OrderProcessor
{
    void processLineItem(String productId, int quantity, Order order);
}
```

Here we see the start of a hypothetical order-processing system, defining interfaces (but not implementations) for the key players: Order, InventoryManager, and OrderProcessor. The implementation of OrderProcessor (shown below) checks with the InventoryManager before adding normal or back-ordered line items to the Order.

`code/hls/OrderProcessorImpl.java`

```java
package com.howardlewisship.easymockexamples;

public class OrderProcessorImpl implements OrderProcessor
{
    private final InventoryManager _manager;

    public OrderProcessorImpl(InventoryManager manager)
    {
        _manager = manager;
    }

    public void processLineItem(String productId, int quantity, Order order)
    {
        int available = _manager.quantityAvailable(productId);

        if (available >= quantity)
        {
            order.addLineItem(productId, quantity, false);
            return;
        }

        if (available > 0)
        {
            order.addLineItem(productId, available, false);
            order.addLineItem(productId, quantity - available, true);
            return;
        }

        order.addLineItem(productId, quantity, true);
    }

}
```

EasyMock and Agility

One of the less obvious advantages of EasyMock is how well it fits into an agile development environment. It lets you build and test one class before building and testing the class's dependencies. If you refactor the interface, the refactorings will simply change how the mocks are trained. Prior to EasyMock, mock object testing required handwritten mock objects, a true maintenance burden.

The separation of code into interfaces and implementations is part of a greater pattern also seen in the use of inversion of control (IoC) containers, such as Spring, HiveMind, and Tapestry 5 IoC. EasyMock makes it simply *possible* to test your code based on interfaces. The IoC containers make it possible to connect many small pieces of code together. It then becomes practical to break monolithic code into small, independently testable classes. The end result is better code: better separation of concerns, fuller testing, greater modularity, and wider reuse.

Let's start by writing a test for the simplest case, when there is sufficient quantity of the product on hand. The sufficient_quantity_available() method shows the basic outline of an EasyMock test. First you create mock objects using the static method EasyMock.createMock(). Then you *train* the mocks, invoking methods on them. The EasyMock.expect() and andReturn() methods are a type-safe way to identify the value returned from some invocation on a mock object.

Once the mocks are fully trained, the EasyMock.replay() call switches them from training mode to replay mode. The test creates an instance of OrderProcessorImpl() and passes in the mock objects (via constructors or via method parameters).

Finally, you invoke EasyMock.verify(), which will ensure that *all* trained methods were invoked and not one was skipped.

Wow! That's a bit of work for just a single test case. Let's look at some refactorings that will make the code easier to read and make it easier to write additional tests.

```
code/hls/OrderProcessorImplTest_1.java
```

```java
package com.howardlewisship.easymockexamples;

import static org.easymock.EasyMock.expect;
import static org.easymock.EasyMock.replay;
import static org.easymock.EasyMock.verify;

import org.easymock.EasyMock;
import org.testng.Assert;
import org.testng.annotations.Test;

public class OrderProcessorImplTest extends Assert
{
    public static final String PRODUCT_ID = "prod-0001";

    @Test
    public void sufficient_quantity_available()
    {
        InventoryManager manager = EasyMock.createMock(InventoryManager.class);
        Order order = EasyMock.createMock(Order.class);

        expect(manager.quantityAvailable(PRODUCT_ID)).andReturn(100);

        order.addLineItem(PRODUCT_ID, 50, false);

        replay(manager, order);

        OrderProcessor processor = new OrderProcessorImpl(manager);

        processor.processLineItem(PRODUCT_ID, 50, order);

        verify(manager, order);
    }
}
```

Basic Test Refactorings

First, rather than having to remember all the different mock objects for the purposes of invoking replay() and verify(), let's see whether I can simplify. This gets even more important when the number of mock objects increase (I've written tests that orchestrate as many as a dozen). As currently coded, each mock object has its own mock control, the object behind the scenes that stores the "script" and verifies method invocations and parameters. The EasyMock API allows a single mock control to control multiple mock objects of different types, so I'll modify the test to create the mock control at the start of the test and add methods to make it easier to create the mock objects using the shared control.

code/hls/OrderProcessorImplTest_2.java

```
package com.howardlewisship.easymockexamples;

import static org.easymock.EasyMock.expect;

import org.easymock.EasyMock;
import org.easymock.IMocksControl;
import org.testng.Assert;
import org.testng.annotations.BeforeMethod;
import org.testng.annotations.Test;

public class OrderProcessorImplTest extends Assert
{
    public static final String PRODUCT_ID = "prod-0001";

►   private IMocksControl _control;
►
►   @BeforeMethod
►   public final void setup()
►   {
►       _control = EasyMock.createControl();
►   }
►
►   protected final <T> T newMock(Class<T> mockClass)
►   {
►       return _control.createMock(mockClass);
►   }
►
►   protected final void replay()
►   {
►       _control.replay();
►   }
►
►   protected final void verify()
►   {
►       _control.verify();
►   }

    @Test
    public void sufficient_quantity_available()
    {
►       InventoryManager manager = newMock(InventoryManager.class);
►       Order order = newMock(Order.class);

        expect(manager.quantityAvailable(PRODUCT_ID)).andReturn(100);

        order.addLineItem(PRODUCT_ID, 50, false);

►       replay();
```

```
        OrderProcessor processor = new OrderProcessorImpl(manager);

        processor.processLineItem(PRODUCT_ID, 50, order);

▶       verify();
    }
}
```

The key is the new method newMock(), which creates a new mock object of the desired class using the single shared mock control.[6] Although the new code bloats the test case a bit, the end result after all test methods have been implemented will be a net gain. Further, many of the methods defined might be moved to a base class and shared between test cases.

More Refactorings

Now, on to the last refactorings and some additional tests to demonstrate their usefulness. Rather than repeated calls to newMock(), I'll create *mock factory methods*, methods that create a new mock object of a given type. Again, these methods tend to bubble up to common base classes.

In addition, I'll create *trainer methods*, methods that wrap around an expect()...andReturn() call. Again, many different tests will often share a single trainer method. These method names are prefixed with "train_" and take the mock object as the first parameter and the return value as the last parameter. The code below shows the results of these refactorings.

```
code/hls/OrderProcessorImplTest_3.java
```

```java
package com.howardlewisship.easymockexamples;

import static org.easymock.EasyMock.expect;

import org.easymock.EasyMock;
import org.easymock.IMocksControl;
import org.testng.Assert;
import org.testng.annotations.BeforeMethod;
import org.testng.annotations.Test;
```

---

6. Of course, this code is not thread-safe, so if TestNG resolves its problems with parallel tests, this will need to be reworked. A base class inside Tapestry, org.apache.tapestry.ioc.test.TestBase, has implemented this idea using a ThreadLocal to store the mock control.

```java
public class OrderProcessorImplTest extends Assert
{
    public static final String PRODUCT_ID = "prod-0001";

    private IMocksControl _control;

    @BeforeMethod
    public final void setup()
    {
        _control = EasyMock.createControl();
    }

    protected final <T> T newMock(Class<T> mockClass)
    {
        return _control.createMock(mockClass);
    }

    protected final void replay()
    {
        _control.replay();
    }

    protected final void verify()
    {
        _control.verify();
    }

    protected final Order newOrder()
    {
        return newMock(Order.class);
    }

    protected final InventoryManager newInventoryManager()
    {
        return newMock(InventoryManager.class);
    }

    protected final void train_quantityAvailable(InventoryManager manager, String productId,
            int quantity)
    {
        expect(manager.quantityAvailable(productId)).andReturn(quantity);
    }

    @Test
    public void sufficient_quantity_available()
    {
        InventoryManager manager = newInventoryManager();
        Order order = newOrder();

        train_quantityAvailable(manager, PRODUCT_ID, 100);
```

```
        order.addLineItem(PRODUCT_ID, 50, false);

        replay();

        OrderProcessor processor = new OrderProcessorImpl(manager);

        processor.processLineItem(PRODUCT_ID, 50, order);

        verify();
    }

    @Test
    public void no_items_available()
    {
        InventoryManager manager = newInventoryManager();
        Order order = newOrder();

        train_quantityAvailable(manager, PRODUCT_ID, 0);

        order.addLineItem(PRODUCT_ID, 75, true);

        replay();

        OrderProcessor processor = new OrderProcessorImpl(manager);

        processor.processLineItem(PRODUCT_ID, 75, order);

        verify();
    }

    @Test
    public void unsufficient_items_available()
    {
        InventoryManager manager = newInventoryManager();
        Order order = newOrder();

        train_quantityAvailable(manager, PRODUCT_ID, 75);

        order.addLineItem(PRODUCT_ID, 75, false);
        order.addLineItem(PRODUCT_ID, 25, true);

        replay();

        OrderProcessor processor = new OrderProcessorImpl(manager);

        processor.processLineItem(PRODUCT_ID, 100, order);

        verify();
    }
}
```

You can see how the code for the individual tests is orderly and readable through the use of the mock factory methods and trainer methods. This is one of the great lessons of testing: treat your test code with the same respect as your production code. If it's broken, ugly, or repetitive, then you should refactor it with the same vigor as you would production code.

Of course, this discussion has been based on the idea that the mocks are trained properly and that the code being tested is correct. More typically, this is a point reached after some effort, small or great. For example, a small change (from quantity/available to available/quantity) breaks the code, and this is reflected in the test with a failure.

Here, EasyMock is attempting to describe what went wrong in terms of which methods were invoked and with which parameters:

```
java.lang.AssertionError:
Unexpected method call addLineItem("prod-0001", -25, true):
addLineItem("prod-0001", 25, true): expected: 1, actual: 0
at org.easymock.internal.MockInvocationHandler.invoke(MockInvocationHandler.java:29)
at org.easymock.internal.ObjectMethodsFilter.invoke(ObjectMethodsFilter.java:45)
at $Proxy6.addLineItem(Unknown Source)
at com.howardlewisship.easymockexamples.OrderProcessorImpl.↩
  processLineItem(OrderProcessorImpl.java:25)
at com.howardlewisship.easymockexamples.OrderProcessorImplTest.↩
  unsufficient_items_available(OrderProcessorImplTest.java:107)
at sun.reflect.NativeMethodAccessorImpl.invoke0(Native Method)
at sun.reflect.NativeMethodAccessorImpl.invoke(NativeMethodAccessorImpl.java:39)
...
```

Here you see that addLineItem() was invoked with a value of -25, when the expected value was 25. That is, the call with the value -25 was unexpected, and the expected (but unsatisfied) call used the value 25. In a more complex test case, with more mock objects, you might see a larger set of expected method calls, but the essence is the same.

More EasyMock Features

Like TestNG, EasyMock has far more features than can be easily covered in this amount of space. Here are a few of the important ones:

- I've shown the default mocks. Other possibilities are *strict mocks*, where the method invocation order counts, and *nice mocks*, where extra method invocations are simply responded to with a default return value.

- Argument matchers allow greater flexibility in how method parameters are verified. For example, you can allow a range of values for a parameter, rather than just a single fixed value, or specify that a String parameter should contain a substring or match a regular expression. You can also create your own argument matchers.

- You have control over call counts. For example, if a method might be invoked multiple times with the same parameters and returns the same value, you can train it with the following: expect(. . .).andReturn(*value*).atLeastOnce()

- You might attach a *callback*, in the form of an org.easymock.IAnswer, to a method call. The callback can analyze the arguments, perform its own validations, and compute a proper return value.

- An extension to EasyMock allows *classes*, not interfaces, to be mocked (with a number of limitations). This allows testing of code that doesn't follow the useful separation of interface and implementation.

7.5 Conclusion

You can use these three tools—Cobertura, TestNG, and EasyMock—together to form a practical infrastructure for testing. Cobertura helps you identify what code needs testing, TestNG provides the facilities for efficiently building test cases, and EasyMock provides the capability to truly unit test your code.

This kind of commitment to testing is not trivial; it can often seem tedious. And yet, every time I reach the point where I ask myself why I bother, I almost immediately find another subtle bug that would have driven me insane in production but stands out like a sore thumb inside my test suite. Once again, I experience the truth that the only way to work fast is to slow down and get disciplined about testing.

7.6 Web Resources

Cobertura. . . . . .http://cobertura.sourceforge.net/
Code coverage tool

EasyMock . . . . http://www.easymock.org/
Mock object testing framework

JUnit . . . . http://www.junit.org/index.htm
Java unit testing tool

Maven . . . . http://maven.apache.org/
High-level Java build tool

Selenium . . . . http://www.openqa.org/selenium/
Browser-based integration test tool

Tapestry http://tapestry.apache.org/tapestry5/
Component-based web application framework (included as a good source of examples)

TestNG . . . . http://testng.org/doc/
Next-generation Java testing framework

## Chapter 8

An Introduction to the Google Web Toolkit

by David Geary

A prominent author, speaker, and consultant, David holds a unique qualification as a Java expert: he wrote best-selling books on both Java component frameworks, Swing and JavaServer Faces (JSF). David's Graphic Java Swing was one of the best-selling Java books of all time, and Core JSF, which David wrote with Cay Horstman, is a best-selling book on JavaServer Faces.

David recently completed an ebook on the Google Web Toolkit (GWT) and is currently working on a pbook (print book) titled GWT Solutions: Cool and Useful Stuff. Both the ebooks and pbooks are published by Prentice Hall.

David served on the JSF and JSTL Expert Groups, has contributed to open source projects, and coauthored Sun's Web Developer Certification Exam. He invented the Struts Template library, which was the precursor to Tiles, a popular framework for composing web pages from JSP fragments; was the second Struts committer; and is currently an Apache Shale committer.

A regular on the NFJS tour since 2003, David loves to interact with attendees and is known for his sense of humor, dazzling demos, and electrifying live-coding sessions. David also speaks at other conferences, including JavaOne and JavaPolis. In 2005, David was awarded a Top Speaker award at JavaOne for his Shale presentation with Craig McClanahan.

8.1 Introduction

Admit it, you're sick and tired of writing boring form-based applications while your desktop-application developer friends build rich, interactive user interfaces. With Google Maps and Gmail, Google showed that it was indeed possible for web app developers to create rich UIs that run in a browser.

But ask the folks at Google if developing Google Maps and Gmail was *easy*, and they will admit it was anything but. By combining a hodge-podge of technologies—JavaScript, XHR, CSS, HTML, and so on—Google was able to pull off some amazing stuff in the confines of the ubiquitous browser, but it was an exercise rooted deep in pain and anguish.

Then Ruby on Rails burst onto the scene, which was ostensibly the first web application framework with Ajax baked in. Not only that, but Rails took things a step further by providing code generators, scaffolding, naming conventions, and instant turnaround after code modifications. As a result, Java developers everywhere were infected with severe cases of Rails-envy.

Out of that crucible (the difficulties of developing Gmail and Google Maps, combined with the Rails influence) emerges the Next Big Thing for web app developers fluent in Java: the Google Web Toolkit (GWT).

The GWT, like Rails, is a web application framework with Ajax support baked in, but unlike Rails, you don't have to learn a new language; in fact, if you are familiar with Java, you're already halfway there. The GWT uses familiar idioms from other Java frameworks such as the Abstract Window Toolkit (AWT), Swing, and the SWT. For example, if you've implemented event handlers using anonymous inner classes with any of those frameworks, then you already know how to handle events with the GWT. The only thing you need to do is learn a new API, which is semantically similar enough to the AWT that you can dive right in and start coding rich UIs. I'll show you how.

8.2 The Example Application

In this chapter, I'll show how to implement a simple login application with the GWT. Along the way, I'll cover GWT basics such as the following:

- Using GWT widgets

- Internationalization

- Implementing remote procedure calls (RPCs)

- Using the GWT's history mechanism

- Using Ajax

- Incorporating the Script.aculo.us JavaScript library

Like Rails, the GWT provides a code generator that will create a starter application. First, create a new project with the projectCreator command, like this: projectCreator -eclipse LoginApplication. That command creates a skeletal Eclipse project with the name LoginApplication.

Next, create your application like this:

```
applicationCreator -eclipse LoginApplication com.acme.client.LoginApplication
```

That command creates a "Hello, World" application in the LoginApplication project, whose application class is com.acme.client.LoginApplication.

At this point, you have a simple "Hello, World" application that you can edit. Figure 8.1, on page 103, shows the login application. This is a view of the application running in hosted mode. In hosted mode, you run the application from Eclipse, which runs the app in the Google browser.

Notice the Compile/Browse button in the Google browser's toolbar. If you click that button, the GWT will compile your Java code to Java-Script and start the resulting application in your default browser.

For the rest of this chapter, I'll walk through the code modifications that you need to make to implement the login application. For invalid logins, I've added an Ajaxian update of the login page with an error message that shakes back and forth a few times to get the user's attention by incorporating the Script.aculo.us JavaScript framework.

Now that you've seen the login application in action, you'll look at its implementation.

8.3 Using GWT Widgets

I'll start by modifying the generated com.acme.client.LoginApplication class to display the login screen:

`code/geary/LoginApplicationBarebones.java`

```
package com.acme.client;

import com.google.gwt.core.client.EntryPoint;
import com.google.gwt.user.client.ui.*;

public class LoginApplication implements EntryPoint {
  public void onModuleLoad() {
    final Label loginPrompt = new Label("Please log in");
    final Grid grid = new Grid(3,2);
    final Label namePrompt = new Label("Name");
    final TextBox nameTextbox = new TextBox();
    final Label passwordPrompt = new Label("Password");
    final PasswordTextBox passwordTextbox = new PasswordTextBox();
    final Button button = new Button("Login");

    loginPrompt.addStyleName("loginPrompt");
    nameTextbox.addStyleName("nameField");
    passwordTextbox.addStyleName("passwordField");

    RootPanel.get().add(loginPrompt);

    grid.setWidget(0, 0, namePrompt); // 0, 0 == row, column
    grid.setWidget(0, 1, nameTextbox);

    grid.setWidget(1, 0, passwordPrompt);
    grid.setWidget(1, 1, passwordTextbox);

    grid.setWidget(2, 0, button);

    RootPanel.get().add(grid);
  }
}
```

This is pretty simple stuff. I created some widgets (labels, textboxes, a button, and a grid) and then set some CSS styles for the login prompt label and the two textboxes. Then I added the login prompt label to the root panel of the window, added labels and textboxes to the grid, and finally added the grid to the root panel. The result looks just like Figure 8.1, on the facing page.

If you've used the AWT, Swing, or the SWT, this code is a yawner. The only really noteworthy thing is that, like all GWT apps, I've implemented the EntryPoint interface, which defines a single method: onModuleLoad().

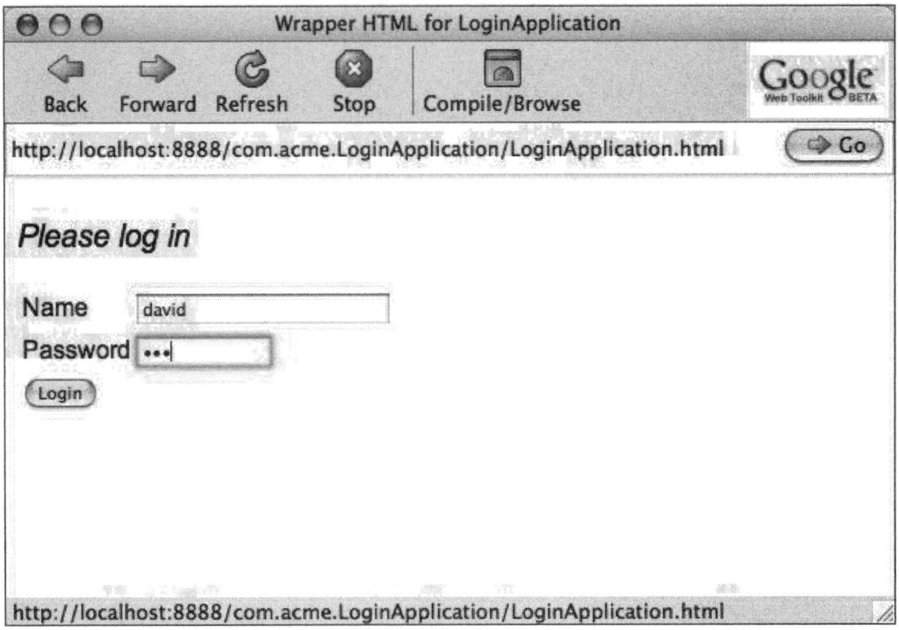

Figure 8.1: The login screen in hosted mode

You can think of that method as essentially the main method that you ordinarily implement in a Java application.

Other than the preceding Java code, the only other piece to the puzzle is the application's HTML file, which was also generated by the GWT. In that file, I define the CSS styles for the login prompt label, the name textbox, and the password textbox. Here's that HTML file:

code/geary/LoginApplication.html

```
<html>
  <head>
    <!-- Any title is fine                    -->
    <title>Wrapper HTML for LoginApplication</title>

    <!-- Use normal html, such as style       -->
    <style>
      body,td,a,div,.p{font-family:arial,sans-serif}
      div,td{color:#000000}
      a:link,.w,.w a:link{color:#0000cc}
      a:visited{color:#551a8b}
      a:active{color:#ff0000}
```

```
        .loginPrompt {
           font-style: italic;
           margin-bottom: 20px;
           font-size: 1.25em;
        }
        .errorMsg {
           padding: 20px;
           margin-bottom: 10px;
           font-style: italic;
           border: thick solid red;
           background: lightGray;
           width: 250px;
           height: 2em;
        }
        .nameField {
           width: 15em;
        }
        .passwordField {
           width: 8em;
        }
        .welcomeMsg {
           margin-bottom: 20px;
           font-style: italic;
           color: blue;
        }
    </style>

    <!-- The module reference below is the link    -->
    <!-- between html and your Web Toolkit module  -->
    <meta name='gwt:module' content='com.acme.LoginApplication'>
    <script language="javascript" src="prototype.js"></script>
    <script language="javascript" src="effects.js"></script>
</head>

<!-- The body can have arbitrary html, or      -->
<!-- you can leave the body empty if you want  -->
<!-- to create a completely dynamic ui         -->
<body>

    <!-- This script is required bootstrap stuff.   -->
    <!-- You can put it in the HEAD, but startup    -->
    <!-- is slightly faster if you include it here. -->
    <script language="javascript" src="gwt.js"></script>

    <!-- OPTIONAL: include this if you want history support -->
    <iframe id="__gwt_historyFrame"
        style="width:0;height:0;border:0"></iframe>
</body>
</html>
```

Rather than tease you with the HTML file piecemeal, as I'm doing with
the Java code, I've just listed the final version of the HTML file. Notice
that besides the CSS styles for the widgets you've seen so far, I have
styles for the welcome and error messages, which you'll see later. Also,
I've included the Prototype JavaScript framework and its sidekick,
Script.aculo.us; I'll show you how to integrate those frameworks in Section 8.8, *JavaScript Integration*, on page 115. At the bottom of the HTML
page is an iframe, which is necessary for the GWT's history mechanism,
which I'll discuss in Section 8.6, *Using the GWT's History Mechanism*,
on page 111. But before all that, I'll talk about internationalization.

8.4 Internationalization

If you've been paying attention, you may have noticed that I mentioned
that the GWT compiles your client-side Java code to JavaScript (OK,
I didn't say client-side, but I'm saying it now). As a result of that chi-
canery, the GWT severely restricts what's available to your client-side
Java code—a few selected classes from java.lang and java.util, and that's
about it. You may think that's an outrage, but in practice, it's not a big
deal. To implement your UI, you typically don't need all that stuff, and
when you do, you can make an RPC to the server, where all of Java is
available to you.

One of the consequences of the GWT's restricted Java on the client is
that you don't have regular i18n capabilities, such as MessageFormat
and friends. So, the GWT implements i18n a little differently. You use
a properties file, coupled with an interface, and then call GWT.create()
to create an implementation of your interface that you can use to pull
values from the properties file. Here's the properties file for the login
application:

code/geary/LoginApplicationConstants.properties
```
loginPrompt=Please log in
namePrompt=Name
passwordPrompt=Password
loginButtonText=Log in
errorMsg=Invalid name/pwd combination. Please try again.
welcomeMsg=Welcome to the GWT!
logoutLinkText=Logout...
```

And here's the corresponding interface:

code/geary/LoginApplicationConstants.java

```java
package com.acme.client;

import com.google.gwt.i18n.client.Constants;

public interface LoginApplicationConstants extends Constants {
    String loginPrompt();
    String namePrompt();
    String passwordPrompt();
    String loginButtonText();
    String errorMsg();
    String welcomeMsg();
    String logoutLinkText();
}
```

Notice that the properties file and interface have the same names (with different suffixes, of course) and that the methods defined in the interface have the same names as the keys in the properties file. You must follow those naming conventions for this all to work. Finally, here's the modified application:

code/geary/LoginApplicationI18N.java

```java
package com.acme.client;

import com.google.gwt.core.client.EntryPoint;
import com.google.gwt.core.client.GWT;
import com.google.gwt.user.client.ui.*;

public class LoginApplication implements EntryPoint {
▶   private static final LoginApplicationConstants constants =
▶           (LoginApplicationConstants)GWT.create
▶               (LoginApplicationConstants.class);

    public void onModuleLoad() {
▶       final Label loginPrompt = new Label(constants.loginPrompt());
        final Grid grid = new Grid(3,2);
▶       final Label namePrompt = new Label(constants.namePrompt());
        final TextBox nameTextbox = new TextBox();
▶       final Label passwordPrompt = new Label(constants.passwordPrompt());
        final PasswordTextBox passwordTextbox = new PasswordTextBox();
        final Button button = new Button("Login");

        loginPrompt.addStyleName("loginPrompt");
        nameTextbox.addStyleName("nameField");
        passwordTextbox.addStyleName("passwordField");

        RootPanel.get().add(loginPrompt);
```

```
    grid.setWidget(0, 0, namePrompt);
    grid.setWidget(0, 1, nameTextbox);

    grid.setWidget(1, 0, passwordPrompt);
    grid.setWidget(1, 1, passwordTextbox);

    grid.setWidget(2, 0, button);

    RootPanel.get().add(grid);
  }
}
```

The GWT.create method creates an object that implements LoginApplicationConstants, which the GWT wires to the corresponding properties file. Then I just call methods whose names correspond to the keys in the properties file to pull out the key's values. Notice that this gives you compile-time checking of the values that you pull from the properties files, not to mention you get method name completion in your IDE. That's pretty cool.

8.5 Remote Procedure Calls

It's time to make the application actually do something. Look:

`code/geary/LoginApplicationRPC.java`

```java
package com.acme.client;

import com.google.gwt.core.client.EntryPoint;
import com.google.gwt.core.client.GWT;
import com.google.gwt.user.client.Window;
import com.google.gwt.user.client.rpc.AsyncCallback;
import com.google.gwt.user.client.rpc.ServiceDefTarget;
import com.google.gwt.user.client.ui.*;

public class LoginApplication implements EntryPoint {
  private static final LoginApplicationConstants constants =
        (LoginApplicationConstants)GWT.create
            (LoginApplicationConstants.class);

  public void onModuleLoad() {
    final Label loginPrompt = new Label(constants.loginPrompt());
    final Grid grid = new Grid(3,2);
    final Label namePrompt = new Label(constants.namePrompt());
    final TextBox nameTextbox = new TextBox();
    final Label passwordPrompt = new Label(constants.passwordPrompt());
    final PasswordTextBox passwordTextbox = new PasswordTextBox();
    final Button button = new Button("Login");
```

```
▶        button.addClickListener(new ClickListener() {
▶          public void onClick(Widget sender) {
▶            LoginServiceAsync ls = (LoginServiceAsync)
▶              GWT.create(LoginService.class);
▶            ServiceDefTarget target = (ServiceDefTarget)ls;
▶            target.setServiceEntryPoint(GWT.getModuleBaseURL() +
▶                                "/loginService");
▶
▶            ls.isValidLogin(nameTextbox.getText(),
▶                      passwordTextbox.getText(),
▶                      new AsyncCallback() {
▶              public void onSuccess(Object result) {
▶                Window.alert("rpc call returned: " + result);
▶              }
▶              public void onFailure(Throwable caught) {
▶                Window.alert("rpc call failed: " + caught.getMessage());
▶              }
▶            });
▶          }
▶        });

        loginPrompt.addStyleName("loginPrompt");
        nameTextbox.addStyleName("nameField");
        passwordTextbox.addStyleName("passwordField");

        RootPanel.get().add(loginPrompt);

        grid.setWidget(0, 0, namePrompt);
        grid.setWidget(0, 1, nameTextbox);

        grid.setWidget(1, 0, passwordPrompt);
        grid.setWidget(1, 1, passwordTextbox);

        grid.setWidget(2, 0, button);

        RootPanel.get().add(grid);
    }
}
```

Here I've added a click listener to the login button that performs an RPC to verify the name/password on the server. If that combination is valid, the RPC returns true; otherwise, it returns false. For the moment, I'm using the GWT's Window class to show an alert that shows the result of the RPC call. In Section 8.6, *Using the GWT's History Mechanism*, on page 111, I'll modify that code so that I load the welcome screen.

Notice that, as was the case for internationalization, I'm using GWT.create() to create an instance of a class, given an interface. That instance implements the LoginServiceAsync interface, whereas the interface passed to GWT.create() is LoginService. I'll show you those interfaces in just a moment.

The object returned by GWT.create() is also an instance of ServiceDefTarget, which is a GWT interface. I call setServiceEntryPoint() to point to a servlet on the server. After I've set the service entry point, I call the only method defined for the service: isValidLogin().

Here are the LoginService and LoginServiceAsync interfaces:

code/geary/LoginService.java

```java
package com.acme.client;

import com.google.gwt.user.client.rpc.RemoteService;

public interface LoginService extends RemoteService {
    public boolean isValidLogin(String username, String pwd);
}
```

code/geary/LoginServiceAsync.java

```java
package com.acme.client;

import com.google.gwt.user.client.rpc.AsyncCallback;

public interface LoginServiceAsync {
    public void isValidLogin(String username, String pwd,
        AsyncCallback callback);
}
```

Once again, I'm using a GWT naming convention. The asynchronous service's name is the same as the service's name with "Async" tacked on the end. And the asynchronous interface's method is the same as the service's method, except for two things: the asynchronous version returns void, whereas the service's method returns boolean. Further, the asynchronous version is passed an instance of AsyncCallback. Who invokes the methods implemented by that callback object? The GWT. When I call the asynchronous version of the method, the GWT calls the actual service, and when the call is complete, the GWT invokes either onSuccess or onFailure on the asynchronous callback, depending upon whether the RPC succeeded or failed.

So far, you've seen the service and asynchronous interfaces and how the service is used in the application.

The next thing is the implementation of the service, which is as follows:

`code/geary/LoginServiceImpl.java`

```java
package com.acme.server;

import com.acme.client.LoginService;
import com.google.gwt.user.server.rpc.RemoteServiceServlet;

public class LoginServiceImpl extends RemoteServiceServlet
                        implements LoginService {
   private static final long serialVersionUID = 1L;
   private static final String VALID_USERNAME = "david";
   private static final String VALID_PWD = "gwt";

   public LoginServiceImpl() { // must have
   }

   public boolean isValidLogin(String name, String pwd) {
      return VALID_USERNAME.equals(name)
             && VALID_PWD.equals(pwd);
   }
}
```

The LoginServiceImpl class extends the service interface (LoginService) and extends the GWT's RemoteServiceServlet. The isValidLogin method determines whether the name and password match the single set of valid values and returns an appropriate boolean value. One potential pitfall when implementing remote services is that you must provide a no-argument constructor; if you neglect to do so, your RPC will fail. Other than that, implementing a service is quite straightforward.

Finally, you must declare the servlet. In hosted mode, you do that in your application's configuration file, which is as follows:

`code/geary/LoginApplication.gwt.xml`

```xml
<module>

    <!-- Inherit the core Web Toolkit stuff.               -->
    <inherits name='com.google.gwt.user.User'/>

    <!-- Specify the app entry point class.                -->
    <entry-point class='com.acme.client.LoginApplication'/>

    <!-- Declare the servlet used for RPCs.                -->
▶    <servlet path="/loginService"
▶            class="com.acme.server.LoginServiceImpl"/>
</module>
```

So, now you have an RPC working to validate the login, but you need to somehow "navigate to the welcome page." I'll show how to do that.

8.6 Using the GWT's History Mechanism

If you've done only web development or it has been awhile since you've developed a desktop application, you might find it vexing to figure out how to "load a new page." The answer is that, with the GWT, you don't. Instead, like Swing and the AWT, you simply clear out the root panel and repopulate it with your new view. Let's see how to do that using the GWT's history mechanism:

```
code/geary/LoginApplicationWithHistory.java
package com.acme.client;

import com.google.gwt.core.client.*;
import com.google.gwt.user.client.ui.*;

public class LoginApplication
►    implements EntryPoint, HistoryListener {
►    private static final String LOGIN_STATE = "login";
►    private static final String WELCOME_STATE = "welcome";

    private static final LoginApplicationConstants constants =
            (LoginApplicationConstants)GWT.create
                (LoginApplicationConstants.class);

►    public void onModuleLoad() {
►      setupHistory();
►    }
►    private void setupHistory() {
►      History.addHistoryListener(this);
►      History.onHistoryChanged(LOGIN_STATE);
►    }
►    public void onHistoryChanged(String historyToken) {
►      if (LOGIN_STATE.equals(historyToken)) {
►        loadLoginView();
►      }
►      else if (WELCOME_STATE.equals(historyToken)) {
►        loadWelcomeView();
►      }
►    }
►    private void loadLoginView() {
        final Label loginPrompt = new Label(constants.loginPrompt());
        final Grid grid = new Grid(3,2);
        final Label namePrompt = new Label(constants.namePrompt());
        final TextBox nameTextbox = new TextBox();
        final Label passwordPrompt = new Label(constants.passwordPrompt());
        final PasswordTextBox passwordTextbox = new PasswordTextBox();
        final Button button = new Button("Login");

        RootPanel.get().clear();
```

```
        button.addClickListener(new ClickListener() {
          public void onClick(Widget sender) {
            LoginServiceAsync ls = (LoginServiceAsync)
              GWT.create(LoginService.class);
            ServiceDefTarget target = (ServiceDefTarget)ls;
            target.setServiceEntryPoint(GWT.getModuleBaseURL() +
                                "/loginService");

            ls.isValidLogin(nameTextbox.getText(),
                        passwordTextbox.getText(),
                        new AsyncCallback() {
          public void onSuccess(Object result) {
            if (true == ((Boolean)result).booleanValue()) {
              History.newItem(WELCOME_STATE);
            }
            else {
              Window.alert("Invalid name/pwd combination. " +
                    "Please try again.");
            }
          }
          public void onFailure(Throwable caught) {
            Window.alert("rpc call failed: " + caught.getMessage());
          }
        });
      }
    });

    loginPrompt.addStyleName("loginPrompt");
    nameTextbox.addStyleName("nameField");
    passwordTextbox.addStyleName("passwordField");

    RootPanel.get().add(loginPrompt);

    grid.setWidget(0, 0, namePrompt);
    grid.setWidget(0, 1, nameTextbox);

    grid.setWidget(1, 0, passwordPrompt);
    grid.setWidget(1, 1, passwordTextbox);

    grid.setWidget(2, 0, button);

    RootPanel.get().add(grid);
  }
  private void loadWelcomeView() {
    final Label welcomeMsg = new Label(constants.welcomeMsg());

    welcomeMsg.addStyleName("welcomeMsg");

    RootPanel.get().clear();
    RootPanel.get().add(welcomeMsg);
    RootPanel.get().add(
```

►   **new** Hyperlink(constants.logoutLinkText(), LOGIN_STATE));
   }
}

Notice that the application class now implements the GWT's HistoryListener interface. Notice also that the onModuleLoad method has shrunk to one line of code, which sets up the history mechanism for the application. The setupHistory method adds the application instance to the GWT's History class, which means the GWT will invoke the onHistoryChanged method anytime the application's history changes. After that registration, I call History.onHistoryChanged() to set the history initially, which results in the History class invoking the application's onHistoryChanged() method, where I load the login screen by calling loadLoginView(), which has subsumed the responsibilities of the previous version of onModuleLoad().

Now take a look at the onSuccess method of the RPC. When the RPC returns true, meaning the login succeeded, I call History.newItem() to add a new item to the history. That item is the string welcome. That call to History.newItem() causes the GWT to once again invoke the application's onHistoryChanged() method, which this time loads the welcome view by invoking the aptly named loadWelcomeView(). That method clears out the root panel and adds the complex array of widgets you see on the welcome screen.

Now you've seen how the login screen gets loaded initially and how the welcome screen is loaded when the user successfully logs in. But how does the user get from the welcome screen back to the login screen? The user gets there with the "logout" link. GWT hyperlinks have a history token associated with them, so when the user clicks a hyperlink, it hooks into the history mechanism. In this case, when the user clicks the logout link, that adds a history item to the application's history, just as if you had manually called History.newItem(). This time, the history token is login, and the application's onHistoryChanged method loads the login screen once again.

8.7 Ajax!

Now you have a fully functioning application, except for one detail: when login fails, you display a JavaScript alert, but that's old-school. Instead, let's integrate an error message into the DOM with some Ajax. That sounds like a considerable task, but with the GWT, it's child's play.

The application class has now grown to more than 100 lines of code, so in the interest of saving space, I'm going to snip out the irrelevant parts of that class. Here's the updated, snipped version with the (ahem) Ajax:

`code/geary/LoginApplicationWithAjax.java`

```java
package com.acme.client;

// [snip]

public class LoginApplication
    implements EntryPoint, HistoryListener {
  // [big snip]

  private void loadLoginView() {
    // [snip]

▶   final Label errorMsg = new Label();
▶   errorMsg.setVisible(false);
▶   RootPanel.get().add(errorMsg);

    // [snip]
    button.addClickListener(new ClickListener() {
      public void onClick(Widget sender) {
        LoginServiceAsync ls = (LoginServiceAsync)
          GWT.create(LoginService.class);
        ServiceDefTarget target = (ServiceDefTarget)ls;
        target.setServiceEntryPoint(GWT.getModuleBaseURL() +
                          "/loginService");

        ls.isValidLogin(nameTextbox.getText(),
                   passwordTextbox.getText(),
                   new AsyncCallback() {
        public void onSuccess(Object result) {
          if (true == ((Boolean)result).booleanValue()) {
            History.newItem(WELCOME_STATE);
          }
          else {
            errorMsg.setText(constants.errorMsg());
▶           errorMsg.setVisible(true);
          }
        }
        public void onFailure(Throwable caught) {
          Window.alert("rpc call failed: " + caught.getMessage());
        }
        });
      }
    });
    // [snip]
  }
}
```

I created a label for the error message, set its visibility to false, and added it to the root panel. When login fails, I set the label's visibility to true. That's all folks!

"But wait," you say, "I thought you were adding elements to the DOM in response to an Ajax call to the server." Well, that's exactly what I just did. The GWT takes care of all the low-level details for me. All I had to do was create a label, initially make it invisible, and then make it visible when login fails.

But I know, you're still not happy, because by now you probably associate Ajax with special effects, such as squishes, puffs, blind-downs, shakes, and the like. Well alright, let's take a look at one more thing: integrating JavaScript, specifically Script.aculo.us, into the application.

8.8 JavaScript Integration

The GWT incorporates JavaScript (Google calls it JavaScript Native Interface [JSNI], which for you old-timers is a take on the Java Native Interface [JNI]) with an ingenious use of Java native methods. Here's how you would incorporate Script.aculo.us into the application:

`code/geary/LoginApplicationWithScriptaculous.java`

```
package com.acme.client;

// [snip]

public class LoginApplication
    implements EntryPoint, HistoryListener {
  // [big snip]

  private void loadLoginView() {
    // [snip]

    final Label errorMsg = new Label();
    errorMsg.setVisible(false);
    RootPanel.get().add(errorMsg);

    // [snip]
    button.addClickListener(new ClickListener() {
      public void onClick(Widget sender) {
        LoginServiceAsync ls = (LoginServiceAsync)
          GWT.create(LoginService.class);
        ServiceDefTarget target = (ServiceDefTarget)ls;
        target.setServiceEntryPoint(GWT.getModuleBaseURL() +
                              "/loginService");
```

```
                ls.isValidLogin(nameTextbox.getText(),
                        passwordTextbox.getText(),
                        new AsyncCallback() {
            public void onSuccess(Object result) {
                if (true == ((Boolean)result).booleanValue()) {
                    History.newItem(WELCOME_STATE);
                }
                else {
                    errorMsg.setText(constants.errorMsg());
                    errorMsg.setVisible(true);
▶                   applyEffect("Shake", errorMsg.getElement());
                }
            }
            public void onFailure(Throwable caught) {
                Window.alert("rpc call failed: " + caught.getMessage());
            }
            });
        }
      });
      // [snip]
    }
▶   private native void applyEffect(String effect, Element element) /*-{
▶       var ne = $wnd._nativeExtensions;
▶       $wnd._nativeExtensions = false;
▶       $wnd.Effect[effect](element);
▶       $wnd._nativeExtensions = ne;
▶   }-*/;
    }
```

When login fails, instead of simply making the error message visible, you'll also shake it. I can't really show you the shaking in figure, but trust me, it rocks. To perform the shaking, I write a native method whose body is commented out. In the commented-out body, I add a few lines of JavaScript to access the Script.aculo.us Effect object to perform the shaking.

Three things are noteworthy here. First, I included Script.aculo.us's effects.js along with prototype.js in the application's HTML file. Second, notice that the native method, which is called in the code just like any other method, is passed the name of the effect and an Element object. That element is a DOM element, which you extract from the error message widget by calling the widget's getElement method. Third, on Windows only, one line of JavaScript is required in the applyEffect method: $wnd.Effect[effect](element); on Mac OS X, the Safari browser requires the other three lines of code because of a conflict with the underlying Prototype library. But hey, that's Prototype's (or Safari's) fault, not the GWT's.

8.9 Conclusion

In this chapter I've shown you the fundamentals of using the GWT. But trust me, this is just the tip of a considerable iceberg. There's a *lot* of stuff in the GWT that I haven't covered here. You may want to check that out for yourself.

Well, that's it for my chapter. Take care, and I hope to see you at NFJS 2007.

8.10 Web Resources

The GWT home page . . . . http://code.google.com/webtoolkit
The Google Web Toolkit home page

The GWT developers' guide . . .
. . . http://code.google.com/webtoolkit/documentation
Developers' guide on the Google website

The GWT blog . . . . http://googlewebtoolkit.blogspot.com
Blog about all things GWT

Ed Burnette's ebook . . .
. . . http://www.pragmaticprogrammer.com/titles/ebgwt/index.html
Ed Burnette's ebook (covers GWT fundamentals)

David Geary's ebook http://my.safaribooksonline.com/0131584650
David Geary's ebook (a look at some of the GWT's more advanced features)

A little Googling shows that selenium. . . is an antidote for mercury poisoning.

> ► Jason Huggins, in an email conversation about what to call the new testing tool

Chapter 9

Web Testing with Selenium

by Neal Ford

Neal Ford is an application architect at ThoughtWorks, a global IT consultancy with an exclusive focus on end-to-end software development and delivery. He is the designer and developer of applications, instructional materials, magazine articles, and video presentations and the author of the books Developing with Delphi: Object-Oriented Techniques [WFW95], JBuilder 3 Unleashed [FWA+99], and Art of Java Web Development [For03]. His language proficiencies include Java, C#/.NET, Ruby, Object Pascal, C++, and C. His primary consulting focus is building large-scale enterprise applications. Neal has taught on-site classes nationally and internationally to all branches of the military and to many Fortune 500 companies. He is also an internationally acclaimed speaker, having spoken at numerous developer conferences worldwide. If you have an insatiable curiosity about Neal, visit his website at http://www.nealford.com. He welcomes feedback and can be reached at mailto:nford@thoughtworks.com.

9.1 Introduction

Selenium is a testing tool for web applications. It is designed for the *user acceptance* portion of the project: Selenium tests the web application from front to back, through all the layers of the architecture. Selenium is the premiere testing tool in its genre, which includes commercial offerings, and Selenium is the only tool that can test all aspects of Ajax behavior. This chapter is all about Selenium: its origins, its behaviors and modes, and the tools that have sprung up in this very active open source project.

Selenium is an open source project created by ThoughtWorks and released to the community. ThoughtWorks did this because Selenium supports testing and agile software development, and we're all about agile development. Selenium is always going to remain open source, so feel free to contribute your ideas and source code to this vibrant project.

9.2 Origins

At ThoughtWorks, we needed a new time and expenses (T&E) system. Like a lot of consulting companies, we suffer from the cobbler's children effect: we write software for clients but can never find time to write it for ourselves. Eventually, we decided we needed to commit resources to this project and make it happen. A resource was made available (which is ice-cold consultant speak for saying that a person was assigned) named Jason Huggins. Jason is a big Python fan, so he wanted to write the new T&E system using the Python portal framework Plone. The choice of tool was fine with ThoughtWorks, but there was a serious problem: we believe that code that isn't tested doesn't exist. The major road block was how to seriously test Plone.

Jason looked around at the current offerings in both the open source and commercial worlds and was underwhelmed. All the tools available at that time had shortcomings of some kind. Probably the closest that met our needs was the Watir framework (incidentally written by a former ThoughtWorker, Brett Petticord), but it worked only in Internet Explorer. ThoughtWorks users almost universally use Firefox, so we needed to be able to test the T&E system in Firefox as well.

So, Jason did what any self-respecting testing fanatic would do: he rolled his own. He created Selenium and started using it to test the new T&E system. Others started looking at what he had done and fell in love with the simplicity and elegance of the tool, so they started adding features. At some point, it was decided that this was too cool to keep within ThoughtWorks, so we decided to open source it.

To open source it, you must have a good name. Lots of names were bounced around, but the one that stuck was Selenium. Why? Well, lots of the contributors had used the commercial Mercury suite of tools and had found it lacking in one way or another. It turns out that, in addition to being the element with the atomic number 34 and being a nontoxic metal related to sulfur and tellurium, selenium is also the cure for mercury poisoning, which was the final straw: the name Selenium stuck.

Selenium is an *acceptance* testing tool for web applications, where the tests run directly in the browser. Selenium is implemented entirely with browser technologies—JavaScript, DHTML, iframes, and so on. It works by directly manipulating the Document Object Model (DOM) of the page shown in the browser. This means that Selenium works with virtually any JavaScript-enabled browser (the entire list of supported browsers appears in the Selenium documentation). You can download Selenium from the web.[1] When you download it, you have a directory structure that includes a bunch of supporting files (including the documentation) and a folder called core (shown in Figure 9.1, on the following page). This core folder contains the guts of Selenium used in TestRunner mode, discussed next.

Selenium features two modes of operation: *TestRunner* and *Remote Control*. We'll look at the simpler of the two, TestRunner, first.

9.3 Using Selenium in TestRunner Mode

In TestRunner mode, you deploy the core folder from the Selenium distribution alongside your application. By "alongside" I mean that you take the entire core folder and deploy it in the root of your web application, in whatever named folder you like (in other words, you can keep the name core if you want, but I frequently rename it Selenium for clarity's sake). For Java applications, this means adding the core folder to the root folder in your WAR file and redeploying your application. Selenium must run in the same web context as your application because of *cross-site scripting* concerns. Cross-site scripting (usually abbreviated XSS) is a hacker trick by which a web application executes malicious

---

1. From either http://selenium.thoughtworks.com or http://www.openqa.org/selenium/

Figure 9.1: SELENIUM FOLDER CONTENTS

code, usually JavaScript. Browsers are designed to deflect XSS attacks by not allowing JavaScript to manipulate a web application outside the context of where the JavaScript is running. Thus, Selenium (which is definitely not a hacker's tool) falls prey to this security restriction.

One of the parts of Selenium you deploy in the core folder is the BrowserBot. It is the piece of Selenium that plays back commands, acting as a virtual user of your application. The BrowserBot is written in JavaScript, so it has full access to the DOM of the page under test. This is what gives Selenium its power: nothing can change in the DOM that Selenium can't see, including background behavior like Ajax calls.

This "alongside" strategy appears in Figure 9.2, on the next page. It is not strictly required that you deploy Selenium in the same WAR file as

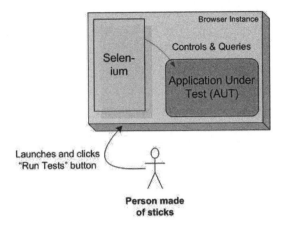

Figure 9.2: SELENIUM DEPLOYED IN TESTRUNNER MODE

your web application. As long as they run in the same web context, your browser should allow Selenium to work. The easiest deployment, though, places the core Selenium folder within your application. All tests and Selenium infrastructure reside solely in that folder, so if you want to remove your tests for production, you can remove this folder and redeploy.

TestRunner Tests

Selenium, like most unit testing frameworks, utilizes two types of testing artifacts: test cases and a test suite. A *test case* is a single interaction scenario with your web application. An example might be a test to log into the application. Another example for an ecommerce site would be to test that a user can select a catalog item and purchase it.

Test cases in Selenium are simple HTML tables with three columns. The first row is ignored (used as a test title), and the following rows consist of either an action/locator/value combination or an assertion/expectation/actual combination. The format of the simple test case appears in Figure 9.3, on the following page.

Test cases are no more complex than these simple HTML tables. You create them in any text editor. The table format is the one expected by the Selenium test runner, but you are allowed to put any additional text on the HTML page that you want. If you are familiar with the FitNesse functional testing tool, the tables here serve the same purpose.

Test Case Title		
action	locator	value
assertion	expectation	actual

Figure 9.3: TEST CASE FORMAT

In fact, you are encouraged to add documentation and other supporting text to the page. The only part that the Selenium test runner cares about is the test case table.

Generally, you have one test scenario per test case. This means you generally have lots of test cases for an application. As you add functionality, you add to your body of tests, which allows you to run the earlier tests as regression tests. Your test cases should remain as cohesive as possible. In other words, don't try to test too much in any one test case: you can have as many as you want.

TestRunner Suites

Once you have a test case or two, you'll want to run them in Selenium's test runner. For that, you'll need a *test suite*. Like test cases, test suites also consist of a simple HTML table. A test suite, though, has a single column. Like test cases, the first row is ignored (good for titling). The remaining rows contain hyperlinks to individual test case files.

Now you are ready to run your tests. Place the test case and test suite files in the Selenium folder you've deployed alongside your application (generally, it's a good idea to create a tests directory underneath the core Selenium stuff, just to keep your stuff separate from the Selenium stuff). Once you've deployed your application, navigate to the file TestRunner.html within the Selenium core folder in your running application. The TestRunner will allow you to browse for your test suite (or it will show it automatically if you've named it TestSuite.html). In either case, once you've selected your test suite, you should see something that looks a lot like Figure 9.4, on the next page.

The TestRunner display is separated into four sections. The upper left contains your test suite. Clicking any of the hyperlinks loads that test case in the upper center pane. As you've probably guessed, the upper center pane shows the current test case. The upper right contains the Selenium console. It allows you to specify the speed of the test (at the

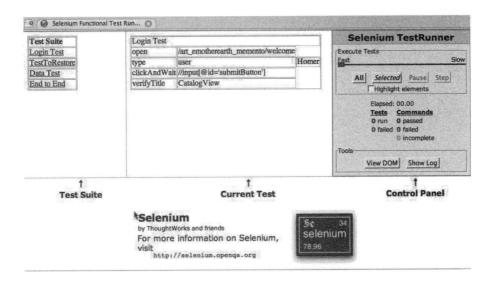

Figure 9.4: Selenium's TestRunner user interface

fastest speed, the application is a blur). This console also shows you statistics and allows you to specify things like which tests to run (All or Selected). The bottom of the frame shows your application as Selenium puts it through its paces. When Selenium runs tests, you see them run in the bottom part of the browser, just as if a user were manipulating the application.

When a test runs, each row is highlighted as the test runs. When that row completes successfully, it turns a light shade of green. Assertion backgrounds turn a darker shade of green. If the entire test case is successful, the title bar also turns green. Even though you can't see the colors in the printed book, Figure 9.5, on the following page, shows the test suite and test case upon successful completion of a test run.

Failed tests are another matter. If a row fails in a test, the failure cascades upward. Test failures are caused by two things: a failed action (which could be a misspelled action name or a failure to locate a control) or a failed assertion. When a row in the test case fails, the row indicates the problem and also turns its background red. This redness also escalates up to the test case title and to the title of the test suite as well. Like unit testing frameworks, red indicates failure and rolls up to the highest level.

Test Suite	Login Test		
Login Test	open	/art_emotherearth_memento/welcome	
TestToRestore	type	user	Homer
Data Test	clickAndWait	//input[@id='submitButton']	
End to End	verifyTitle	CatalogView	

Figure 9.5: SUCCESSFUL TEST CASE COMPLETION

This is as complex as TestRunner mode gets. Green means good; red means bad. You can run these tests over and over, putting your web application through its paces. You can also tie the TestRunner into a continuous integration environment (discussed in Section 9.6, *Tools*, on page 135). Before you start writing tests, though, you must master certain Selenium concepts.

9.4 Selenium Concepts

Selenium has five important concepts that represent everything you need to know about it: locators, patterns, actions, assertions, and accessors.

Locators

Locators tell Selenium how to find things on a web page. They live in the middle column of your test cases. Locating elements on a web page is tricky, so Selenium provides a bunch of ways to do it. The locators appear in Figure 9.6, on the facing page.

Locators start with the type of locator followed by = followed by the value you are trying to find. For example, to locate a table using XPath, you would use the locator xpath=//html/body/table. Without an explicit locator prefix, Selenium uses the following default strategies:

- *dom* for locators starting with "document."

- *xpath* for locators starting with "//"

- *identifier* otherwise

Type	Meaning
identifier=*id*	Select the element with the specified @id attribute. If no match is found, select the first element whose @name attribute is id.
id=*id*	Select the element with the specified @id attribute.
name=*name*	Select the first element with the specified @name attribute.
dom=*javascript expr*	Find an element using JavaScript traversal of the HTML Document Object Model. DOM locators must begin with "document.". • dom=document.forms['frm'].Drpdwn • dom=document.images[56]
xpath=*xpath expr*	Locate an element using an XPath expression. • xpath=//img[@alt='The image alt text'] • xpath=//table[@id='table1']//tr[4]/td[2]
link=*textPattern*	Select the link (anchor) element that contains text matching the specified pattern.
css=cssSelectorSyntax	Select the element using CSS selectors. • css=a[href="#id3"] • css=span#firstChild + span

Figure 9.6: LOCATOR TYPES

Because Selenium provides so many options, you have a huge number of locator strategies. *id* is by far the best; its uniqueness is encouraged by the HTML standard. Unfortunately, most HTML elements (such as tables) aren't considered first-class citizens enough to warrant *id* attributes. Thus, you are left with *DOM* and *xpath*. Although both of these options allow you to find anything on the page, they tend to be brittle: changes to the page will break these relative locators. This is one of the reasons that Selenium is designed for testing late in the life cycle of the project, when changes are less pervasive.

glob:pattern	Match a string against a glob (a.k.a. " wildmat") pattern. *Glob* is a kind of limited regular expression syntax typically used in command-line shells. In a glob pattern, * represents any sequence of characters, and ? represents any single character. Glob patterns match against the entire string.
regexp:regexp	Match a string using a regular expression. The full power of JavaScript regular expressions is available.
exact:string	Match a string exactly, verbatim, without any of that fancy wildcard stuff.

Figure 9.7: String-matching patterns

Patterns

Patterns describe how Selenium matches strings, so they concern the third column in test cases, where you specify the value you want to match. Selenium supports the patterns shown in Figure 9.7.

If no pattern prefix is specified, Selenium assumes that it's a glob pattern.

Actions

An *action* is something a user might do with the application. Actions represent the verbs in Selenium. The list of actions defines the kind of behaviors you can tell Selenium to perform. Actually, the list of actions encompasses more capabilities than users typically have. For example, Selenium includes a set of actions that allow you to manipulate cookies directly in tests (adding cookies, deleting them, and so on).

The list of actions is much too long to list here; actions make up the base API of Selenium. The complete list with descriptions appears in the Selenium documentation, which resides in a single HTML file named reference.html in the Selenium distribution.

Actions come in two forms: *action* and *actionAndWait*. The *action* performs the function of that action. For example, the *type* action types a value into a field. The *AndWait* version of an action does the same thing, but it assumes that the action will perform a call to the server, so it will wait for a response before continuing the test case. All actions (except *open*) have both an *action* and *actionAndWait* version.

End 2 End Scenario		
open	http://localhost:8080/art_emotherearth_memento/welcome	
type	user	Homer
clickAndWait	//input[@id='submitButton']	
assertLocation	glob:*art_emotherearth_memento/catalog	
assertTitle	CatalogView	
assertTextPresent	Catalog of Items	
assertElementPresent	//html/body/table/	
assertTable	//html/body/table/.1.1	Ocean
type	document.forms[1].quantity	3
clickAndWait	//input[@id='submit2']	
assertLocation	*art_emotherearth_memento/showcart	
assertTitle	ShowCart	
assertElementPresent	link=Click here for more shopping	
assertTextPresent	*, here is your cart:	
clickAndWait	link=Click here for more shopping	
assertLocation	*/art_emotherearth_memento/catalog	
type	document.forms[3].quantity	2
clickAndWait	//input[@id='submit4']	
click	//html/body/input[1]	
assertConfirmation	Do you * want to check out?	
type	ccNum	444444444444
select	ccType	label=Amex
type	ccExp	12/10
clickAndWait	//input[@value='Check out']	
assertTextPresent	*, Thank you for shopping at eMotherEarth.com	
assertTextPresent	regexp:Your confirmation number is \d?	

Figure 9.8: A REALISTIC SELENIUM TEST CASE

To provide a flavor of actions (and a realistic test), see the test in Figure 9.8. That test case shows a mix of locator and pattern-matching strategies. In addition, it illustrates a variety of actions, mixing both the *action* and *actionAndWait* variations. It also illustrates Selenium's ability to handle elements such as confirmation dialog boxes and popups. Notice the *assertConfirmation* action toward the bottom of the test. This is expecting the web application to provide the user with a confirmation dialog box (in this case, to make the checkout form available). Selenium automatically clicks the OK button of the confirmation dialog box (unless you've previously issued a *chooseCancelOnNextConfirmation* action). If the confirmation dialog box doesn't appear, the test fails. If a confirmation dialog box appears that had no assertion expecting it, the test will also fail. This illustrates Selenium's ability to interact with the web application at every level. Selenium handles pop-up alerts, confirmations, pop-up JavaScript windows, and frames. Because Selenium interacts directly with the DOM, it "sees" everything the browser sees and can therefore test it.

Assertions

Assertions allow you to verify the state of the application. They come in three forms:

- assert*Condition*
- verify*Condition*
- waitFor*Condition*

The "assert" version for a given condition fails the test if the assertion is incorrect, which stops the running of this test case (meaning that the test suite will continue to the next test case in the list).

The "verify" version will mark the row as a failure (which escalates to the test case title and test suite title) but allows the test case to continue running. Note that the test row, case, and suite are still marked as failures, but the test case continues to run so that you can test the other behavior in the test case.

The "waitFor" version of assertions is primarily designed to support Ajax operations. Frequently, Ajax calls take place in the background, issuing a call to the server to harvest some value. The "waitFor" version of an assertion will wait a specified amount of time for the condition to become true (the timeout period is set via the *setTimeout* action). If the value doesn't appear before the timeout, the test row fails. If the condition becomes true before the timeout, the row is marked as a success, and the test continues. In the "success" case, it doesn't wait the entire timeout amount of time.

Accessors and Variables

Selenium includes the ability to save variable values harvested or generated in one test and use them in another test. Internally, Selenium creates a JavaScript map called storedVars. Selenium includes a set of commands to populate this variable store. For example, the *storeAllButtons* action stores the names of all the buttons on the current page in the variable map.

You can also store your own variables in this map, using one of several store commands. For example, the store(variable_name, value) command allows you to store an arbitrary value in a variable, which might include JavaScript. As an example, web applications frequently require unique values for input fields. Using code like the following, you can generate a unique value and retrieve it later:

```
javascript{ "merchant " + (new Date().getTime()) }
```

To retrieve variables in later test rows, use the syntax ${variable_name}. Alternatively, because you know the internal representation, you can use a JavaScript expression directly:

```
javascript{ storedVars['name'].toUpperCase() }
```

Selenium allows you to store virtually any information harvested from the page for later comparisons. You can think of the variable collection as a global variable store, scoped at the test suite level.

9.5 Remote Control Selenium

Up until now, I've been talking about Selenium in TestRunner mode. The benefit of TestRunner mode is its simplicity: even nontechnical people (such as business analysts) can understand the syntax of the test cases and test suites. This is on purpose: Selenium was designed so that nondevelopers could write and execute tests. However, TestRunner mode has a serious constraint: you must deploy the Selenium core folder alongside your application. As mentioned, this restriction exists because of XSS concerns. But, it also means you can't test public websites such as Google or your own site in production.

Two other restrictions exist for TestRunner mode: the HTML format of the tests and the requirement that you must deploy the tests to the web application. As everyone knows, "real" developers don't write HTML, so another, more macho format must exist. Some ThoughtWorkers, led by Really Smart Guy Paul Hammant, decided to fix these problems, so they created Remote Control Selenium.

Remote Control Selenium solves all these problems. Remote Control gets around the requirement that you deploy the BrowserBot by deploying it on a proxy server. The contents of the application under test are pulled down to the proxy server, and the tests run there. To set up Remote Control, you must run the proxy server (which is a slightly modified version of the open source Jetty servlet engine).

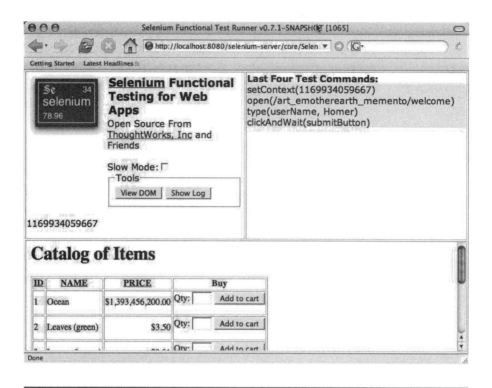

Figure 9.9: REMOTE CONTROL INSTANCE OF A BROWSER

Remote Control Selenium allows you to write tests in your base language as run-of-the-mill unit tests.

When Remote Control Selenium starts, it must still start an instance of a browser. One of the major strong points of Selenium is its ability to run tests directly in the browser, and Remote Control doesn't change that. The difference is that the controlling process is now a unit test, and the browser just runs the tests, not the TestRunner itself. Figure 9.9, shows an instance of the browser started from Remote Control.

Because the proxy handles the BrowserBot functionality, you can write your tests as "normal" JUnit tests. The following test shows a JUnit test written in Java that drives Remote Control Selenium:

```
code/ford/SeleniumRemoteControlTest.java
```

```java
package com.nealford.art.memento.emotherearth.test;

/**
 * User: Neal Ford
 * <cite>Incidentally, created by IntelliJ IDEA.</cite>
 */

import com.thoughtworks.selenium.DefaultSelenium;
import com.thoughtworks.selenium.Selenium;
import junit.framework.TestCase;

public class SeleniumRemoteControlTest extends TestCase {
        private Selenium s;

    public void setUp() {
        s = new DefaultSelenium("localhost", 4444, "*firefox",
                "http://localhost:8080/");
        s.start();
    }

    public void testEMotherEarthEnd2End() {
        s.open("/art_emotherearth_memento/welcome");
        s.type("user", "Homer");
        s.click("//input[@id='submitButton']");
        s.waitForPageToLoad("30000");
        assertTrue(s.getLocation().
                matches(".*art_emotherearth_memento/catalog"));
        assertEquals("CatalogView", s.getTitle());
        assertTrue(s.isTextPresent("Catalog of Items"));
        assertTrue(s.isElementPresent("//html/body/table/"));
        assertEquals("Ocean", s.getTable("//html/body/table/.1.1"));
        s.type("document.forms[1].quantity", "3");
        s.click("//input[@id='submit2']");
        s.waitForPageToLoad("30000");
        assertTrue(s.getLocation().
                matches(".*art_emotherearth_memento/showcart"));
        assertEquals("ShowCart", s.getTitle());
        assertTrue(s.isElementPresent("link=Click here for more shopping"));
        assertTrue(s.isTextPresent("*, here is your cart:"));
        s.click("link=Click here for more shopping");
        s.waitForPageToLoad("30000");
        assertTrue(s.getLocation().
                matches(".*art_emotherearth_memento/catalog"));
        s.type("document.forms[3].quantity", "2");
        s.click("//input[@id='submit4']");
        s.waitForPageToLoad("30000");
        s.type("ccNum", "444444444444");
        s.select("ccType", "label=Amex");
        s.type("ccExp", "12/10");
```

```
        s.click("//input[@value='Check out']");
        s.waitForPageToLoad("30000");
        assertTrue(
            s.isTextPresent("*, Thank you for shopping at eMotherEarth.com"));
        assertTrue(
            s.isTextPresent("regexp:Your confirmation number is \\d?"));
    }

    public void tearDown() {
        s.stop();
    }
}
```

Java is far from the only supported language. As I mentioned in Section 9.1, *Introduction*, on page 120, the original author of Selenium was (and is) a huge Python fan. Selenium supports tests written in Java, Python, Ruby, .NET, and Perl (and someone from the community has added support for Squeak, the open source dialect of Smalltalk). Here is the same unit test as earlier, implemented in Ruby instead of Java:

code/ford/SeleniumRemoteControl.rb

```
require 'test/unit'
require 'selenium'

class SeleniumRemoteControlTest < Test::Unit::TestCase

  def setup
    @s = Selenium::SeleneseInterpreter.new("localhost", 4444, "*chrome",
          "http://localhost:8080/", 15000)
    @s.start
  end

  def test_emotherearth_end_to_end
    @s.open "http://localhost:8080/art_emotherearth_memento/welcome"
    @s.type "user", "Homer"
    @s.click "//input[@id='submitButton']"
    @s.wait_for_page_to_load "30000"
    assert @s.get_location =~ /.*art_emotherearth_memento\/catalog/
    assert_equal "CatalogView", @s.get_title
    assert @s.is_text_present("Catalog of Items")
    assert @s.is_element_present("//html/body/table/")
    assert_equal "Ocean", @s.get_table("//html/body/table/.1.1")
    @s.type "document.forms[1].quantity", "3"
    @s.click "//input[@id='submit2']"
    @s.wait_for_page_to_load "30000"
    assert @s.get_location =~ /.*art_emotherearth_memento\/showcart/
    assert_equal "ShowCart", @s.get_title
    assert @s.is_element_present("link=Click here for more shopping")
    assert @s.is_text_present("*, here is your cart:")
    @s.click "link=Click here for more shopping"
    @s.wait_for_page_to_load "30000"
```

```
    assert @s.get_location =~ /.*art_emotherearth_memento\/catalog/
    @s.type "document.forms[3].quantity", "2"
    @s.click "//input[@id='submit4']"
    @s.wait_for_page_to_load "30000"
    @s.type "ccNum", "444444444444"
    @s.select "ccType", "label=Amex"
    @s.type "ccExp", "12/10"
    @s.click "//input[@value='Check out']"
    @s.wait_for_page_to_load "30000"
    assert @s.is_text_present("*, Thank you for shopping at eMotherEarth.com")
    assert @s.is_text_present("regexp:Your confirmation number is \d?")
  end

  def teardown
    @s.stop
  end
end
```

All the Selenium concepts discussed earlier apply equally in Remote Control mode. In fact, the Selenium API is completely agnostic as to how it is run. Anything supported by TestRunner mode is intrinsically supported by RemoteControl Selenium. As you will see in Section 9.6, *Tools*, it even offers ways to translate the two formats back and forth.

Remote Control Selenium is much more of a developer's tool, but it offers great flexibility and power. Notice that you can run Selenium tests against any site by pulling the contents down to the proxy server that runs the Selenium BrowserBot. This allows you to test public websites and your own websites in production upon which you don't want the BrowserBot deployed. Remote Control also allows you to keep your tests in your regular testing infrastructure (including version control).

9.6 Tools

Creating tests in Selenium was designed to be as simple as possible. However, you still must create the HTML tables and files. As mentioned previously, the intent of Selenium was to create a testing tool that non-developers could use. Some developers decided that it was still too hard to create the tests, so the Selenium IDE was born.

The Selenium IDE is a Firefox plug-in that allows you to record Test-Runner Selenium tests directly from your interaction with the web application. The Selenium IDE in action appears in Figure 9.10, on the following page.

The IDE records your interaction with the web application, creating test cases for you. You can also run the tests directly from the IDE or push

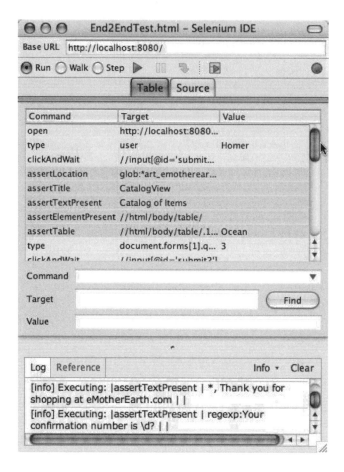

Figure 9.10: The Selenium IDE

the tests over into TestRunner mode from the IDE. The goal of the IDE is to create a real development environment for Selenium tests. You can set breakpoints, look at log messages, add and remove test rows, and even get code completion for Selenium commands.

The IDE is primarily designed to make TestRunner tests trivially easy to create. But it will also allow you to convert recorded TestRunner tests to Remote Control tests in all the currently supported languages.

As you can see, the Selenium IDE is the icing on the cake. It makes it easy for *anyone* to generate Selenium tests. For projects on which I've worked, we had the business analysts record their acceptance tests using the Selenium IDE, which we then saved as Remote Control tests and ran as part of our continuous integration process. This allowed us to get regression testing for acceptance tests. And it paid off handsomely: several tests unexpectedly broke after changes that shouldn't have affected them, alerting us to problems *as soon as they happened*, not a week later. That made Selenium worth its weight in gold for us.

9.7 Summary

This chapter only scratched the surface of the capabilities of Selenium. Room won't permit a discussion of extending Selenium (which is easy, using JavaScript to add you own actions, locators, and patterns). I also don't have room to talk about incorporating Selenium into a continuous integration process. It would be odd indeed for the company that created CruiseControl to build a tool that didn't play nice with it, and trust me, we didn't. Selenium is supported by all major continuous integration servers; the documentation includes setup information to get it to work. I also don't have room to talk about sexy Selenium tricks, such as creating data-driven tests. (The tests themselves, because they are HTML, can be generated by a JSP. The test suite includes only hyperlinks, so nothing says you can't have a hyperlink to a JSP.)

Selenium is an awesome testing tool. It shows how a vibrant open source community can come together and create something great that benefits everyone. Selenium is the only tool that can test every possible Ajax behavior because Selenium runs alongside the DOM. There are no competitors for what Selenium does, commercial or otherwise. Do your project a favor: go download Selenium right now, and start using it to improve your project life cycle via testing. It's so easy now you can't have an excuse not to do it.

9.8 Web Resources

Selenium . . . . .http://www.openqa.org/selenium/
Selenium's home page

The Selenium IDE . . . . .http://www.openqa.org/selenium-ide/
The Firefox plug-in for recording and playing tests

XPather https://addons.mozilla.org/firefox/1192/
Firefox plug-in that makes it easy to grab XPath expressions by pointing to resources

Samples .http://www.nealford.com/index.html\#NFJS_Selenium
Downloadable samples from this chapter

If I couldn't get an IntelliJ license through my work, I would
give blood once a week until I could save up enough money
to buy one of my own.
► Neal Ford, IntelliJ junkie since 2001

Chapter 10

IntelliJ Tips, Tricks, and Techniques

10.1 Introduction

There are two primary religions in the Java world: Eclipse and IntelliJ.
Or, as one of our colleagues puts it: "There are two kinds of developers:
those with IDEA and those with no idea." Of course, there are lots of
secondary camps, filled with pagan Emacs and vi users and the occa-
sional NetBeans or JBuilder refugee, but mostly you have the Eclipse
camp and the IntelliJ camp. At a few of the No Fluff Just Stuff shows
last year, we did an "IDE Productivity" Birds of a Feather (BOF) session, where adherents from each camp came together to learn keyboard
shortcuts and tips about their favorite IDEs. Those BOFs turned out to
be some of the most popular of the year, and it was fun for the speakers as well. The tips that follow are just some favorite little tricks and
techniques that some speaker uses all the time and is spreading to the
rest of the world.

10.2 Stop Typing the Left Side

This tip works in any modern IDE that includes the "Introduce Variable"
refactoring. Typing the left side of any expression is totally passe—let
the tool do it for you. For example, if you need to create a new Date
object, like this:

```
new Date();
```

just type the right side, and let IntelliJ do the hard work by invoking the "Introduce Variable" refactoring. IntelliJ will look at the type and suggest a variable name, which is generally about what you would put anyway:

```
Date date = new Date();
```

Learn the keyboard shortcut for 'Introduce Variable," and you'll never type the left side of an expression again.

10.3 Remote Debugging Setup

All major IDEs support remote debugging by relying on facilities built into the Java platform (the Java Debug Wire Protocol and related APIs have been around since the introduction of Java 2). One of the headaches of setting up remote debugging is making sure that the *debugger* (that is, the IDE) and the *debuggee* (that is, the virtual machine running the application you are trying to remote debug) agree on their settings. If you specify a port number of 8001 on the debugger and a port number of 8002 on the debuggee, the magic just doesn't work.

IntelliJ knows that this is a problem, so it helps you keep track of the myriad settings required to make remote debugging work. Figure 10.1, on the next page, shows the remote debugging dialog box with the helper section outlined at the top.

The box highlighted in red indicates what debugger settings you've set up in the fields below it. As you change those values, the ones in the text field at the top change to reflect the settings you've made below. When you have completed configuring the debugger, you can copy and paste those settings to the debuggee. This means you can never get the settings out of sync: IntelliJ becomes the single place where the settings are defined, allowing you to paste them into the start-up script of your servlet engine/application server.

10.4 The IDE That Reads Your Mind

IntelliJ users are used to an IDE that reads your mind. It just seems to know what you want to do before you realize it yourself. IntelliJ is one of the few pieces of software that has actually made us stop in midwork to speculate on how it figured out exactly want we wanted. It is so uncannily smart that we have to mentally reverse engineer how the IntelliJ developers did it. Here are a couple of examples.

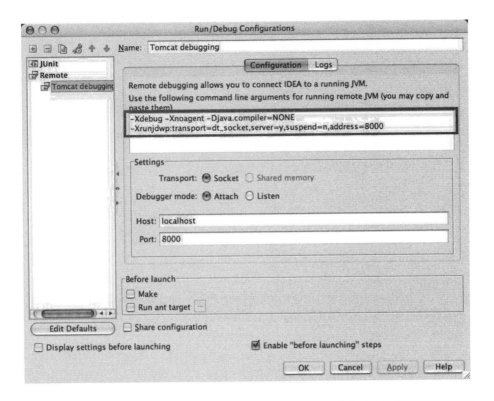

Figure 10.1: INTELLIJ'S REMOTE DEBUGGING SETUP DIALOG BOX

Smart Extract Interface

When writing code in the proper agile way, you tend to refactor your code a lot. Although the tools have gotten much better at assisting you, you still do some *aggregate refactorings* by hand. Aggregate refactorings are refactoring steps that require a combination of the atomic refactorings mention in Martin Fowler's *Refactoring* [FBB+99] book. For example, *extract interface* refactoring frequently takes multiple steps, especially if you are trying to extract an interface with the name of the current concrete class and replace the current concrete class with a new name:

1. Rename the current class.
2. Extract interface with the old class name.
3. Make the old class implement the new interface.

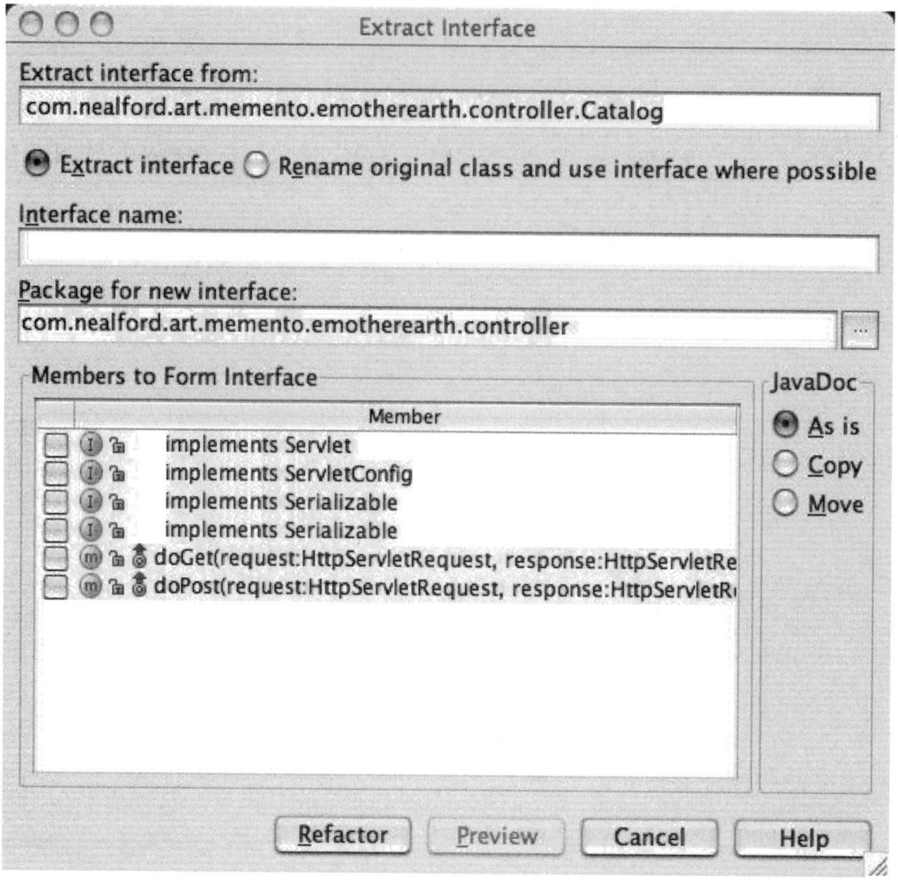

Figure 10.2: INTELLIJ'S SMART EXTRACT INTERFACE DIALOG BOX

IntelliJ "understands" that this is the typical need when you *extract interface*, so it collapses this into a single step. This option is highlighted in Figure 10.2. This is one of the options that make you realize the makers of IntelliJ actually *use* their tool for everyday coding.

IntelliJ is sometimes so smart that it's like having a pair programmer always watching out to make sure you are doing the right thing. Here's a perfect example: you're doing Swing development and need to set the width and height for a component. It's easy to get the parameters transposed. IntelliJ knows this and tips you off as shown in Figure 10.3, on the next page.

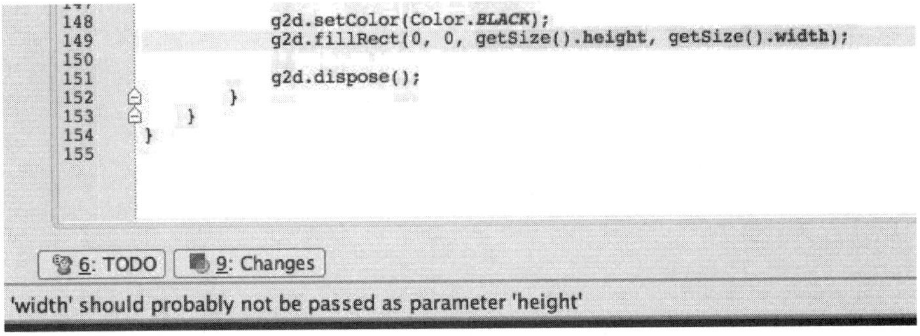

```
147
148         g2d.setColor(Color.BLACK);
149         g2d.fillRect(0, 0, getSize().height, getSize().width);
150
151         g2d.dispose();
152    ⌂  }
153    ⌂ }
154  }
155
```

6: TODO   9: Changes

'width' should probably not be passed as parameter 'height'

Figure 10.3: INTELLIJ AS A PAIR PROGRAMMER

The Magic Lightbulb

IntelliJ users get used to seeing the lightbulb icon pop up in the left margin. This is IntelliJ's polite way of telling you that there is a better way to do what you are trying to do or to automatically fix something for you. Of course, most of the major IDEs are smart enough to fix little things like package imports. IntelliJ's lightbulb is a scary-smart pair programmer.

Here is a good example of just how far the lightbulb can take you. We were refactoring the following code:

```
Timer timer = new Timer("message timer");
final int countdownToNextMessage = 0;
timer.scheduleAtFixedRate(new TimerTask() {
    public void run() {
        if (countdownToNextMessage >= 0) {
            playback.playback();
        }
    }
}, 100, 100);
```

In this code, we are creating an anonymous inner class to handle counting down to the next timed event. The rule on anonymous inner classes in Java states that all external variables accessed in the inner class method must be final. In this case, we already had countdownToNextMessage declared as **final**. Earlier in the code, we assigned the instance of the playback object. As soon as we put playback inside the run() method, our friend the lightbulb popped up, as shown in Figure 10.4, on the following page. IntelliJ knew that it must be **final** to work and that it couldn't be changed to **final** because of the earlier assignment.

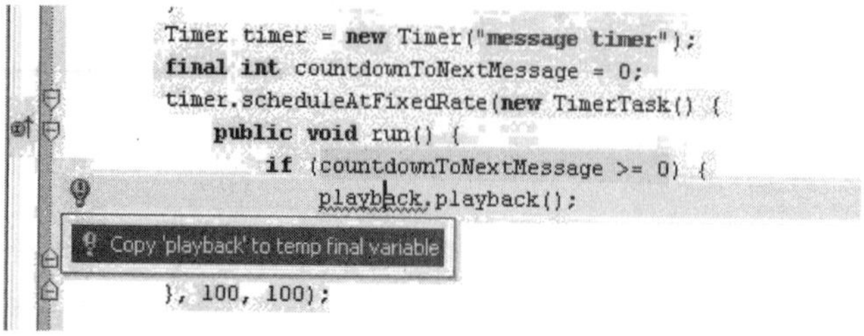

Figure 10.4: Intellij's smart lightbulb

Thus, it correctly changed the code to this:

```
Timer timer = new Timer("message timer");
final int countdownToNextMessage = 0;
final Playback playback1 = playback;
timer.scheduleAtFixedRate(new TimerTask() {
    public void run() {
        if (countdownToNextMessage >= 0) {
            playback1.playback();
        }
    }
}, 100, 100);
```

IntelliJ does this mind-reading trick all the time. It understands really obscure things about Java that a lot of developers don't even know. That the developers of IntelliJ anticipated this situation and provided an automatic fix for it is just stunning.

10.5 Quick File Finding

Hierarchies have gotten too deep to be useful. File systems, package structures, and other hierarchical systems, once they reach a certain size, become too deep for effective navigation. Large Java projects suffer from this because the package structure is tied to the directory structure. Even for a small project, you must dig through trees, expanding nodes as you go, to find a file to open, even if you already know the name of the file. If you find yourself doing this, you are working too hard for your computer.

IntelliJ allows you to quickly find any Java source files within the current project by pressing Ctrl+N on Windows or Apple+N on the Mac. It opens a text box in the editor, allowing you to type the name of the file you want. This is shown in Figure 10.5, on the next page.

```
   24            ServletExcep  Enter class name: (☐ Include non-project classes)
   25            doPost(request,  Shopp
   26        }
⊙ ShoppingCart (com.nealford.art.memento.emotherearth.util)
⊙ ShoppingCartMemento in ShoppingCart (com.nealford.art.memento.emotherearth.util)
   30            ServletException, IOException {
   31
```

Figure 10.5: INTELLIJ'S "FIND FILE" TEXT FIELD

```
   23                    HttpServletResponse response) throws
   24            ServletExcep  Enter class name: (☐ Include non-project classes)
   25            doPost(request,  SCM
   26        }
⊙ ShoppingCartMemento in ShoppingCart (com.nealford.art.memento.emotherearth.util)
   29                    HttpServletResponse response) throws
   30            ServletException, IOException {
   31
```

Figure 10.6: INTELLIJ'S SMART PATTERN MATCHING FOR NAMES

Typing the entire name (or even a significant portion of it) is cumbersome. It would be nice if IntelliJ was even smarter about how you specify names. And it is. Instead of typing the name of the file, if you start typing capital letters, IntelliJ looks for names that have that same pattern of capital letters. For example, if you are looking for the file ShoppingCartMemento, you can type *SCM*, and IntelliJ will ignore the intervening lowercase letters and find the matching pattern of capital letters, as shown in Figure 10.6.

This find-finding magic works with non-Java source files, too. Instead of Ctrl+N (or Apple+N), add a Shift to it. This is the "find resources" text field, and it works just like the "find files" one. We never go slogging through the huge tree of source files anymore: we know what we want, and we go directly to it.

10.6 Quick Navigation

To navigate to a class whose name you have in the code, press Ctrl+B on Windows or Apple+B on the Mac, and the class source file opens. Instead of going to the source of a class, what if you want to find all the derived classes (or navigate to a particular derived class) of a class? Instead of the previous key sequence, press Ctrl+Alt+B on Windows or Apple+Option+B on the Mac, and you will get a list of classes that derive (or implement in the case of an interface) from the class. If only one class derives (or implements), then you're directly taken to it. And, last but not least, `Ctrl+U` on Windows or `Apple+U` on the Mac takes you to the superclass method of the method within which your cursor currently resides. The code navigation features of IntelliJ are awesome.

When working on a class, you can navigate to various methods of the class by pressing `Ctrl+F12` on Windows or `Apple+F12` on the Mac. Wait, what if you want to go to a method that is part of another class, one that might not even be open in the IDE? Press `Ctrl+Shift+Alt+N` on Windows or `Apple+Shift+Option+N` on the Mac, and start entering the method (or symbol) name. You will be presented with a list of all methods (or symbols) and where they belong. Pretty cool, eh?

When you have multiple files open in the IDE, you of course can click the Tab key to navigate between them. But that takes way too much effort (and the use of mouse) for your humble speakers. Simply press `Alt+right arrow` on Windows or `Option+right arrow` (or left arrow) on the Mac to navigate. And what if you want to bring that project window up again? Simply press `Alt+1` on Windows or `Option+1` on the Mac, and you can make it appear and disappear. This is useful to maximize your code real estate but quickly bring the project window when needed.

Often we find ourselves looking for stuff (variables, declarations, comments, and so on) in the code or documents. Incremental search (`Alt+F3` on Windows or `Option+F3` on the Mac) allows you to search as you type what you want to find. Once you find what you desire, you can find the next or previous occurrence of the same word in the file using the down or up arrow, respectively.

10.7 Column Select and Replace

One of the main reasons to use a editor is to make it easier to manipulate text. You can select a column of text and replace its content. To start selecting a column of text, press `Alt+Shift+Insert` on Windows or `Shift+Apple+*` on the Mac, as shown in Figure 10.7, on the next page. Now you can select a column of text using the mouse or the keyboard arrows. Whatever you type now will replace that column in each row. Press the previously mentioned keystroke combination to end the column select.

```
public FunWithInitializers() {
    List<String> movieList = new ArrayList<String>() {
        { add("The Godfather");
          add("The Shawshank Redemption");
          add("The Godfather Part II");
          add("The Lord of the Rings: The Return of the King"); }
    };
    for (String s : movieList)
        System.out.println(s);
}
```

Figure 10.7: COLUMN SELECTION

10.8 Super-Smart Live Templates

Live templates, which provide automatic insertion of snippets of code
you constantly reuse, are one of the most productivity-enhancing features of modern IDEs. IntelliJ obviously includes this feature, in three
different forms: simple, parameterized, and surround.

Templates are chunks of code, either static code that never changes
(simple templates) or code that includes *variables* (parameterized templates). IntelliJ uses the Velocity template engine internally, so the variables in templates take the form $<variable-name>$. Everywhere that
the variable appears, it takes on the value you give it while typing. For
example, consider the *itar* template (for creating iterations over collections), shown here:

```
for(int $INDEX$ = 0; $INDEX$ < $ARRAY$.length; $INDEX$++) {
  $ELEMENT_TYPE$ $VAR$ = $ARRAY$[$INDEX$];
  $END$
}
```

Notice that the variable $INDEX$ appears more than once in the template. As you expand the template, whatever value you type for $INDEX$
in the first instance is automatically replaced everywhere that variable
appears. When the template expands, IntelliJ goes into template editing mode, which allows you to tab between variable declarations. It also
allows you to choose from appropriate variables in scope, shown in Figure 10.8, on the following page.

The third type of template in IntelliJ is a *surround template*. This is
a template that surrounds existing code, using the specially defined
$SELECTION$ variable. For example, the template <TAG>$SELECTION$
</$TAGNAME$> surrounds the selected text in an XML tag, which you
type after the surround operation (the tag and matching end tag insert
in unison).

```
public class LiveTemplateTester {
    public LiveTemplateTester() {
        int[] integerArray = new int[] {1,2,3,4,5};
        char[] charArrray = new char[] {'c', 'd', 'e'};
        for (int i = 0; i < charArrray.length; i++) {
            char c = char  charArrray        char[]
                           integerArray      int[]
        }
    }
}
```

Figure 10.8: INTELLIJ SUPPLIES VARIABLES DURING TEMPLATE EXPAN-
SION

Using live templates is one of the most important steps you can take
as a developer to greatly increase your productivity. By typing repetitive code for you, it cuts down on mistakes and the sheer number of
characters you must type. Don't be shy about adding new ones: every
time you find yourself typing something for the second time, make it a
template. Chances are good that if you type it twice, you'll type it 100
times. Let IntelliJ do that work for you.

10.9 Macro Recorder

One of the most underutilized tools for raw developer productivity is
the *macro recorder*. The ability to record a series of keystrokes and play
them back can save huge amounts of time. As you record more and
more macros, it becomes easier to see tasks as repeatable series of
steps. For example, if you need to perform a similar change to multiple
lines, do it once with the macro recorder running, making sure you
understand at what position you start and stop. Then you can replay
the macro for each line. Part of the learning curve to really leverage a
macro recorder is to *think* in a way that facilitates using it.

The lack of a macro recorder is our number-one complaint about
Eclipse. IntelliJ has a decent macro recorder and playback behavior,
found under Tools and the menu options Start Macro Recording, Playback Last Macro, and Edit Macros. The Edit Macros menu option allows
you to look at the list of named macros you've saved along with the editor commands captured by that macro.

IntelliJ allows you to assign macros you've recorded to keystrokes
(through the keystroke editor in the Preferences pane). You can also
share macros across your development team: the macros reside in the

```
34      }
35
36      public Object[] toArray() {
37          return _set.toArray();
38      }
39
    ⌘⇧⌥C (Copy Reference)    ject[] a) {
                4 time(s)
44      public boolean add(Object o) {
45          _count++;
46          return _set.add(o);
47      }
```

Figure 10.9: THE KEY PROMOTER POP-UP

file IDEA_HOME/config/options/macros.xml, which can be copied into the same location on each developer's machine. Or, if you are clever, you can create a *symbolic link* to a copy of this file in version control, placing the link in the required location from IntelliJ. Then, if one person adds a new macro, a quick synchronization with version control updates everyone on the team.

Sharing a resource across the team with a well-chosen link is an example of the *indirection* principle, one of five techniques to improve developer productivity found in *The Productive Programmer* [DB07].

10.10 Key Promoter Plug-In

Of course, one of the nice features of the Eclipse ecosystem is the sheer number of plug-ins available for the platform. IntelliJ also has a pretty vibrant community, with some slick plug-ins. One of our favorites is the Key Promoter plug-in. We're fanatics about using keyboard shortcuts for everything because it makes us orders of magnitude more productive. The Key Promoter plug-in for IntelliJ encourages you to use the equivalent keyboard shortcuts for any menu or mouse operation you perform. Not only that, but it tells you how many times it has reminded you to use the keyboard for this particular shortcut. It shows its reminder in a pop-up window at the bottom of the editor anytime you use the menu or mouse to perform something that already has a keyboard shortcut defined. It is shown in Figure 10.9, complaining that we've used the menu for Copy Reference four times now when the perfectly good keyboard shortcut is going to waste.

It can get overwhelming when you have so many keyboard shortcuts to master. The best way to remember a shortcut is to use it frequently.

The next time you are performing a frequent operation or navigation, stop for a second, and ask whether there is a keyboard shortcut for it. But, how do you know? Click Help and the (appropriately named) productivity guide. Not only will you see a list of shortcuts and description, but you will realize that IntelliJ has been keeping an eye on you, quietly monitoring when and how frequently you use certain features!

We like tools like this that encourage good behavior and punish (or at least ridicule) bad behavior. This plug-in has taught us tons of keyboard shortcuts in IntelliJ.

10.11 Summary

A lot of the NFJS attendees ask why so many of the speakers on the tour use IntelliJ, because polls of the room typically indicate a huge number of Eclipse users. We've used all the major Java IDEs "in anger," and for the authors of this chapter, IntelliJ is simply the best. In fact, in our opinion, IntelliJ is in the top-five best-written pieces of software ever created, considering how well suited it is to the task for which is was designed. It has the uncanny ability to read your mind. Few pieces of software have made us stop in mid-action and ask, to no one in particular, "How did it know to do *that*?" and then sit around for fifteen minutes figuring out how it figured out to do the Right Thing.

We greatly admire Eclipse and the effort that has made Eclipse into the tool it is. It is a shining example of how far open source can go (especially with funding from a large company like IBM with a chip on its shoulder—do you think it is a coincidence that the tool is called Eclipse?). Eclipse shows what a strong, vibrant community can create. And, it would be our favorite IDE. . . if it weren't for IntelliJ. IntelliJ on the Mac is the best programming experience we've encountered thus far, and we hope the JetBrains crew can keep it coming.

10.12 Web Resources

JetBrains . . . . www.jetbrains.com
IntelliJ's home page

IntelliJ Plugins . . . . http://www.jetbrains.com/idea/plugins/plugins.html
IntelliJ's official plug-ins page

IntelliJ's Plugin Repository . . . . http://plugins.intellij.net/
IntelliJ's plug-in repository (including Key Promoter)

## Chapter 11

Pragmatic Tips, Tricks, and Techniques: Eclipse

11.1 Introduction

Eclipse is one of the most successful open source projects ever. We frequently take a poll at No Fluff Just Stuff shows to ask the participants which IDE they use, and the overwhelming response is always Eclipse. And it's not just because it's free (although that certainly doesn't hurt). NetBeans is also free, yet it trails Eclipse considerably in popularity. Eclipse is both free and just plain *good*! We've gathered some handy tips, tricks, information, and plug-ins from No Fluff Just Stuff speakers.

11.2 Generating by Your Own Rules

Eclipse, like most IDEs, can autogenerate the get/set methods for a particular field when requested. By default, it generates the names of those get/set methods around the name of the field itself. This means if you create a field _foo, Eclipse wants to generate get_foo() and set_foo() for you. Although simple to understand, this is somewhat counter-intuitive—after all, the field name shouldn't really be at all important, and truthfully, proper encapsulation suggests that we should think of the public API in terms divorced from the internal implementation, including the name. Fortunately, Eclipse allows for this; see under Window –> Preferences –> Java –> Code Style, where you can specify prefixes or suffixes for fields of different types. Note that this can be either a project-wide or global setting.

Code completion	<A few starting characters or CamelCaseAbbreviation>+Ctrl+space
Complete identifier	<zero or more starting characters>+Ctrl+space Text completion or Alt+/
Open declaration	`F3`
Open type hierarchy	`F4`
Open a type	`Ctrl+Shift+T`
Open a file (resource)	`Ctrl+Shift+R`
Open type hierarchy	`Ctrl+Shift+H`
<`Ctrl+Shift+L`>	Lists all keyboard shortcuts (for the current context)

Figure 11.1: CHOICE ECLIPSE SHORTCUTS

11.3 Pasty-White Pasting

Like most languages, Java has some specific rules around character strings. String literals can contain any character, but certain character combinations are used to create "effects" within the text string; for example, \t embeds a tab character into the stream, \r embeds a carriage return, and so on. When copying text from outside sources (such as a shell prompt or other editor) into a Java string literal (such as when writing unit tests and assert()ing the results), these special characters can get lost. Fortunately, Eclipse has a nifty editor setting to recognize these special characters when pasting and will automatically add the necessary escape sequences (the backslash-character combinations) for you. Look for Escape Text Pasted into Java Strings in the Eclipse editor settings.

11.4 Tickling the Keys

There is no better way to improve your productivity than to master shortcuts and key bindings. In Figure 11.1, you can see a list of rather simple but very useful operations.

Of course, there are many more key bindings to make you productive, and time spent learning them is time well spent. One of the best ways to learn features such as keyboard shortcuts are flash cards. The book *The Productive Programmer* [DB07] includes flash cards for both Eclipse and IntelliJ so you can torture your co-workers with questions like "Which keystroke lets you search for resources?" instead of arguing about where curly braces should go.

11.5   Filtration

If you are working on a server-side project, it is quite unlikely that when you type *List* you mean java.awt.List. Yet, Eclipse will ask you which List you meant when you use any code completion feature (organize imports, for example). Type filters help you avoid this nuisance by specifying types that you will not need in your workspace.

To define a type filter, open the Type Filters window by selecting Preferences –> Java –> Appearance –> Type Filters, and add any packages you will not or don't want to use (for example, java.awt.*, javax,*, com.sun.*, or sun.*).

11.6   Blinded by Source Code

If you are trying to understand a functionality in a complex project or fixing a bug, it is not uncommon to start navigating at an element and then get distracted by elements unrelated to the functionality being examined. The result is spending too much time wandering around without any focus. Further, if you have to leave the exploration because of any interruptions, coming back to the same activity is difficult because you may not remember your prior exploration.

The Mylar plug-in (http://eclipse.org/mylar), named because mylar is used to safely view eclipses, helps you manage explorations in a complex project. Once you install the plug-in, all you need to do before any exploration is to create a new task. Mylar will track your activities and create a view of elements that are most relevant to the current task. You can come to a task any time, and it will show the related elements to get you started quickly with further exploration. If you can't see what you need, then you'll want to click the plug-in to see all non-task-oriented files (at first we lost track of our files because of this plug-in, not realizing that's what was happening).

11.7   Managing Plug-Ins

Although we don't necessarily like to admit it, upgrading versions of the IDE is a necessary evil in software development, and although the Eclipse environment provides a phenomenal amount of support for managing plug-ins, it can still be a little rocky to upgrade Eclipse itself and keep all the plug-ins and their settings in line. To make it easier, create two "extension locations" where plug-ins are installed, outside the main Eclipse subdirectory tree. Create one for the majority of plug-ins (managed by the Plugin Manager), and create the second for those oddball plug-ins that require manual downloading/installing. Now you can blow away your entire Eclipse subdirectory tree, install a new version, and point the new version at the two extension locations, and all your old plug-ins are ready and waiting for you.

11.8 Just Browsing

One of Eclipse's little-known skeletons hiding in the closet is that Eclipse was born of the same folks who gave us Visual Age for Java, which in turn was a direct descendant of Visual Age for Smalltalk. Although much of Visual Age for Java's "quirks" aren't present in Eclipse, one of its more powerful features remains in the Java Browser mode, a multipaneled view of all the packages, classes, and methods present in the code base on which you're working, complete with easy-to-use navigation features. Next time you're in Java Editor mode, take a moment and switch over to Java Browser mode and wander around a bit.

11.9 Window Shopping

Find yourself flipping back and forth between two different views? Or between two different editor windows? Point the mouse at the Window menu, and click the New Window menu item, which brings up an entirely new Eclipse window. Now, when working on a two-monitor setup, you can have one Eclipse window in Java Browser mode (see the preceding tip) and put the other in Resource mode. You can also right-click a tab and select New Windows to open a new window for the current view. Then, by clicking and dragging that tab down toward the bottom, you have two simultaneous views of the same file in case you need to look at two different portions of the file at the same time.

11.10 Do-It-Yourself DBA

Ever want to tell a DBA to take a flying leap off a short pier? We hope not—that kind of interdepartmental behavior isn't good for your career.

You can, however, perform some of your own database-related tasks (SQL queries, browse database tables, and so on) from within Eclipse and leave the poor DBA alone.

From within Eclipse, you can connect to a database and perform all of your database-related work without having to leave Eclipse. If the filename you have open in the editor ends with .sql, then you can right-click in the editor and select Use Database Connection. This option will open a dialog box where you can add a database connection. Simply specify all the usual JDBC pertinent information: the database type, the name of the database, the driver class, the location where Eclipse can find the drivers, and finally the database URL. This information needs to be entered only once. Once connected, the connection information will appear on the lower-right corner of the screen.

To execute a query, simply open a .sql file (or create a new one), and enter your query. Then right-click the file in the editor, and select Run SQL. This will execute your SQL statement and open the Data Output view showing the results of the query. You can also open up the Database Explorer view once connected and drill down to browse database tables, stored procs, functions, types, and views.

11.11 Emacs Key Bindings

We mentioned learning the key bindings for Eclipse functionality earlier, but what about simple text editing? Developers do the same thing over and over all day. We wear grooves into our brains and muscles for particular actions: jumping to the beginning of the line, moving up and down, copying rectangular blocks of text, and so on. This muscle memory becomes ingrained and automatic. Moving to a different editor is a painful process.

Luckily, Eclipse does a satisfactory job of emulating the Emacs key bindings.[1] To activate them, go to the Window -> Preferences menu. Open the General node, and select Keys. From there, select Edit. Change the Scheme option menu to Emacs, and click the Apply button. The keys should now function properly. You will obviously still miss some features, but this should at least feel more comfortable.

---

1. We don't believe Eclipse supports vi bindings by default, but several plug-ins purport to add these capabilities. There are also deeper Emacs integration plug-ins available as well. Please see http://swik.net/Eclipse+vi for more information.

11.12 Summary

Developers spend so much of their time working with code that they need a top-notch editor to efficiently manipulate their text. Ever the hopeless romantics, they tend to fall early and hard for sexy beasts like vi and Emacs. Developers love these tools because there is a low impedance between thinking through a solution and expressing it in code. Any tool that wants to be used must not get in between developers and their first loves.

Eclipse was one of the first Java development environments that offered enough features to catch our attention and could be made to feel enough like editors such as Emacs that we lost track of the fact that we weren't using it. Beyond distracting us with shiny features, Eclipse was one of the first actual Java *environments* where the acts of editing, debugging, designing, and refactoring (not in that order!) were seamless and a joy to use. Newer environments such as IntelliJ have seduced many developers away, but Eclipse remains a solid, powerful, and easy-to-use environment based on years of solid engineering. It has a vibrant community always looking to the next version and for new plug-ins to make the environment richer, more efficient, and powerful. Although IntelliJ has a great plug-in infrastructure and a suite of useful tools, the sheer volume of the Eclipse user base keeps it the focus of plug-in development for Java-based IDE environments.

11.13 Web Resources

Eclipse home page . . . . http://www.eclipse.org
The Eclipse home page

Eclipse plug-ins . . . . http://www.eclipseplugincentral.com/
The official Eclipse plug-in repository

More Eclipse plug-ins http://eclipse-plugins.2y.net/eclipse/index.jsp
The Eclipse plug-in site

Notes on the Eclipse plug-in architecture. . .
. . . www.eclipse.org/articles/Article-Plug-in-architecture/plugin_architecture.html
Article describing the architecture and design of Eclipse plug-ins

There's no such thing as a free lunch, and even if there were, there's no guarantee that it would be any good. Software development is a far cry from haute cuisine, however, and software quality is unusual in a significant way. The General Principle of Software Quality is that improving quality reduces development costs.
► Steve McConnell, Code Complete 2

## Chapter 12

Improving Code Quality Using Automation

by Paul M. Duvall

Paul M. Duvall is the CTO of Stelligent Incorporated, a consulting firm and thought leader that helps organizations quantify development efforts so that they can reliably and rapidly produce better software. Paul has worked in virtually every role on software development projects: developer, tester, architect, and project manager.

Paul has consulted for clients in various industries such as finance, housing, government, health care, and large independent software vendors. He is a featured speaker at many leading software conferences. He authors a series for IBM developerWorks called "Automation for the People," is a contributing author to UML 2 Toolkit, and is an author of Continuous Integration: Improving Software Quality and Reducing Risk (Addison-Wesley, 2007). He actively blogs on http://www.testearly.com/.

12.1 Introduction

Code quality is a term that is often misused, misconstrued, and simply *missed* when software is developed. I can't tell you what it looks like, but I can paraphrase Justice Potter Stewart who says, "You know (quality code) when you see it." Fortunately, we can speak concretely about how to get there. You can improve code quality—measurably—by reducing complexity, reducing code duplication, adhering to coding standards, adhering to a robust software architecture, and measuring code coverage of tests to analyze and improve the code quality.

In this chapter, the tools I'll cover are available as Maven 2 plug-ins. I tend toward utility tools that are free and open source. Most of these tools provide the features I am seeking, and I'm not bothered with download or license hassles. Specifically, I'll cover tools such as Cobertura, JavaNCSS, CheckStyle, CPD, and JDepend.

12.2 Code Quality

At Stelligent, one of our services is analyzing code bases and development processes for clients in varied industries and on different platforms. We use automated tools to speed up the process and "save our energy" to focus on specific areas within the code base that are flagged by the automated tools. At a minimum, we want to know that the code:

- is adhering to the project's coding standards,

- is following an architecture that is not fragile,

- is not too complex,

- has minimal code duplication, and

- has tests with a good amount of code coverage.

These are the "big five" code quality metrics. Their importance isn't new, but only recently has it become relatively simple to obtain good results quickly. On projects over the years, I've created Ant scripts to obtain these metrics, but the results often did not justify the effort. Fortunately for you, these metrics are easy to obtain using Maven and its assortment of code quality metrics plug-ins (largely dependent on you using Maven's approach to building and managing your Java projects).

Cyclomatic Complexity

Cyclomatic complexity[1] is a big phrase for a simple concept indicating the number of unique paths in a method. It was defined by Thomas McCabe in 1976. It has been generally accepted that any method with a Cyclomatic Complexity Number (CCN) greater than 10 is too complex and, thus, must be reduced. Any if, while, and for statements increase the CCN in a method. A method with a CCN greater than 10 is considered to have "too many moving parts," and many studies confirm that defects often correlate to methods with high cyclomatic complexity. So to improve code quality, look into using refactorings that can reduce CCN for overly complex methods, such as *extract method*, *extract class*, and *replace conditional with polymorphism.*

Code Duplication

Code duplication refers to code that is the same (or similar) in a code base. Tools that analyze code duplication can be set to analyze duplication for as little as two lines of code. Code will be flagged as duplicate if a set of two lines of code is the same or similar to another set of two lines of code anywhere else in the analyzed code base. Duplicate code has a big negative effect on reusability. Refactorings that reduce duplicate code may include Pull Up Method and Extract Method. Tools such as Simian and PMD's CPD help determine the amount of code duplication in a code base.

Coding Standards

Defining a *coding standard* on your project leads to fewer headaches. You can improve the maintainability of software by defining a simple coding standard that works for your team. A technique I like to use that I learned from William Wake[2] is to annotate a single class with the project's coding standards. I've found this works much better than a detailed thirty-page coding standards document. Furthermore, I like to incorporate the project coding standards into the build process with tools such as PMD and CheckStyle so that I can have automatic checks run every time the software is built (or on whatever schedule I choose).

---

1. See http://en.wikipedia.org/wiki/Cyclomatic_complexity.
2. See http://www.xp123.com/xplor/xp0002f/codingstd.gif.

Dependency Analysis

A software architect may define the most elegant software architecture on paper, but the architecture brings value only through its implementation in the actual code. The code might do one or more of the following as it relates to the software architecture:

- Adhere to a well-designed architecture
- Violate a well-designed architecture
- Expose the flaws of a poorly designed architecture

An architecture is by and large made up of decisions to which the development team(s) agree to adhere. This does not suggest that you should define a UML diagram down to the class and method level, but there are still a number of ways you agree to what the architecture "is" throughout the development process. This is why it can be useful to determine whether the architecture you believe to be present is *actually* present in the code. In particular, there are object-oriented metrics such as *afferent coupling, efferent coupling, abstractness, instability,* and *distance to main sequence* that can be extremely useful in determining the robustness or brittleness of your software architecture. The analysis feedback can assist developers in evaluating and deciding which code to improve or in creating estimates for subsystems that may be negatively susceptible to change.

Code Coverage

Perception and reality don't always match. When we analyze code for clients who have written automated tests, we often find that their perception of code coverage is considerably larger than the *actual* code coverage.

Code coverage measures the amount of code that has corresponding tests. For the purposes of this chapter, I am referring to coverage by automated tests written by the developers using tools such as JUnit and TestNG, although there are certainly ways to determine the code coverage of manual tests as well.

The main measures of code coverage are line coverage and path/branch coverage. Line coverage refers to whether there is a test that executes a line of code. Path/branch coverage indicates whether there is an associated test for every path (think CCN). Ideally, you'll need one test for every path in your code base. (Note: I've never *actually* seen this happen; it's just an ideal.)

12.3 Maven

On its website, *Maven*[3] is described as a tool that "can manage a project's build, reporting, and documentation from a central piece of information."

I will not describe all the features of Maven in this chapter. There are books[4] and articles that thoroughly cover the topic. Instead, I will demonstrate how to get Maven up and running and how to use and customize some of the code quality plug-ins. After that, you'll be able to run the Maven code quality plug-ins to measure the "big five" metrics in your source code.

Step 1: Download Maven

The first step is to download Maven.[5] Extract the Maven zip (that is, maven-2.0.4-bin.zip) to your preferred install location, such as C:\dev\ tools\maven-2.0.4 on Windows or /usr/local/maven-2.0.4 on Unix-based operating systems.

Step 2: Place Maven in Classpath

Add the bin directory to your system's path. In Windows, go to Environment Variables (from your System Properties window), and add a variable called MAVEN_HOME that points to C:\dev\tools\maven-2.0.4 (or the directory location of your Maven install from Section 12.3, *Step 1: Download Maven*). Next, add %MAVEN_HOME%\bin; to your system's PATH environment variable. Ensure that your JAVA_HOME environment variable is set correctly in your system's path as well. For Unix-based operating systems, add the bin directory to your path (that is, export PATH=/usr/local/maven-2.0.4:$PATH).[6] To test your Maven 2 install on either operating system, type this from the command line:

```
mvn --version
```

You should see something like this:

```
Maven version: 2.0.4
```

---

3. Maven is available for download at http://maven.apache.org.
4. You can download *Better Builds with Maven* for free at http://www.mergere.com/m2book_download.jsp.
5. See http://maven.apache.org/download.html.
6. Go to http://maven.apache.org/ for more information about installing and configuring Maven.

Now, you're ready to create an *archetype*, which enables you to create a Maven project very quickly.

Step 3: Create Archetype

Have you ever wished you could work with a tool immediately, without the hassle of setup and configuration? Maven 2 makes this happen with its archetype feature. After installing and configuring Maven, open a command prompt in a directory where you want to create a new Maven project. Type the following:

```
mvn archetype:create -DgroupId=com.brewery.app -DartifactId=my-brewery
```

archetype:create is the command for creating an archetype. -D indicates you are passing system parameters to the command line. groupId is the unique identifiable name, and artifactId is the name that will be used as the top-level directory.

12.4 Code Quality Plug-ins for Maven

When I was first learning how to program, an instructor used to say "You eat an elephant one bite at a time." I don't know much about eating elephants, but it still made sense. The same goes for code quality; the best way to improve code is by coding a little, testing a little, and *inspecting* a little. The more rapid the feedback, the more likely you are to fix the defect or the *potential* defect. By running code quality plug-ins as part of your build process, you increase your chances of finding potentially defective code such as those exhibiting *code smells*. A code smell is "...any symptom (in code) that indicates something may be wrong."[7] Example code smells include conditional complexity, duplicated code, large classes, and shotgun surgery. Using a code inspection tool can help you find areas that might have more code smells than others—areas of risk. Armed with this knowledge, you can make better decisions on estimates and refactorings. Tools such as Cobertura, JDepend, CheckStyle, JavaNCSS, and CPD can provide you with this targeted insight into your code.

Cobertura

Imagine you've written some automated developer tests and want to know which sections of your code do *not* have corresponding tests. A

---

7. See http://en.wikipedia.org/wiki/Code_smell.

code coverage tool such as Cobertura can help you determine which code areas lack tests. Cobertura[8] is an open-source tool that reports on code coverage in Java code. This tool is my favorite because of its useful graphs.[9] It's easy to get Maven to generate a Cobertura report for a code base. Simply type the following from your command line:

```
mvn cobertura:cobertura
```

This creates a report like the one shown in Figure 12.1, on the following page. To contrast, let's see what it would take to generate the same Cobertura report using Ant; it's a little longer:

```
<target name="run-instrumented-tests">
  <mkdir dir="${logs.junit.dir}" />
  <junit fork="yes" haltonfailure="true" dir="${basedir}" printsummary="yes">
    <sysproperty key="net.sourceforge.cobertura.datafile" file="cobertura.ser" />
    <classpath location="${instrumented.dir}" />
    <classpath location="${classes.dir}" />
    <classpath refid="test.class.path" />
    <classpath refid="project.class.path"/>
    <formatter type="plain" usefile="true" />
    <formatter type="xml" usefile="true" />
    <batchtest fork="yes" todir="${logs.junit.dir}">
      <fileset dir="${test.component.dir}">
    <patternset refid="test.sources.pattern"/>
  </fileset>
    </batchtest>
  </junit>
</target>
```

Not only is it long, it's full of variables, so if a property attribute or filename changed, you would need to change the script. The power of Maven is realized when you need to use more features and tools in your build scripts.

JDepend

When it comes to software architecture, our best intentions don't always translate into reality. A dependency analysis tool such as JDepend shows the stability of an architecture and, specifically, how it manifests in the code—are you flexible, are you fragile, and, if so, how fragile? JDepend[10] is a free open source tool that provides dependency

---

8. You can find more information about the Maven 2 plug-in for Cobertura at http://mojo. codehaus.org/cobertura-maven-plugin/.

9. EMMA (http://emma.sourceforge.net/) is another freely available open source code coverage tool.

10. You can find more information about the Maven 2 plug-in for JDepend at http://mojo. codehaus.org/jdepend-maven-plugin/.

Figure 12.1: COBERTURA REPORT GENERATED FROM MAVEN

analysis at any point in time. JDepend provides information on key object-oriented metrics such as number of concrete classes, number of abstract classes, afferent coupling, efferent coupling, instability, and distance to the main sequence. To generate the JDepend report using Maven 2, type this:

```
mvn jdepend:generate
```

For each package, JDepend identifies the number of other packages the analyzed package relies upon (efferent coupling), the number of packages that rely on the analyzed package (afferent coupling), the number of abstract classes, and other useful coupling metrics. These help you make decisions about which packages can be changed easily and which might prove to be more difficult.

CheckStyle

Have you ever sat through anything more boring than a code review where you spend most of your time speaking about naming conventions, spacing rules, use of modifiers, and so on? It's not that these coding standards aren't important to the maintainability and readability of the source code, but a static analysis tool such as CheckStyle

can help find these sorts of issues and free up more of your brain and
your time for discussing more substantive design issues. What's more,
when you incorporate this into your build process, you can find and
fix these coding standard violations incrementally rather than wast-
ing precious time during a manual code review.[11] CheckStyle[12] is an
open-source tool that provides information on any violations to a coding standard. Remember the project with the thirty-page coding standards document? It may have been the most well-written prose, but
most of your team will probably not read it. Static code analyzers such
as CheckStyle provide a way to augment human code reviews so that
you are focusing on the more important issues. You type this from the
command line to get a CheckStyle report:

```
mvn checkstyle:checkstyle
```

But if you needed to create a report for CheckStyle using Ant, you might
need to create a script like the one shown here:

```
<target name="run-checkstyle" unless="ran.checks" description="Coding Standard adherence">
  <property name="checkstyle.rules.dir" value="${config.dir}" />
  <echo> lib.dir/checkstyle.file is: ${lib.dir}/${checkstyle.file} </echo>
  <taskdef classpath="${lib.dir}/${checkstyle.file}" resource="checkstyletask.properties" />
  <delete dir="${reports.checkstyle.dir}" quiet="true" />
  <mkdir dir="${reports.checkstyle.dir}" />
  <path id="checkstyle.cache.file" location="${reports.checkstyle.dir}/cache.file"/>
  <property name="checkstyle.cache.file" refid="checkstyle.cache.file"/>
  <touch file="${checkstyle.cache.file}"/>
  <checkstyle
    config="${checkstyle.rules.dir}/cs_checks.xml"
    failOnViolation="false"
    failureProperty="checks.failed"
    classpathref="lib.path">
    <property key="checkstyle.cacheFile" value="${checkstyle.cache.file}"/>
    <property key="checkstyle.tabWidth" value="4"/>
    <property key="checkstyle.supressions.xml"
          value="${basedir}/config/checkstyle/suppressions.xml"/>
    <fileset casesensitive="yes" dir="${src.dir}" includes="**/*.java" />
    <formatter toFile="${reports.checkstyle.dir}/checkstyle_errors.xml" type="xml" />
  </checkstyle>
  <antcall target="checkstyle-report"/>
</target>
```

---

11. This does not imply manual code reviews aren't important. In fact, they are extremely
beneficial especially when augmented with static analysis.
12. You can find more information about the Maven 2 plug-in for CheckStyle at http:
//maven.apache.org/plugins/maven-checkstyle-plugin/.

```
<target name="checkstyle-report" if="checks.failed">
  <property name="checkstyle.data.file"
        value="${reports.checkstyle.dir}/checkstyle_errors.xml" />
  <property name="checkstyle.report.file"
        value="${reports.checkstyle.dir}/checkstyle_report.html" />
  <property name="checkstyle.xsl.file"
        value="${checkstyle.rules.dir}/checkstyle-frames.xsl" />
  <xslt taskname="checkstyle"
    in="${checkstyle.data.file}"
    out="${checkstyle.report.file}"
    style="${checkstyle.xsl.file}" />
</target>
```

You can see that as long as you adhere to Maven's conventions, you can save a considerable amount of time and effort in writing build scripts so many of the useful processes don't have to be written.

JavaNCSS

They say that a human can keep track of only about seven things at a time. This is why it's easy to remember phone numbers while it's difficult to remember things like credit card numbers or, say, launch sequences.[13] This is why we start to lose track of methods with many conditional statements, especially when these conditionals are deeply nested. Ever notice that many defects occur in methods like these? This is not a coincidence. It's useful to determine which methods are overly complex. JavaNCSS[14] provides visibility into per-method metrics on cyclomatic complexity. Other tools will provide aggregated CCN metrics (at the package or system level), but there is little value in averaged CCNs; if you have many methods with a CCN of 1, it can skew the average. Instead, we want tools that provide method-level CCNs, such as JavaNCSS. This is the simple command:

```
mvn javancss:javancss-report
```

A JavaNCSS report is generated showing NCSS averages, methods that contain the most NCSS, and then a list of methods each with its own CCN.

---

13. Anecdote provided by Andy Glover of Stelligent.
14. You can find more information about the Maven 2 plug-in for JavaNCSS at http://mojo.codehaus.org/javancss-maven-plugin/.

CPD

CPD[15] is part of the PMD code analysis tool. CPD reports on source code blocks that have been copied and pasted, which as we all know reduces code maintainability and reusability. Once these areas are targeted, you can refactor and increase maintainability. One of PMD's goals in Maven is called cpd-check:

```
mvn pmd:cpd-check
```

When using this Maven goal, you can configure it to fail the Maven if the violations exceed the established duplication threshold.

12.5 Summary

Code quality can be more than something you "know when you see it." If you incorporate Maven 2 code quality plug-ins into your build processes, you have tangible ways to determine which parts of your code might be overly complex, copied and pasted, instable, not following project coding standards, or lacking developer tests. And when you integrate these code quality plug-ins into your build process, you can incrementally improve your code, one byte at a time. Now that's the way to eat an elephant.

12.6 Web Resources

Cyclomatic complexity...
. . . http://www.sei.cmu.edu/str/descriptions/cyclomatic_body.html
The Software Engineering Institute's description of cyclomatic complexity

JUnit . . . . http://www.junit.org
The JUnit testing framework home page

TestNG . . . . http://testng.org/doc/
The TestNG home page

Maven . . . . http://maven.apache.org/
The Maven home page

Cobertura . . . . http://cobertura.sourceforge.net/
Cobertura, the open source code coverage framework

---

15. You can find more information about the Maven 2 plug-in for PMD's CPD goal at http://maven.apache.org/plugins/maven-pmd-plugin/cpd-mojo.html.

JDepend .... http://clarkware.com/software/JDepend.html
JDepend, the open source dependency analysis tool

CheckStyle .... http://checkstyle.sourceforge.net/
A development tool to help programmers write Java code that adheres to a coding standard

JavaNCSS .... http://www.kclee.de/clemens/java/javancss/
A source measurement suite for Java

CPD .... http://pmd.sourceforge.net/cpd.html
The Cut and Paste Detector (part of the PMD project)

Don't use manual procedures: A shell script or batch file
will execute the same instructions, in the same order, time
after time.

Use the power of command shells: Use the shell when
graphical user interfaces don't cut it.
   ► Tips 21 and 61, *The Pragmatic Programmer*

Chapter 13

Capistrano: Application Deployment and More

by David Bock

David Bock is the technical director of federal and commercial systems at FGM,
Inc., a government contractor in Northern Virginia. He is also president of the
Northern Virginia Java Users' Group. You can find out more about David at his
website, http://www.javaguy.org.

13.1 Introduction

Capistrano started life as a command-line tool for deploying web applications written in Rails, but it has grown into much more than that. Today, Capistrano's capabilities make it an excellent tool for performing routine administration tasks on one or more computers, administering a server farm, monitoring your production app, and, of course, setting up and deploying applications written in Ruby as well as other languages.

Capistrano (also known just as Cap, because it is invoked from the command line as cap) is a tool that lets you define one or more computers that are related to each other in a project and lets you define tasks that can be run on them individually, in groups, or all at once. Anyplace you might want to write a shell script or log into a computer to check some status, Capistrano can be a useful tool in your toolbox. This chapter won't cover all the nitty-gritty details available in the docs available with the tool; instead, I'll give you enough to get started and then talk about some of the features you'll need a little experience with—the kinds of tips you might find out about if you were to sit down at lunch with a couple of the NFJS speakers.

13.2 Capistrano's Assumptions

Before you can even think about using Cap, you need to make sure it fits in with the other tools you are using for your project. Capistrano doesn't make too many assumptions about your environment, but it does make a few assumptions in order to get off the ground. Of course, you already know you are planning to talk to a remote server; the requirements are largely around this communication:

- Cap needs to use secure shell (SSH) to talk to the machines you are going to be controlling.

- It also expects that there will be a POSIX shell on the other end ready to execute the commands it gives. For most Linux/Unix/Mac users, this isn't a problem. If you are deploying to a Windows server, take a look at installing Cygwin (http://www.cygwin.com).

- Cap expects to be able to use the same name and password to connect to all the servers (although there are clever ways around this assumption).

The default tasks make other reasonable assumptions (such as the use of version control), but those aren't of interest at the moment; you want to learn how to make Cap do *your own* bidding.

People generally assume that since Capistrano is written in Ruby, Ruby will need to be installed on the remote machines. This is *not the case*. Neither Ruby nor Capistrano needs to be installed on the machines being controlled. They need only to be on the machine doing the controlling.

13.3 Concepts

Cap is actually a pretty simple tool. Starting with some pretty simple ideas and building other constructs on top of those, you end up with some really cool capabilities. I'll cover those fundamentals first so we have a common vocabulary.

Recipe

A Capistrano *recipe* is simple a Ruby program, although you wouldn't know it from looking at it. In typical Rubyesque fashion, Cap defines a domain-specific language for the kinds of things it knows. This file contains all the "stuff" you need to define for your project.

By default, Cap expects this file to be in conf/deploy.rb, but you can change this to anything you want (much like Ant expects a build.xml file):

`code/dbock/SampleRecipe.rb`

```
# VARIABLES
set :application, "main_website"
set :repository, "http://svn.davebock.com/projects/#{application}

# ROLES
role :web, "www.davebock.com"
role :app, "www.davebock.com"
role :db, "databases.davebock.com"

# TASKS
task :restart_apache, :role => :web do
  run "/sbin/service httpd restart"
end

task :clear_sessions, :role => :db do
  run "cd #{current_path} && rake db:sessions:clear"
end
```

Role

Looking back at that sample recipe file, you will notice a line that says role :web, "www.davebock.com". A role is simply a machine or group of machines named for the function they are performing in this system's architecture. In this case, the machine is www.davebock.com, and the function is web. You can create a role of whatever name you want; :app, :web, and :db are common, but I have also seen :ldap and :j2ee-server for more complex setups.

Task

A task is a set of commands to be performed on a target machine. In some cases you will specify what roles the task will be performed on, and in other cases, Cap will figure it out based on other information. These tasks are ultimately shell commands that will be executed on the remote machines over SSH.

Capistrano provides a whole bunch of default tasks for deploying Rails applications and has some extensions for doing some routine system monitoring. In addition, dozens of projects have released recipes for database administration, Apache administration, PHP app deployment, virtual machine provisioning, and so on, and of course, you can easily write your own.

Variables

As you would expect, you have the ability to execute things conditionally and create tasks that depend on something specific (such as a Subversion repository) with the ability to define that specific resource later. Capistrano lets you define variables that you can use in your tasks. Cap also includes a bunch of default variables that you will need to specify in order to use the default tasks.

And now with those fundamentals, I can give a pretty good definition: Capistrano is a tool that lets you define your system architecture as a number of physical machines, group those machines into the functional roles they perform, and write administrative tasks that will be executed on those machines. As you can see, deploying Rails apps is just a little piece of that capability.

13.4 Kick-Starting Your Own Recipe File

Capistrano is easy to install; if you already have RubyGems on your machine, simply type this:

```
gem install capistrano
```

You might also want to install capistrano-ext (extended tasks) and termios (prevents echoing of passwords). If you do not have RubyGems on your machine, check out http://www.rubygems.org for further instructions.

If you are using Capistrano with a Rails app, there is a built-in command to kick-start you. From a command line at the top of your project structure, simply type this:

```
cap --apply-to .
```

This will create several files for you, the most important being a file in config/deploy.rb. Capistrano is showing its legacy here, but that's OK. If you want to use Cap outside a Rails app, you just need your own deployment recipe file, which you can create by hand with your favorite text editor. The boilerplate recipe file isn't very useful anyway, besides being full of comments that tell you what is happening. You still have to edit it to have reasonable values for all the variables and roles, and the included tasks are just samples; all the interesting Rails-related tasks are baked into Cap.

So, start with your own file, with the following simple contents:

code/dbock/recipe1.rb

```
# VARIABLES
set :application, "cap-examples"
set :repository, "http://svn.davebock.com/projects/#{application}"
set :user, "dbock"

# ROLES
role :web, "www.davebock.com"
```

Feel free to substitute your own server and username in there for a server to which you have SSH access. That will make some of the following examples more interesting.

13.5 Capistrano's Standard Tasks

If you intend to use Cap to deploy Rails applications, then these standard tasks are for you. They contain all the nitty-gritty details for setting up a server, deploying your code to it, restarting, running database migrations, and so on. If you plan on using Cap to manage something other than a Rails app, then these are still an excellent source of inspiration; some of the conventions here (especially the setup and symlink tasks) can be useful in other contexts.

show_tasks

As obvious as it sounds, show_tasks lists all the current tasks that Cap is currently capable of executing.

setup

The setup task creates several directories under the deploy_to path you set in your recipe. There is a releases directory, which will contain one or more versions of your web app, and a shared directory, which will contain logs and other files. Why "one or more" versions? you ask. The Capistrano deployment convention is to check out the "next" version of your app into the releases directory, with a directory named with today's date and time. You might have several versions of your application in this directory and be able to switch between them. I'll talk more about this in some of the other task descriptions.

deploy

This is where some real magic happens. If you have everything set up correctly, the deploy task—which is one command—will deploy the latest version of your application by checking it out of source code control, creating a link called current to it under the deployment root, restarting the application server, and doing anything else necessary (depending on what variables you provide and what other customizations you make). It will do this on one machine or several. If it fails, there are even options for recovery (and I will talk about transaction support a little later).

rollback

If your last deployment went a little awry or your clients just decided they don't like the new purple blob on the navigation bar, you are one command away from restoring your application to the previous version. The rollback capability alone makes Capistrano worth using.

symlink

You probably won't have to run the symlink command yourself, but it is worth knowing about so you understand how the magic of deploy and rollback work.

When you deploy your application, it is checked out under the releases directory. symlink is then executed, which makes the symbolic link current point to this release. It also updates several other symlinks so that any shared resources (such as logs or uploaded files) are available to the new application (these things, quite sensibly, live under the shared directory). The rollback command simply adjusts these symlinks and restarts the application server.

cleanup

With all of this rapid application deployment, you can end up with a lot of copies of your application. The cleanup task simply gets rid of all but the last five versions.

Several other default tasks exist, but these are the bread and butter of your typical Rails deployment. The other tasks are used internally to these, in support of restarting application servers, performing migrations, and doing other tasks.

The whole support of deploy and rollback tied in with Subversion, along with the minimal yet sufficient directory structure, is very elegant. I have been waiting to see someone take these ideas and repurpose them into deployment recipes for Tomcat or JBoss in the Java world.

13.6 Extending Capistrano

Writing new tasks is easy, but before you do that, it is worth taking note of some of the kinds of tasks that are already available in the Capistrano community. More are appearing every day.

capistrano-ext

Jamis Buck, the author of Capistrano, also maintains a set of tasks called capistrano-ext for other server maintenance. They are useful little utilities for monitoring the uptime of your servers and watching server loads and requests per second being served by your application servers. This library also serves as an example of how to package your own tasks as a Capistrano extension library.

vmbuilder

http://vmbuilder.rubyforge.org/

Neil Wilson has released some Capistrano recipes for building Xen-based virtual machines on top of Debian.

deprec

http://deprec.rubyforge.org/

This is a collection of recipes for setting up production-ready Rails servers based on a standard Ubuntu 6.06 Linux server. Starting with a clean Ubuntu install, it sets up Apache 2.2 for load balancing and static content, forwarding to a Mongrel process for serving up Rails applications.

Deploying PHP Apps

http://preview.tinyurl.com/y67sex

A blog entry over at Simplistic Complexity shows how easy it is to adapt the existing Cap deployment recipes to deploy PHP apps instead.

Tom Ward's Doing Bad Things with Capistrano

Oddly, I haven't been able to find these packages as a library, but they are available in slide form as a PDF file from a presentation given to the London Ruby Users' Group. In these slides, Tom shows examples of tasks that control Apache as well as Mongrel (a web server written in Ruby) and tasks for performing some basic PostgreSQL administration. You can easily copy them into your own recipe files, and they show clearly how to turn your own command-line judo into Capistrano tasks.

Rails Machine Recipes

Rails Machine is a hosting service provider that publishes Capistrano recipes to allow you to administer your hosted environment, easily deploy your Rails apps, and even easily get your projects into Subversion. They even have a video to show you how to do it.

A quick search of Google, RubyForge, or Freshmeat shows dozens of other projects in the works. There are also dozens if not hundreds of small tasks shared as code snippets in blogs and on mailing lists such as the Capistrano List at Google.[1] Like most new open source projects,

---

1. The Capistrano Mailing List is available at http://groups.google.com/group/capistrano.

most of what I could catalog here would be outdated by the time you read it.

13.7 Rolling Your Own Tasks

You have already seen a couple of simple task definitions. Tasks have a pretty simple structure. Just define the name of the task, any machine roles the task should run on, and then some Ruby code defining what the task should be.

That's right, these tasks are just bits of Ruby code. In most cases, they are simply lists of other tasks to call or possibly some of the convenience methods you are about to see. In other cases, they can contain conditional logic based on variables defined in the environment, passed in on the command line, or provided by the output of other tasks.

The workhorse of Cap is the run command. This takes a shell command that will be executed on the appropriate machines. Any shell command can be run, and the output will be directed to your local terminal window.

```
task list_ruby_processes do
  run "ps aux | grep ruby"
end
```

If you know you are expecting a program that requires interaction, you can actually pass a Ruby code block to the run method that will be invoked with every line of output from the process. This is a pretty useful capability but is a little beyond the scope of this chapter. The Capistrano documentation[2] includes information about this.

The sudo command is another workhorse and does exactly what you would expect if you are used to writing shell scripts—it executes a task with the permissions of the superuser. The syntax is the same as run, and the user must be in the sudoers file on the remote machine for this to work.

Capistrano also has a facility for copying files to the remote host: put. Actually, put doesn't quite copy files; it creates a file with whatever content you feed into it. This might be another file, or this might be the output of another method, such as an XML renderer. This is typically used for creating configuration files on the fly, based on values provided

---

2. The Capistrano manual is available at http://manuals.rubyonrails.com/read/chapter/97.

at runtime. If you are thinking this would be a great way to set things such as database passwords at runtime, you are right. This is often used for exactly that purpose so you don't have passwords checked into configuration files in your version control tool. You will see an example of that later.

```
task hello_world do
  put "Hello World", "~/hello.txt"
end
```

Capistrano has a handful of other built-in methods, but you will learn more about them in the next section.

If you have done any kind of system administration work, you should be seeing the possibilities by now. Anything you can do from the command line, you can now automate and run across multiple machines in your environment with just one command. This is great stuff, but it gets better.

13.8 Advanced Concepts

By now, you might be thinking of all the things you might want to automate around your office. Have you ever had a new person join your team and had to create accounts across seven computers, a couple of Subversion repositories, and a MySQL database, with sudo access to the continuous integration server? You can set that up into a repeatable task that won't need any maintenance beyond the definition of the roles section of your recipe as machines come and go. But a capable tool always has nooks and crannies with some impressive capabilities. You'll now look at some of them.

Extending Tasks with before and after

Sometimes you will need to attach some new behavior to an existing task without writing an entirely new one. I had this problem on a deployment where I had to change the value of one environment variable after the deployment, and I couldn't have the value as part of the original file for various content management reasons. This issue came up in only one of three different places I needed to deploy this application.

I solved this problem by creating a task named after_deploy. This task will run every time and immediately after the deploy task is run. My task used patch and a second file to solve the problem, and it looked something like this:

```
task :after_deploy, :role => :app do
  if rails_env == "acceptance")
    run "patch #{deploy_to}/current/config/environment.rb
                #{deploy_to}/current/config/environments/patches/acceptance.patch
  end
end
```

Notice the use of the :role declaration; this prevents it from running on machines other than the application server. Also notice the use of the deploy_to variable so that this code survives any changes in deployment location. This is similar to the use of variables in tools such as Ant.

Before and after filters are a kind of aspect-oriented control over your existing tasks. You can get carried away with this; it is possible to chain these and write a before_after_deploy task, but if you actually do, the refactoring police will take away your keyboard. Used sparingly, these leave your code clean and full of intent. Used to be "too clever," they can create quite a mess of things.

Chaining Tasks

It is possible to give Capistrano more than one task to execute. You can chain commands like cap setup deploy and have both tasks execute. You can use this to your advantage, because the first task can actually set variables that can then be used for the next task. So if you create task definitions that contain all your configuration, you can chain them to do some interesting things:

```
task :acceptance do
  role :app, "acceptancetest.davebock.com"
  set :deploy_to, "~/projects/sampleproject"
  set :user, "dbock"
end

task :production do
  role :app, "www.thecustomersite.com"
  set :deploy_to, "/var/www/website"
  set :user, "secure_user"
end
```

You can now execute commands like cap acceptance deploy and have the customer look at and approve the work at an acceptance test site, and then you can deploy it by typing cap production deploy and have it deploy onto the production environment. Best of all, the deployment to the acceptance test site has also been a decent smoke test of a successful deployment to the production environment (especially if the two environments are actually the same machine, just responding as different virtual servers). I have used this technique in deployments of real-world web applications.

Transactions

Once you start writing more complex recipes and performing activities across multiple machines, you begin to worry, "What would happen if one of these tasks failed on one of these machines? My cluster would be left in a strange in-between state!"

Transactions to the rescue.

To prevent the in-between state caused by a failure on some arbitrary task and machine, you need some ability to "roll back" the changes that have been made so far. Capistrano keeps track of the tasks that have succeeded on each machine, so you just need to tell it what to do when something fails. The first part of this is the transaction keyword:

```
task :create_accounts do
  transaction do
    create_user_accounts
        make_su_on_development
        create_email_account
        create_mysql_account
  end
end
```

The tasks called in the transaction/end block are grouped together in a transaction scope. If, for some unforeseen reason, the create_email_account task fails, you want to undo all the tasks that have succeeded on all the machines on which they succeeded. The transaction block is the first part of performing this magic:

So, how does Capistrano know how to undo the successful tasks? Enter the *rollback handler*:

```
task :make_su_on_development, roles => :development do
  on_rollback {run "gpasswd -d #{the_user} wheel"}

  run "gpasswd -a #{ths_user} wheel"
end
```

If this task ever needs to be undone (as determined by Capistrano, the transaction blocks, and the failures of other tasks), this rollback handler will be executed. Each task needs to define its own on_rollback handler.

So, what happens if a failure occurs while rolling back? At that point, you are on your own; the strategies for dealing with this get complex and depend on the situation.

Note that it can be difficult to test your rollback handlers, but it can be well worth the effort. When you need them, you will *really need them*. An ounce of prevention now is worth a pound of cure.

The disable_web/enable_web Tasks

These tasks are pretty simple, but they require a little bit of web server configuration to work correctly. disable_web provides a quick and simple command to force the web server to show a "down for maintenance" message to any visitors; enable_web simply makes the web server start serving files normally.

The message displayed by disable_web has reasonable defaults but can be customized with some command-line parameters:

```
cap disable_web
```

```
cap disable_web UNTIL="Monday afternoon" REASON="routine server upgrades"
```

Note that this is not stopping the web server; if it did that, the maintenance message couldn't be displayed. Instead, this relies on a little bit of server configuration magic. In the case of Apache, some rewrite directives are added to httpd.conf that make the server ignore all file requests when the maintenance file is present:

```
RewriteCond %{DOCUMENT_ROOT}/system/maintenance.html -f
RewriteCond %{SCRIPT_FILENAME} !maintenance.html
RewriteRule ^.*$ /system/maintenance.html [L]
```

The disable_web task simply creates the maintenance.html file with the provided message, and the enable_web task simply deletes the file.

The Capistrano Shell

Introduced in 1.2 and still considered experimental, the Capistrano shell lets you execute commands across your entire set of machines interactively from the command line. There are some limitations, and this can be a little dangerous, but it sure is cool to see:

```
cap -v shell
```

Or if you have chaining set up as described earlier, you can do this:

```
cap -v acceptance shell
```

This starts the shell and sits you at a blinking cursor, ready for your army of slave machines to do your bidding. Your commands can be executed across all your machines or can be scoped using the with and on keywords:

```
with servers uptime

on app1 ps ax | grep apache
```

In addition to running shell commands, you can also run tasks defined in your recipe by using the task name prefixed with an exclamation point:

```
with database !run_backup
```

This is pretty cool stuff, but it is no replacement for a real shell. First, it is stateless, so you can't go navigating around the filesystem and expect to maintain a path to a current directory. Second, it isn't possible to interact with commands across multiple machines. Still, for keeping an eye on your production environment, whether it is one server or fifty, this is a nice tool in your toolbox.

This tool can be a little dangerous in the wrong hands. Quoting Jamis Buck, the author of Capistrano, "If you thought rm -rf / was dangerous when connected to a single host, imagine the damage you could do with Cap shell! This is probably one of the biggest reasons it is still experimental. Until I can find a way to make it less likely to accidentally wipe an entire cluster with a single command, you ought to go into using this with caution."

13.9 Tricks of the Trade

So far, what you have seen and done with Cap has been pretty straightforward once you get your head around the concepts and the existing documentation. With a little experience, though, you'll find yourself wanting to do something a little off the beaten path. The following is a small collection of some things I have run across and added to my bag of tricks.

Monitoring Traffic on your Web Servers

The tasks included in capistrano-ext have some great little tasks for monitoring your web servers. These are easy to use; you just have to install the capistrano-ext gem and then, in your deployment.rb file, include the following line at the top:

```
require 'capitrano/ext/monitor'
```

After you have that in your recipe, you can type commands such as these to get some real-time stats from your servers:

```
cap watch_load

cap watch_requests

cap uptime
```

Creating Files on Remote Machines

I talked briefly about the put command in Capistrano that lets you dump a stream into a file on the server. I'll show how to combine that with another command, render. render lets you take a local file that is an *ERB template* and substitute values in that file with your own. For instance, here is an example that builds a new httpd.conf file from a template for Apache and then restarts the server:

```
task :add_virtual_server, :roles => :web do
  put render(File.read("virtual_server.template")),
      "/etc/httpd/conf.d/#{server_name}.conf"
      sudo "/etc/init.d/apache2 restart"
  end
```

And the template file you are using would look something like this:

```
&lt;VirtualHost #{ip_address}:80&gt;
  ServerName #{virtual_server}
  DocumentRoot /var/www/#{virtual_server}/current/public
  # other setting ommited for space
&lt;/VirtualHost&gt;
```

If everything else about the server was configured correctly, the template contained all the necessary details, and the Capistrano recipe contained (or asked the user for) all relevant variables, this would automatically provision a new virtual server in Apache.

Prompting for a Different Password

Earlier, I mentioned that Cap expects all the usernames and passwords to be the same. More often than not, I have a different username/password combination for my Subversion repository than I do for the machine to which I am deploying. This little bit of code saves the day in this situation. Notice it isn't even defined as a task; this is just defining some variables, but one of the variables is a Ruby Proc that will prompt me for a password:

```
set :svn_repo, "svn.davebock.com/projects"
set :svn_user, ENV['svn_user'] || "dbock"
set :svn_pwd, Proc.new{Capistrano::CLI.password_prompt('SVN Password: ')}
set :repository, Proc.new { "--username #{svn_user} " +
                           "--password #{svn_pwd} " +
                           "http://#{svn_repo}/#application}/trunk/" }
```

You can now type commands such as this:

```
svn_user="production_user" cap deploy
```

You will be prompted for a Subversion password different from the one used to log into the machines in your cluster.

Avoiding Passwords in Configuration Files

Often you need to have a password to some asset (like a database) stored in a plain-text configuration file. Although this isn't necessarily a *bad* thing as long as the file permissions are set so random users can't read the file, it *is a bad thing* if these passwords end up checked into version control for a larger number of people. Call me old-fashioned, but I just don't like large numbers of people being able to log into a single account.

This should seem like an easy one to solve now...you know how to create files on the fly, and you know how to prompt for passwords; therefore, it seems like you should just prompt for the password and write it out into a template file that contains everything else you need.

Automatically Tagging Releases

This tip comes courtesy of François Beausoleil's blog.[3]

When Cap deploys your application, it deploys right off the trunk. Where I work, we have a content management policy that requires we keep track of which versions are deployed to production. We keep track of this with tags in our version control program.

This nice little task hooks into deploy with the after_ hook and tags the exact release:

---

3. See François Beausoleil's blog at http://blog.teksol.info/articles/2006/10/20/.

```
require 'uri'
  task :after_deploy do
  source = repository
  dest = URI.parse(repository).merge
        ("../releases/#{File.basename(release_path)}")
  cmd = "svn copy --revision=#{revision}
    --quiet --message \"Auto tagging release #{release_path}\" #{source} #{dest}"
  puts cmd
  '#{cmd}'
end
```

Create a version.txt File for Your Web App

Along the lines of the previous tip, I also like to be able to tell at a glance which version of an application is currently in production. If you are using Subversion, you are probably already aware that the repository has a version number that increments with each check-in. If you can just create a file with this number in it, you can serve it up via the web server:

```
task :label_version, :role => :web do
  revision = source.latest_revision
  file = rendeer :template => "#{revision}"
  put file, "#{current_path}/public/version.txt", :mode => 644
end
```

Of course, you could also render this into an HTML file that you also insert other variables into, giving a nice summary of your application environment.

You'll find dozens if not hundreds of tips like this on mailing lists, in blogs, and in how-to articles with a simple Google search. Where possible, I've given sources in the footnotes. Capistrano is getting a lot of attention lately, and capabilities are maturing around it quickly.

13.10 Automation Redux

Automation is such a useful concept that the Pragmatic Bookshelf published a book about it.[4] Capistrano is an excellent automation tool because it doesn't try to do "too much"; it simply takes something that is already done well (shell scripting) and applies a few conventions to it to leverage it across a collection of computers operating as a group.

---

4. See *Pragmatic Project Automation* by Mike Clark.

It then adds some useful concepts for handling issues such as rollbacks and helps enforce conventions that make developers do the Right Thing (like source code control).

Once you can do it, automate it. You will be able to amplify your effectiveness as well as the effectiveness of those who work with you. Getting more done in less time is what makes good developers great.

13.11 Web Resources

Capistrano manual http://manuals.rubyonrails.com/read/book/17
The source for all the basic information about Capistrano

Capistrano discussion group . . . . . http://groups.google.com/group/capistrano
Capistrano discussion group at Google

vmbuilder . . . . .http://vmbuilder.rubyforge.org
Provisioning Xen-based virtual machines

deprec . . . . .http://deprec.rubyforge.org
Using Capistrano to provision Ubuntu 6.0.6 servers

PHP and Capistrano http://preview/tinyurl/com/y67sex
Deploying PHP apps with Capistrano

Chapter 14

Bootstrapping Agility

by Venkat Subramaniam

Venkat Subramaniam, founder of Agile Developer, Inc., has trained and mentored thousands of software developers in the United States, Canada, and Europe. Venkat helps his clients effectively apply and succeed with agile practices on their software projects, and he speaks frequently at international conferences. He is author of .NET Gotchas and coauthor of Practices of an Agile Developer.

14.1 What's Agility?

You get your requirements. You go off for a year or two to develop your application. Finally, one day you show up in front of your customers to deliver what you've done. Your customers receive it with excitement. You walk away with a very happy customer on your resume. If this is your typical project, stop reading further—you don't need this chapter! The reality is different for most of us software developers, however. You struggle to meet the customers' expectations. They often are shocked at what's delivered. You are genuinely interested in ways to improve.

What's agility, and why should you care? Merriam-Webster's dictionary defines agility as "the quality or state of being agile: nimbleness, dexterity." That begs the question then, what's agile? Being agile is to be quick, adaptive, flexible, and at ease to do so. A number of activities in our lives need agility (I am sure you've seen your share of agile drivers on the streets!). Sport is an area that requires agility—swimming, surfing, tennis...and so on.

But what does that have to do with software development? It's quite related. For instance, Cockburn views software development more as cooperative gaming than engineering.[1] Heraclitus said, "There is nothing permanent except change," (the only constant is change). He added, "Everything flows, nothing stands still." This is true for software projects—from requirements, challenges, expectations, and complexity to our ability to comprehend and communicate.

Your goal is simple and clear: to succeed in software development. You want to develop software on time, within budget, and with high quality so that it meets your users' needs and functions reasonably well within realistic expectations.

Software projects heavily depend on the skills, training, and competence of the developers. To succeed in this ever-changing field, your practices, process, attitude, and approach should favor, not resist, change. The tools and techniques you adopt must work in your favor, accommodating your limitations instead of working against your nature.

How can you be agile? How do you move toward agility? That'll be the focus in this chapter. I'll discuss ways you can improve your chances of success in delivering working software.

---

1. See http://www.comsis.fon.bg.ac.yu/ComSISpdf/Volume01/InvitedPapers/AlistairCockburn.pdf. Alistair Cockburn, "The End of Software Engineering and the Start of Economic-Cooperative Gaming," ComSIS Vol. 1, No. 1, February 2004.

14.2   Status of Development

Often time, software development is compared to other fields, such as engineering, business process, and construction. These comparisons miss two important considerations. First, software development is a nascent field when compared to several other human activities. Second, software development is a different problem from most of these activities. Let's take a look at some of the fields.

Construction

In the early days we constructed bridges with wood and stone. Then we took up iron and steel. Concrete bridges then came about.

Constructing a bridge is a nontrivial task. When constructing the Brooklyn Bridge, many people lost their lives. We are fortunate; no one loses their life building software (we could jeopardize lives with software we build, but let's not go there!).

When a bridge is under construction, assume one using stones, no one walks up to say, "Hey, I've got an idea; you want to try some iron?" In other words, engineers do not innovate in the middle of construction project—that happens separately. During construction, they follow standards, well-established metrics, and rigor. Yet, when we develop software, it is not unusual for us to hear new-fangled ideas and suggestions. In software development, innovation happens along with construction.

Medicine

You can probably agree that medicine is one of the most important fields for human survival. Until the early 1900s, starving, vomiting, and bloodletting were considered ways to restore health. For example, the first president of the United States, George Washington, had 9 pints of blood taken out before his death. Surgeons and barbers widely practiced with leaches and knives until the practice was declared quackery!

As a child, I remember reading about Joseph Lister. Before his time, doctors did not understand germ theory. The doctor's reputation was proportional to the amount of blood on his coat. However, rate of infection was high—if a patient survived surgery, he was sure to die from infection. Thanks to Lister, we now understand infection. What does this teach us? It tells us that we could be wrong for a long time. Have we gotten things right for software development?

Flying

Back in 400 B.C. Chinese people made kites to show that it's possible to make heavier-than-air man-made objects fly. We tried to fly like birds. We used stream power, hot air, and several other disastrous attempts, some ending with loss of life. Centuries went by before we could complain about the food in airplanes. This shows us that we can't simply duplicate nature or other approaches—laws of physics are complex and varied. Things don't scale the way we want.

Mobile Phones

Mobile phones are commonplace today. We live in the days of quick, short, cryptic instant messaging. We want to be able to reach anyone, anytime, instantly. If you ask how much time and money you need to make 10,000 phones, I can give you a fairly decent estimate. However, how long did it take to create the first commercial mobile phone? That took more than three decades of effort! You can estimate predictive manufacturing; however, it is hard to do that on innovation. Most software development effort is innovative and not predictive manufacturing, observes Craig Larman [Lar04].

Software development is a nascent field compared to other fields of human endeavor. Software development is a complex business. We use software in different fields. We have people with different backgrounds and training involved in software development. Computers and software are critical to businesses.

In the late 70s and early 80s, managers and experts were trying to get a grip on the software development process. They saw continued high rates of failure. They wanted to find ways to improve software development and success rates. They looked at how engineers operate—obviously, they were successful. They thought, if we do what they do, we will be successful as well. So, they devised processes and practices that resembled engineering. We were given guidelines and guidance. We were told what kind of models, diagrams, and documents we must create. Although these models and documents have use, the process we followed through the 80s and into the 90s, however, did not bring success.

Capers Jones[2] observes that only 10% of large software projects are

---

2. See http://www.stsc.hill.af.mil/crosstalk/2004/10/0410Jones.html. Capers Jones, "Software Project Management Practices: Failure Versus Success."

successful. He defines a project successful if it is completed on time, is within budget, meets user's expectations, and functions without major flaws. That is, it meets the "schedule, cost, and quality objectives." Even if we lower some of these standards, the success rate is not great. The only other human activity where we have come to accept such abysmal success rates is politics.

When we consider software development, we generally think about taking requirements, specifying these requirements clearly, analyzing these requirements, designing, implementing, and testing. These steps are part of a series of activities we know as the Waterfall method.[3] Winston Royce, however, did not mean this to be a single pass-lock-step process, though that is how most people took it. The problem is requirements for any nontrivial software projects can't be clearly specified up front. Our understanding of what needs to be developed gets better as the project progresses, with little clarity in the beginning. However, we often do up-front design when we understand the least and hold ourselves to follow that in the rest of the development. The process we've followed for decades doesn't work. We need to rethink the approach.

14.3 Agile Movement

Conventional approaches haven't set us on the path of success. Experience has shown that developing applications in isolation and showing up in front of users a year later is a recipe for disaster. However, it takes courage to take an unconventional approach.

From February 11 to 13, 2001, seventeen software gurus[4] met—in Snowbird, Utah—to discuss the trend in software development.[5] They found there was a lot in common among the lightweight processes they practiced and coined a common name for the processes: agile. They expressed their beliefs in the Agile Manifesto (copyright © 2001, the Agile Manifesto authors): "We are uncovering better ways of developing software by doing it and helping others do it. Through this work we have come to value:

- Individuals and interactions over processes and tools
- Working software over comprehensive documentation

---

3. See http://www.cs.umd.edu/class/spring2003/cmsc838p/Process/waterfall.pdf. Winston W. Royce, "Managing the Development of Large Software Systems."
4. See http://www.agilemanifesto.org/authors.html.
5. See http://www.martinfowler.com/articles/agileStory.html.

- Customer collaboration over contract negotiation
- Responding to change over following a plan

That is, while there is value in the items on the right, we value the items on the left more."[6]

In agile processes, people and interaction are valued more than tools. Tools help us to be productive, no doubt. However, "a fool with a tool is a dangerous fool" goes a saying. Competent, skillful people put tools to good use. A tool serves better in the hands of a craftsperson. Skillful people, not tools, help projects succeed. Documentation is necessary but can't replace real software. One problem with diagrams and models is they are hard to validate. How do you evaluate whether a design is adequate and meets the needs? You do so only by implementing it and executing the code. The code either solves your problem or doesn't. Working software is considered the true measure of progress in agile development.

Why do developers fear change? Some developers are worried that users keep changing their minds, and it gets harder and expensive to accommodate. Instead of resisting change, how can you accommodate change? One of the key factors that influences this is reversibility ([HT00]). When the decisions you make (design, choice of framework, tools, and so on) are written on stone, change becomes prohibitive, and you have irreversibility. You try to get things right up front (and fail trying). By working in reversibility, you allow things to evolve and attain maturity. This is the evolutionary approach of agile development.

14.4 Adaptive Planning

Planning is an important activity in software development. However, when was the last time your plan went as...planned?

Dwight D. Eisenhower said, "Plans are nothing; planning is everything." What you can learn from the planning game is important. We gain insight into the problem we are on. It helps you understand the risks and the amount of resources you need to allocate. However, we typically do this type of planning fairly early in the project development—a state when we understand the least about the project. Relying heavily on this

---

6. See http://agilemanifesto.org.

early plan, and sticking with it, is one of the risks in itself. The insight gained from this planning is more important that the plan itself.

As Helmuth von Moltke, a German general and field marshal, succinctly put it, "No plan survives contact with the enemy." Who's the enemy in our case? No, it's not the customer I'm talking about! The enemy is the change itself [Sub06]. Our requirements change; our understanding of the requirements changes. What our customers come to expect of our system changes. The technology we use changes. With everything around us changing, how can the plan we developed way in the beginning still hold strong?

Failure from poor planning is not new to humans. For one of the worst cases of poor planning and the result of sticking to a bad plan, see details about the Battle of Somme.[7] Thousands of lives were lost because the officers foolishly held to the poor plan they devised—making this one of the worst battles in human history. You learn more about a project as you progress with it. You need to consider three qualities: scope, time, and quality. You may suggest that quality is really not something that can be compromised. That is not true always, however. If you are trying to bring a proof of concept to the market and trying to establish market dominance by being the first to deliver it, there are higher priorities from the business point of view. Considering these three—scope, time, and quality; you let your customers pick two, and you decide the third. If they demand a certain quality within a certain time period, you will have to decide and educate them on the scope that can be realized with that time and quality. Similarly, if your customers demand a certain scope and quality, you will have to help them realize the time it takes to deliver that.

You should devise a good plan to start with. At the same time, you need to evolve and adapt the plan over time, through the iterations and increments. "It is more important to succeed than to stick with a plan."

14.5 Agility and Architecture

Architecture is something we all give a lot of importance. We all quickly agree that developing a good architecture is critical to any application we develop. Put this book down, walk over to your developers/col-

---

7. See http://www.worldwar1.com/sfsomme.htm.

leagues, and ask, "What's architecture?" Go ahead—try it now, before you read further.

OK, what were the answers you got? Chances are you got a few minutes of silence. Then maybe a few developers started giving their definitions. You probably got as many different definitions for architecture as the number of people who spoke.

We will not argue that architecture is important. It actually is very important. When do you develop the architecture for your projects? It's typically in the beginning of the project, isn't it? We pay a lot of attention to details and want to make sure we get the architecture right. Let's put that thought aside for a minute.

Let's switch gears to think about software development. When you're developing applications, you typically gain a better understanding of the application as the development continues. You get a better handle on things as you progress, much better than what you know when you start the project. So, we can agree that we know the least when we start and know the most when we finish.

That's right. Now, isn't it ironic that we, as software developers, insist on developing a right, robust architecture in the beginning of the project —at a time when we have the least understanding of what the project really is? That is one of the biggest risks in project management— committing to develop something when you haven't the slightest clue of what you're doing.

By the way, I almost forgot to give you my definition of architecture! I consider architecture as a high-level, highly granular, system-level design that tells you what components your system is comprised of; how these components communicate; and what frameworks, tools, techniques, and languages you will use.

Oftentimes, teams decide these issues too early. In fact, it's not unusual for teams to pick these even before the start of the project.

Why is there such a hurry to commit to a solid architecture? Why not let the architecture evolve? What if you take a few iterations to create your architecture? You give your team the option to evaluate ideas, let them understand trade-offs, and provide a platform for them to choose what's right, based on their growing understanding of the project needs.

Of course, I am not suggesting that it is easy to do this. However, I am suggesting that it's critical to do that for the success of the project. How do you achieve that? That's where the skills of a good architect come in. Who is a good architect? That, I'll discuss next.

14.6 Agility and the Architect

I argued that a good architecture is evolutionary and needs the hard work and talent of a good architect. What makes a good architect?

The job title "software architect" carries a lot of prestige. You have probably come across people who are eager to call themselves architects rather than programmers or developers.

Often, we look up to an architect to provide us solutions to hard problems. Architects often hope to quickly arrive at that elegant, most extensible, efficient, and maintainable architecture.

The job of a software architect is highly technical—there's no doubt about that. Yet, some architects claim that all they will do is draw pretty pictures, speak confusing jargons, make presentations, and then let those lowly programmers take the great ideas and code them. On projects these "PowerPoint architects" don't last too long. They may quit before anything substantially is achieved, often leaving the project and its architecture in pretty bad shape.

If an architect proposes an idea, how does he or she evaluate its merits? If this architect can't roll up the sleeves and code a certain idea in order to illustrate or to validate, how effective can this architect be?

Sadly, I've come across architects who refuse to code. Donald Knuth puts it aptly, "The designer of a new kind of system must participate fully in the implementation." I've also come across programmers who refuse to design (or participate in design activities). A programmer who refuses to design is a programmer who refuses to think, and that is trouble.

In a fantastic article entitled "Who Needs an Architect?"[8] Martin Fowler describes the true qualities of a good architect. He says that a good architect does not try to dominate in solving hard problems; he instead motivates and mentors the team to solve those problems. He constantly works toward improving the team's capabilities. A good architect realizes that the architecture needs to be evolutionary.

---

8. See Martin Fowler's "Who Needs an Architect?" article at http://www.martinfowler.com/ieeeSoftware/whoNeedsArchitect.pdf.

In [Sub06], Andy and I claim in Practice #39 that an "Architect Must Write Code." In that book, our angel whispers: "Good design evolves from active programmers. Real insight comes from active coding. Don't use architects who don't code—they can't design without knowing the realities of your system."

An agile architect is not someone who takes pride in the title but who focuses more on technical and professional accomplishments. An agile architect wears multiple hats, performs multiple duties, is technically savvy, and is a great mentor.

14.7 Agility and Modeling

We discussed architecture and the role played by an architect in an agile project. What about modeling and documentation? How're they related? And where does UML fit in?

Modeling is what you do when you analyze the requirements and synthesize possible solutions or design ideas. Documentation, on the other hand, is used to communicate what you've done, to explain how you've done it, and to explain why it was done that way.

Modeling is essential. Some developers use agile as an excuse to avoid modeling and design. They use it as a free ticket to start hacking the code. Agile development can't produce successful working software if we ignore modeling.

You need to take the time to analyze and understand the requirements. You then explore possible solutions, their merits, their drawbacks, and their trade-offs. It's true that you'll face certain situations or change in requirements that you didn't anticipate. However, going through this will help you understand the scope and magnitude of what's ahead. It will minimize the surprises.

I often use UML (or UML-like) notation to represent my ideas as they emerge. I may draw these on a piece of paper or a board so I can solicit input from my fellow developers involved in the modeling session (an agile developer never models alone). I don't like to get bogged down with heavyweight design or modeling tools. If a pencil and paper (or board and marker) work for you, don't feel compelled to use some fancy tool.

Some developers tend to deemphasize documentation. They say, it's hard to keep up with documentation when you're progressing at a rapid pace. However, entirely avoiding documentation is not a good idea. Documentation can make the difference between clarity and chaos when a project moves into maintenance, for instance.

Imagine your project is nearing the end of its development phase and you decide to move developers to other projects/teams. You plan on using a small set of developers for maintenance, possibly a different set of people than the original developers. How can these people come up to speed on the project quickly if there's no documentation?

OK, we agree that it is essential to document. But, how much documentation should we aim to create? I often find that organizations create extensive documentation. However, when asked (a) if they keep the document updated and (b) how often developers actually refer to these documents, the answer is often not what you would desire.

Creating and keeping the document up-to-date can become very ceremonial. You don't possibly need all notations and diagrams prescribed in UML, at least not all possibly in the same project. The more detailed and lengthy your document is, the less it is generally used.

Imagine that I give you a five- to ten-page document, call it document A. It quickly brings you up to speed on the overall architecture and key high-level design details you need to know. It may refer you to other documents or related parts of the application code or unit tests for specific details.

Now imagine I give you a lengthy, highly descriptive document, call it document B, that's more than 100 pages. It goes into explaining details of several classes, their attributes (fields), methods, relationships, and so on.

Are you more likely to read document A or document B? Which one might be most useful? You might argue that since document B has more details, it might be more useful. However, the length and depth of the concepts described often turn away readers, and unfortunately, these documents often become dumping grounds for ideas rarely looked up or maintained.[9]

Instead of spending time transcribing your ideas into documents, consider taking digital photographs of your diagrams (UML or otherwise)

---

9. "I've never met a human being who would want to read 17,000 pages of documentation, and if there was, I'd kill him to get him out of the gene pool." — Joseph Costello

and checking them into your repository and/or attaching them to a wiki. The wiki can also contain any discussions about why certain decisions were made. These can be useful later.

In an agile project, the documentation should strive to be minimal yet sufficient. It should help the reader grasp important concepts, keep their attention, and lead them to other documents or unit tests that can help them gain deeper understanding. It should be like the water fountain that quenches your thirst, not a high-pressure water hose that blows you away.

14.8 Evolutionary Design

Agile development practices recommend that we start coding early. That doesn't mean avoiding design—some developers use this as a free ticket to start hacking code. In fact, design is a critical part of agile development.

In the beginning of the project, you don't have a good understanding of the requirements and the scope. At this time, any effort you put in to specify the requirements thoroughly and to arrive at a complete design is futile. Up-front design is not effective. "No up-front design," however, doesn't mean "no design." However inaccurate this design might be, there is certainly value in it. We learn a great deal from the design activity; the insights you gain from this help shape your understanding of the system you've set out to develop.

Two kinds of design exist: strategic and tactical.

Strategic design is often done up front or early enough. It should give you a broad idea of classes and components that you might use. This design is somewhat high level and coarse grain in nature.

You should perform a more detailed, fine-grained, tactical design as you get ready to implement functionality or a user story. During this design, you might delve into details on method signatures, fields, relationship between objects, actual algorithms to use, types of unit tests to write, and so on.

You need to strike a good balance between time and effort in developing this design vs. documenting it. Although developing this design is critical, how much of this you document and how you document varies. Instead of lengthy textual documentation, consider writing code in a

way that it is self-explanatory, and write unit tests that can help understand the expectations. The idea is to write executable documentation
instead of stale documentation that quickly becomes obsolete and out
of sync with code.

A design is an idea that you arrive at based on what you know. As
what you know changes, the design will have to change as well. This is
the evolutionary nature of design. You constantly evaluate your design
and make adjustments. Refactoring is a continuous activity. Since the
design depends on your knowledge and perspective, you have a better shot at arriving at a good design when you involve multiple people
in the design activity—never design alone. Design must be carried out *Never design alone.*
by a small group of developers working closely with each other. A bet-
ter design emerges when intelligent people are involved in passionate
discussions.

How do you know whether your evolutionary design is right and whether it is suitable for the problem on hand? What if it keeps changing
all the time and gets cost prohibitive? A good design should converge
toward stability quickly, and you should be able to keep up with some
minor modifications after that. If it does not, chances are you are expe-
riencing fragility and not agility.

14.9 Evolving the Design

Development done while ignoring good design principles ends up as a
mere act of hacking and leads to fragility and not agility. Let's discuss
design principles that, when followed not all up front but during the
evolutionary phases of design, can lead to better quality of software.

One of the key recommendations of agile development is simplicity. Why
should we keep things simple? Developers often fear simplicity. Some
of us think if we make things simple, our work may not be valued. We
try to impress our boss, colleagues, and friends by creating complex
things. If they scratch their head saying "Wow, that looks hard," we feel
content!

Unfortunately, by building complexity, we are making it harder to extend and maintain our application. We often throw in code, frameworks,
classes, components, and so on, with perceived extensibility in mind.
However, these tend to complicate things, and in the end, this ends up
defeating the very purpose for which we added these complexities.

Simplicity is not simplistic. Einstein said, "Any intelligent fool can make things bigger, more complex, and more violent. It takes a touch of genius—and a lot of courage—to move in the opposite direction." Ron Jeffries calls for "simple code that works." He coined the YAGNI principle. It stands for "You Aren't Gonna Need It." The next time you are in a design meeting and someone convinces you that a remoting architecture is needed, a major XML configuration is needed, and so on, ask loudly whether you are going to need it. If the need is perceived, ask whether it is OK to wait before committing to that complexity. There has to be forces (real evidence) that you will actually benefit from the additional complexity. Generally, it takes a couple of iterations to figure that out. Commit to building something that you know you absolutely need and will benefit from having. This applies to the use of databases, frameworks, multithreading your application, and so on.

Assume you are sitting on code that is a nightmare to maintain. Anytime you touch it, something breaks, and it is hard to get it working again. You can put on a smiling face for agility, but your code won't allow you to be agile. That's why during development, we constantly reevaluate the design and make changes along the way. During refactoring you need to keep an eye on duplication or redundancy. Assume a piece of code that validates a phone number is duplicated in twenty places. When the rules for validation change, you'll have to find all these places and fix them. Chances are you will fix a few places and wait for others to be discovered as bugs.

Duplication does not mean only redundant code. It may also be duplication of effort. If you modify a database schema, do you have to make seven changes for that change to take effect in your application? Consider duplication of effort as much as duplication of code. The DRY principle [HT00], which stands for "Don't Repeat Yourself" says that "Every piece of knowledge must have a single authoritative representation in the system."

Another consideration while refactoring is cohesion. Cohesion is a property of a class or component to be focused and narrow—it does one thing and only one thing well. If a class, component, package, or subsystem does too many things, it will have many reasons to change and will not be stable. It also becomes hard to maintain. The single responsibility principle (SRP) [Mar02] states that a class should have only one reason to change.

Robert Martin discusses seven signs of bad design: rigidity, fragility, immobility, viscosity, needless redundancy, needless complexity, and opacity. He further discusses the following principles in great detail and clarity.

What is extensibility? It is the ability to accommodate change in requirements by adding small modules of code and not changing existing code. Bertrand Meyer proposed the open closed principles (OCP). He says that modules (functions, classes, components, and so on) must be open for extension but closed from modification. How can you do that? Well, you can realize that by carefully relying on abstraction and polymorphism.

Inheritance is one of the most abused concepts in object-oriented modeling. Oftentimes, it's better to use delegation (containment) instead of inheritance. When should you use inheritance? Use inheritance if an instance of your class might be used in place of an instance of the class it derives. If that's not the intent, you're better off using containment. Not every nonfinal (Java) class is inheritable (sealed in C#). Barbara Liskov emphasizes this in the Liskov substitution principle (LSP). She states that the services of a class must be substitutable to the corresponding services of its base class. "The derived class services should require no more and promise no less than the corresponding services of the base class."

A class has both interface and implementation. A class that depends on another class has coincidental coupling to the implementation of the dependent class. It's not easy to use an alternate implementation without having to modify the dependency. Alternately, if a class depends on an interface, then it can easily utilize any implementation of that interface. The dependency inversion principle (DIP) says that a class must not depend on a concrete class; instead, both the classes must depend on an interface.

Several other useful object-oriented design principles are discussed in Martin's book.

These principles influence your agile development and evolutionary design. However, these principles have to be used where they make sense, when you see a clear force that calls for the use of each. Otherwise, you will end up with one of the perils of bad design—needless complexity.

14.10 Testing and Integration

Change is the only constant in software systems. We constantly face change in requirements, request for enhancements, and addition of features. That often results in design changes. So, you think through the change, modify the code accordingly, compile your code, and check it into the repository.

What happens next? Maybe nothing happens for a few days or even weeks sometimes. Then one quiet afternoon you hear a boom. You lean over and look at your colleague. He says—with shirt torn, smoke coming out of his computer—that he just checked out your code and was integrating when it blew up. You walk over, take a look at the code, and try to understand what went wrong. In the meantime, while you're tending to the code that was "done" a while ago, your current task is on hold. It might take you a few minutes to hours to figure out what went wrong. Then you say you will fix it and walk back thinking, "That's interesting...I wonder what else is broken and I don't know." Is this the way to develop software? What does it mean when you say you're "done" with a task? "Done" should mean that the code is written, compiled, and tested reasonably well that it does what you expect it to do.

Testing the code to make sure it meets your expectations is part of your job. Why do you have to do that? The human mind is very creative, but to err is also human. Our minds play lots of tricks on us. For instance, we really mean <=100, but our fingers typed < instead.

That is only part of the reason to test the code. A more important reason is to make sure the code continues to meet our expectations as we modify it, as our design changes.

Test-driven development (TDD) ([Bec02] and [HT03]) or unit testing is an approach where we write code to test whether the code under development meets our expectations. Unit testing has several benefits:

- It gives you confidence in your code.

- It helps you identify problems quickly when things fall apart.

- When a test is written before the code, it can serve to help you with design.

- It provides a safety net while refactoring.

- It serves as a form of documentation.

Tools such as JUnit, TestNG (Section 7.1, *Introduction*, on page 68), NUnit, and mock object frameworks facilitate creating and exercising unit tests. For a detailed example of TDD, refer to my three-part article.[10]

As a side note, let's consider another important tool that promotes agility. Having a good source control system is absolutely essential. Although it is unthinkable, I've come across teams that don't have a good system in place. I am a big fan of Subversion (SVN). If you have to choose, choose one that is lightweight and allows multiple developers to simultaneously check out files and work concurrently. As Neal Ford mentioned once, "What's good about SVN is it favors you when you do the right thing and severely punishes you when you do the wrong thing." Developers using SVN quickly realize that frequent check-in can avoid merge hell for them. Frequently checking in code is a good thing, because the longer we hold on to our code, the more complicated and irrelevant it becomes. Checking in frequently opens it for review, integration, and feedback.

You will probably agree that checking in code that fails to compile should be considered an act of criminal negligence. Similarly, you must make it a point to not check in code that doesn't pass your unit tests. OK, you're doing that. That doesn't, however, tell you whether you're breaking the expectations of code that depends on your code. This you will come to know only when tests are run on the code that uses your code. But, you have no way to say when the developer using your code will do that.

This is where continuous integration[11] comes in (see [Cla04]). How often should the code be built and tested? Once a week? At least once a day? Why not each time the code is checked in?

You may say, "But I am the person in charge of the build. I don't have time to run to the build machine each time someone checks in the code to build and run all the tests." You shouldn't. If you are that build monkey on projects (I used to be one), ask yourself how you can automate it [Cla04] so you don't have to do this manually. By setting an automated build process (using tools such as CruiseControl), you can have the code built and tested automatically as code is modified and checked in.

---

10. See http://www.agiledeveloper.com/download.aspx.
11. See "Continuous Integration" by Martin Fowler at http://www.martinfowler.com/articles/continuousIntegration.html.

What is the benefit of doing that so aggressively? For one thing, if the code checked in does not work properly, your team is notified immediately. What is the point in writing more code when the code you've completed and checked in is not good? You need to keep the code that's checked in to the source control in good shape. If the application starts to fall apart, you immediately put in effort to bring it back to shape. This ensures that your application is good at all times and is releasable (for demo and testing) at all times.

I don't recommend that all code in an application must be unit tested. However, I do recommend that all code in an application must be tested. It is sad to deploy applications where some part of the code never actually got exercised, even once, during development and testing. These parts of the system pose a significant risk in production.

Although manual testing is needed for some parts of the system (for instance, to qualitatively evaluate usability), relying on manually testing your entire application is not prudent. As a change is made, you want to get quick feedback that the application is continuing to meet the users' expectations and the application level.

Certain tools can help automate integration testing. Consider using Framework for Integration Testing[12] (FIT). (See also *Fit for Developing Software: Framework for Integrated Tests* [MC05] by Rick Mugridge and Ward Cunningham.) FIT allows you to specify a set of input and expected output. You write a test fixture that will exercise the code, send in the specified input, and assert to make sure the expected output was received. The expectations are specified in a tabular form. FIT-Ness[13] allows you to express these using a HTML form or a wiki.

If you are developing a web application, Selenium (see Chapter 9 on page 119) can help automate the testing of your web application. It allows you to record interaction with a web application and then run it automatically to make sure your application continues to behave the way you expect it to behave.

By employing automated unit testing and automated integration testing, you can benefit from the feedback you get about the health of your application as your design and code evolves. And evolution is the name of the game in agile development.

---

12. See http://fit.c2.com.
13. See http://www.fitnesse.org.

14.11 Agile Team

Some managers ask, "What process can we use to be agile?" Others ask "What tools can we use to succeed with agility?" You can't simply apply process and tool and expect to succeed. It takes more than that.

If given a choice between having exceptional people and mediocre tools and having mediocre people with exceptional tools, I prefer the latter.

It is not the question of if, but how and when, things will go wrong on a project. What happens when things go wrong? Are the people in the team quick to solve the problem or quick to lay blame on someone else? The team should work toward a quick solution rather than brooding over a problem with the intent to affix blame on someone.

Developing software is a highly collaborative effort. We need to interact frequently with other developers and key customer representatives. This is easier when we share a good attitude and the friction is low. How do we make that happen? We need to keep an eye on how we—each one of us—communicate. We need to focus on criticizing ideas and not people [Sub06]. Rather than slamming the door on someone by saying "Your idea is bad and will not work for concurrency," try promoting a healthy conversation with a question such as "If we use this, how can we handle concurrency?" You are giving an opportunity for everyone on the team to come up with solutions without being defensive.

An agile team consists of motivated individuals who are self-managed, competent, and responsible. The manager, in such a team, focuses more on managing the project than the people.

Each person on the team has a great deal of respect for each other—respect is valuing the time and effort of others by being prompt to meetings, delivering what you promise, and being dependable. Each person takes responsibility for keeping others informed on their progress. If anything is blocking their ability to fulfill their responsibility, they work proactively toward removing those obstacles instead of using those as an excuse for not getting work done.

The team has great value for the code being developed; they don't let the application fall apart. The team owns [Bec00] the code; no one takes territorial ownership of the code, and anyone on the team can take the responsibility to edit any code.

The team invests in learning [Sch04]. They court criticism and are willing to adjust behavior to become more effective.

Agility requires that you invest in your team. Shared success is the return on that investment.

14.12 Essence of Agility

What does it really take to be agile?

We've found a number of ways to make our development approach agile. Which one of those, in particular, is absolutely essential?

Is it unit testing? Certainly TDD is an important activity in agile development. It provides a number of advantages, helping you check whether the code meets your (programmer's) expectations. However, it tells you that you have the code right, but it does not tell you whether you have the right code.

Is it continuous integration (CI)? CI is an excellent way to receive quick feedback when the code begins to fall apart. As your team continues to evolve the code, you can be notified instantly if any change breaks any expectation. So, certainly it's a key tool to realize agility, but that's not enough.

What about collective ownership? In an agile team, no single person takes territorial ownership of any area of code. The team collectively owns the code. Anyone on the team can take responsibility to modify any code. You reduce risk if multiple developers take turns to review and maintain code—you keep the code from becoming overly complex and hard to understand.

Am I agile if I follow an iterative and incremental development (IID) cycle? IID is a necessary condition but not a sufficient condition to be agile. So, certainly for us to be agile, we must follow IID, but that's not enough. Why not? I heard some one say, "We used IID, and it did not help." When I asked how long the iteration was, he replied, "About a month; and we sent a copy of the application to the customers at the end of each iteration." When I asked what the customer's response was, he replied, "They said thank you!" When all the iterations were over, the customer apparently was not happy with what was delivered. That should come as no surprise. You get the true benefit of IID only if you actively seek your customer's feedback.

One of the key reasons to be agile is to make sure you're developing an application that's relevant to your customers. Surveys have shown that only about 7% of the features in software developed in conventional ways are frequently used. What a waste of effort and time the rest of the features represent.

So, the topmost activity in agile development is to have active communication with key customers. Have them on-site. Interact with them on a daily basis. Actively seek their feedback. And then respond to them in a timely manner with details on what you did or why you did things differently. When it comes to agility and success in developing software, all other agile activities come second to active customer-developer interaction and participation.

14.13 Web Resources

"The End of Software Engineering and the Start of Economic-Cooperative Gaming"...

... www.comsis.fon.bg.ac.yu/ComSISpdf/Volume01/InvitedPapers/AlistairCockburn.pdf
Alistair Cockburn's essay about agile software development and software engineering

"Software Project Management Practices: Failure Versus Success"...

... http://www.stsc.hill.af.mil/crosstalk/2004/10/0410Jones.html
Capers Jones's article about success

"Managing the Development of Large Software Systems"...

... http://www.cs.umd.edu/class/spring2003/cmsc838p/Process/waterfall.pdf
Winston W. Royce's article about process

The Agile Manifesto .... http://www.agilemanifesto.org/authors.html
The consolidation of agile thinking by luminaries meeting in Colorado

"Who Needs an Architect?"...

... http://www.martinfowler.com/ieeeSoftware/whoNeedsArchitect.pdf
Martin Fowler's perceptive article about software and architecture

The most common user action on a website is to flee.
  ► Edward Tufte

## Chapter 15

The Software Engineer's Guide to Usability

by Nathaniel T. Schutta

Nathaniel T. Schutta is a software engineer, speaker, and author based in the Twin Cities area of Minnesota with extensive experience developing Java Enterprise Edition–based web applications. For the past several years, he has focused on user interface design, contributed to corporate interface guidelines, and consulted on a variety of web-based applications. A longtime member of the Association for Computing Machinery's Computer-Human Interaction Special Interest Group, Nathaniel believes that if the user can't figure out your application, then you've done something wrong. Along with his user interface work, Nathaniel is the cocreator of the open source Taconite framework (http://taconite.sf.net), has contributed to two corporate Java frameworks, has developed training material, and has led several study groups. During the brief moments of warm weather found in his home state of Minnesota, he spends as much time on the golf course as his wife will tolerate. He's currently exploring Ruby, Rails, and other dynamic languages.

He has spoken at several conferences around the country, including the No Fluff Just Stuff Symposium conferences, Twin Cities Java Users' Group, Object Technology Users' Group, and various colleges and universities. For more of his random thoughts, check out his blog at http://www.ntschutta.com/jat.

15.1 Introduction

Unless you want your users to flee screaming from your application, you better pay attention to usability. Unfortunately, usability is the software equivalent of flossing:[1] everyone knows it is a good idea, yet it's often one of the first things to get cut from a typical project. Part of the problem is lack of understanding—the average software engineer is schooled in algorithms and compiler theory, but rarely is a class on interaction design part of the curriculum. Add to this the long-standing misconception that usability is the exclusive domain of PhDs and "designers," and it's no wonder most developers would rather write up a status report than deal with the touchy-feely "ility."

Usability is pretty straightforward, as you'll discover over the next few pages; after defining the basics, I'll explore a number of usability myths. Once I've addressed the most common reasons projects forgo usability, I'll cover a simple approach to creating usable applications. As you'll soon see, usability isn't nearly as challenging as you might have thought.

15.2 What Is Usability?

When all is said and done, usability boils down to this: how easy is your application to use? To a certain extent, this question is pretty easy to answer (especially in the negative category), but ultimately, the definition consists of a set of concepts:

- Learnability: Can new users master your application in an afternoon, or do they require years to grasp it?

- Efficiency: Does your application require the fewest clicks possible, or does even the most basic feature involve ten screens?

- Memorability: Does your application leave a lasting impression, or have your users forgotten everything by the time they close down?

- Errors: How does your application handle and recover from errors?

- User satisfaction: Does your application leave users with a happy feeling, or are they hurling expletives in your direction?

Before you run off and try to maximize each of these principles, you have to ask yourself some questions about your users—the relative

---

1. Alternatively, insert regular exercise, eating right, or getting plenty of sleep. . . .

importance of each concept depends highly upon how your application will be used. If your users will be in your app all day every day, chances are factoring in a couple of days (or even a few weeks) of training might provide a higher return on investment than spending several weeks tweaking the interface. On the flip side, if you're building the next great Web 2.0 app where people won't hesitate to move on in a millisecond, there's no chance people will take the time to "learn"—it better just work they way they expect.

The story on efficiency is pretty similar to that of learnability—if an application is used constantly throughout the day (think call center employees), even small improvements in efficiency can have a dramatic impact on the bottom line. Shaving just a few seconds off every interaction might allow a rep to help one or two more customers a day. If your customers use an application only sporadically, efficiency might not be that important.

The importance of memorability is generally the inverse of learnability. A system that is used constantly will be remembered—even if it doesn't deserve to be. In this case, we might get away with a system that isn't as obvious. However, if most users won't interact with the system long enough to remember all the tricks of the trade, it better make a lasting impression.

No matter how good a designer you are, users will make mistakes. How your system responds to these missteps goes a long way toward determining its overall usability. Ideally, you should prevent errors before they happen—if you know the user can't select a value, don't let them! We all know that error messages need to be helpful (and no, "E5432: Illegal State" isn't very useful), but more important, your application must recover gracefully from errors. A well-designed application encourages users to explore, safe in the knowledge that if they step off the happy path, the result won't be a reformatted hard drive. Just think of the warm fuzzy blanket of security that is version control.

User satisfaction gets a bad rap—developers who mostly work with inward-facing customers might openly scoff at the idea that this factor even matters. I hope those of you developing for an external audience are trying for happy users, but, hey, even people who are forced to use what you create are humans too, and they deserve better! Never underestimate the power of a satisfied customer.

Now that you have an idea of what usability is, I can start to debunk the typical usability myths.

15.3 Usability Myths

There are some commonly held misconceptions about usability. Many think it's not that important or that it'll cost too much. Others think testing will take too much time or that focus groups are sufficient. Though these reasons seem valid on the surface, dig a little deeper, and you'll see that they just don't hold water.

Does It Matter?

The first question developers often ask is "Does usability really matter?" It's tempting to think that usability isn't as important as using the latest and greatest database or the newest flashiest web framework, but poor usability costs companies a tremendous amount of money—estimates put the annual cost at $30–100 billion. Although a click here and there might not seem very important, a small number times a big number equals a big number! These days developer productivity is a hot topic, but let's not forget that our counterparts on the business side are constantly being asked to do more with less. Saving our customers even a few minutes a day might make a huge impact on their job performance.

It's important to remember that, to the user, the interface *is* the system. You might be able to impress your software buddies by describing how you leveraged some arcane technology to solve some issue, but chances are your users don't have a clue what reporting engine you're using. That said, if your interface sucks, they will be sure to notice.

Isn't Usability Expensive?

Most managers have a near allergic reaction to anything that costs money, and to many people, usability is just another expense to be cut. At one time, usability was synonymous with pricey labs complete with two way mirrors, cameras, and elaborate equipment for tracking eye movements. Although a usability lab can certainly be useful, it's not required to make a good product.

This notion faded after the publication of usability pioneer Jakob Nielson's paper "Usability Engineering at a Discount" where he introduced the world to usability on the cheap. His results proved that with minimum investment, you could make significant improvements in the usability of a product. You can use a number of discount techniques, and ultimately, you can conduct useful tests with little more than the following:

- Paper and pencil

- A couple of users

- A conference room

If even this is too much for your superiors, you might want to ask what the cost of a poor product is. A product with poor usability can cost a company serious cash. Recently, Joel Spolsky discussed a cell phone that a leading provider sent him (and other popular bloggers) in an effort to garner some publicity. Something tells me they got more than they bargained for with Joel's piece.[2]

After reading the article, I was hard-pressed to figure out how the product ever made it out of the lab and into the public's hands. Joel on Software is widely read by the very people who the company in question was targeting—many of whom will now look askance at the company's offerings. Of course, it's hard to put a precise dollar figure on the effect of one blog post, but I suspect this particular phone will not exceed the expectations of its creators.

I Don't Have Time!

Usability testing doesn't take that much time. In fact, Steven Krug recommends that you spend a morning a month on usability. Creating a paper-based prototype takes an hour or two—running a few users through it takes another couple of hours. You don't need dozens of users either; the most glaring issues will be found with as few as half a dozen users.

Have you ever spent hours (or days) arguing with your co-workers about what a user *might* do? Rather than rehash the same tired argument again and again, simply test it—you'll find out pretty quickly what your users think, and the argument will be over. We've all heard the agile mantra of shortening feedback loops, and usability is no different. It's much easier to fix a problem you find early in development than after your product is released and suffers a scathing review on a popular website.

---

2. See http://www.joelonsoftware.com/items/2006/09/19b.html.

But We Use Focus Groups

When you bring the topic of usability up at some companies, you'll often get a smiling face saying "Our products are usable; the focus group said so." Focus groups are useful, but they can't really tell you whether your application works. *Demoing* your application is no substitute for testing—when presented with an interface, most users will agree it works (especially if driven by someone who stays on the happy path).

15.4 Creating a Usable Interface

Now that I've dispelled some common usability myths, I'll talk about a process for designing a more usable system. Although you can certainly embellish any of these steps, it basically boils down to this:

1. Know your users.
2. Sketch up some screens.
3. Test and refine.
4. Rinse and repeat.
5. Create wireframes.
6. Test and refine.
7. Rinse and repeat.

As you would expect, this is a very iterative process—you're constantly refining the interface as you know more. Now that you have the overall picture, I'll cover the individual steps.

Know Your Users

To create a usable application, you must know your users—real users. Don't be swayed by the vice president or manager who says "I can speak for my people." Unless you are designing a system that is going to be used by them, they're not the people who can help you build a better system. As much as manager types like to think their opinions are gold, they often write the manual on how their employees *should* be doing their tasks. Occasionally, people might actually follow the manual, but more often than not, they won't. So, you can develop an application that supports the "right" model, or you can match what people do.

Management usually has a preconceived notion of how the work in their areas should be done, and again, sometimes they are right. But don't take their word for it. Their people might tell the boss what he wants to hear, but when you actually watch them work, you will likely see

\\// Joe Asks...
 ⁀⁀   **What If I Can't Get to Real Users?**

Occasionally, you will find yourself in a situation where you can't actually work with end users. Perhaps you work for a huge software company that has product managers who serve as stand-ins for the end user. Though not ideal, work with the constraints you have—chances are you have conferences or other customer gatherings, so see whether you can't take advantage of that time to test with real users.

something completely different. It's also important to remember that many people in a supervisor role were promoted because they were particularly good at doing what they are now managing—and they often got there doing it their way. Now this might even be the best way to do things, but maybe not. You'll get much better results if you watch real end users in their typical environment.

If you *really* want to get a sense of what your users do, well, try their jobs for a couple of days. Though not always practical, it's an invaluable way to learn how the business works. The next best thing is to observe your users for a day or two. Watch them work—in their normal environment. You need to understand what your users face every day. Do they have private offices? Are their workspaces quiet? Are they constantly on the phone? Are they interrupted throughout the day?

It's important to remember that designers aren't real users (unless, of course, you are creating an application for designers). As much as we want to think that most people are just like us—they're not. Just because something makes perfect sense to you and the rest of your team doesn't mean it will resonate with your users.

Users Lie

It's vital to actually watch users perform their duties—interviews yield valuable insights, but there is almost always a difference between what a user says they do and what they actually do. Sometimes people will just tell you what they think their boss (or you) wants them to say, but more often than not, what they do is so ingrained that they can't really describe it. At best, they will leave out key details; at worst they will completely fabricate their typical day.

Personas

After studying your users, patterns will emerge. There will naturally be groups of users that form. Although you can talk about them in abstract terms, it can help to use formal personas. Originally coined by Alan Cooper, the concept is pretty simple. Rather than deal with nebulous representations of users, create a set of "imaginary" users with the characteristics typical of representative users. Give the persona a name, and toss in a few personal tidbits—this gives you a more concrete handle when discussing different design issues. Personas are kind of like patterns; they capture a lot of information in a single name.

A typical persona might sound something like this: Mike is a 42-year-old portfolio manager responsible for 3.2 billion in fixed-income assets. He began his career as an analyst, and he has an MBA. On a typical day, he arrives early in the morning, and after reading through several news sources, he maps out the trades he wants to make for the day. Though he has a private office, he spends most of his time in the noisy "bullpen" shouting trade orders to his staff. He has a constant feed of information—while checking prices, he keeps an eye on the plasma TVs that are tuned to financial news networks....

Keep in mind that personas are a design artifact—your sales force might try to steer you toward market segments, and managers will often trot out job descriptions. Don't be surprised if your personas sound nothing like either.

For more on personas, see http://www.cooper.com/content/insights/newsletters_personas.asp.

When watching users, get them to talk about what they are doing. Ask them what they are trying to do, and ask about their goals. Get them to describe what they are ultimately trying to accomplish and describe what stands in their way in the current design. Frustration is also a key marker—ask what really bugs them.

You should be on the lookout for impedance mismatches. Watch for times when they write something down or switch systems. Do they need to skip through three or four screens to find what they want? Is a bit of information copied from one system to another? Are there steps in their process that aren't necessary? These are all cues to places where an improved design can have a huge impact.

Tasks and Scenarios

By now you know your users, and you have an idea what they are trying to accomplish. Now, I'll start talking about tasks and scenarios. A task is a description of a complete job (what users actually do—not what the book says they do). Tasks are coarse-grained descriptions of a user goal that isn't tied to a specific interface.

A typical task from a financial application might sound something like this. A trader gets a sales order from a portfolio manager instructing them to dispose of a position at the best possible price on the open market using the company's preferred broker. Since the company owns multiple lots, the trader must make a tax-efficient trade.

There are a couple of things to notice here. First, things like "logging on" are not user goals—disposing of a bond is. The details here matter: how can the system help the user pick the proper lots to sell? We haven't talked at all about *how* the system is going to do any of this, we've just discussed *what* users need to do.

Once we have a set of tasks, we create a set of scenarios. Scenarios are particular to a task and an interface—at this point, details about the user interface appear. These are step-by-step instructions of how a user will accomplish part or all of a particular task. At this point, you can start sketching up possible interface designs.

Paper Prototyping

It's time to design! Though it might seem odd, start with paper prototypes. Paper has a number of advantages: every office has it, there are no costly licensing agreements or steep learning curves, and, most important, paper allows you to iterate. It might seem like kindergarten, but take a stack of paper and some colored pencils (or pens), and sketch up some designs. Try different approaches—the more ideas, the better. Your designs should be fairly sloppy (no rulers, seriously): if you invest too much time in making everything perfect, you'll be hesitant to throw them away, and your users might not think they can change anything. Paper prototyping is one of the only times in software when quick and dirty is good.

The three most important words in paper prototyping are iterate, iterate, iterate; you won't get the interface right the first time, so don't try. You'll want to consider implementation details, but don't let that restrict your imagination. Move quickly—if you're spending more than ten or fifteen minutes per page, you're trying to be too perfect. You should be able to create a full deck for testing in an hour or two.

Testing the Prototype

Once you have a design, it's time to test it with real users. A typical test covers one or two scenarios, so you'll need to create a test deck—in other words a set of paper-based interfaces covering the parts of the application needed for the test. Typically, this deck will be pretty shallow, meaning it won't have pages for every possible interaction. Sticky notes represent drop-down lists, and you'll need a teammate to "play computer" (changing pages, swapping out drop-downs, and so on). You'll need some space to conduct the test—a conference room is ideal.

Obviously you'll need a user or two, someone to moderate the tests, and another person to take notes. In a pinch, the moderator can also play computer, but it's key to have someone else take notes (alternatively you can record the session, though some users might object or suffer performance anxiety). Testing two users at a time can help people talk aloud—they can discuss with each other what they would do next or why they think they should click a certain button.

You might have noticed someone missing from the previous list—managers. Users must feel comfortable, and having supervisors present (even if it's your manager, not theirs) can skew the results the tests. In general, people are less free with their opinions when the folks who decide pay raises are around.

It might seem a bit silly at first, but you want your user to interact with the paper prototype as if it were the real system. After some initial hesitation, virtually every user will suspend their disbelief. Tell them to pretend they have a keyboard in front of them and that their finger is the mouse pointer. Other than that, have them interact with the prototype as if it were the real system.

Moderating a Test

Other than the end user, the moderator is the most important role in a usability test. The moderator's primary job is to put the user at ease. When moderating, emphasize that the user isn't being tested—the interface is. Once you've explained the scenario, you want to encourage the user to think out loud. Explain that the design is evolving, and their input will directly influence the direction the interface takes. During the test, keep them talking by asking leading questions like "Why did you click there?" and "What do you expect that to do?" Keep them engaged in the test.

When moderating, you want to guide the user, but don't just tell them what to do. Remember, you're testing the interface! If the user is confused or they don't know what to do next, you've got some work to do on the interface. Occasionally, little hints might be needed to keep the test moving, but if the user is clearly getting exasperated, you might need to be more direct.

Users Say the Darndest Things

Testing provides invaluable feedback on your design; things you think are obvious won't be—expect to be surprised. The user's mental model will be revealed as you test with multiple users. When testing, you'll want to watch where users go off the happy path: did they click somewhere you didn't expect? Note their questions, and if they don't understand a term, figure out why. Did you use their language or yours?

When Cancel Doesn't Mean Cancel

One day I was moderating a test and I asked the user what she would do if she discovered she had modified some data on the page but quickly realized she was in the wrong account—basically, I was testing the Cancel button prominently displayed on the page. She immediately froze and said she didn't think she could do anything at that point. I asked her to look around and see whether there was anything on the page that suggested she could abort the page.

When it was clear she wasn't going to click anything, I asked her about the aforementioned Cancel button. She exclaimed, "Oh that, I'd never touch that." I was quite surprised (none of my other tests found this term problematic), and I asked her why not. She went on to explain: "That button would cancel their account." I was testing a billing system, and if you didn't pay your bill, you would find your account canceled. I had discovered an overloaded term—needless to say, we changed the label on the button.

How many users should you test? More is better (up to a point), but in general, four to eight will be enough. In some cases, you can repeat until you aren't finding any new issues. Don't worry about finding the perfect user—they should be representative of your user population, but don't get too caught up in making sure every single one exactly fits your user profile.

Inevitably, you will find flaws in your design—this is a feature, not a bug! Take it in stride, iterate the interface, and test it again. Continue this process until you're out of time or the issues you're finding are minimal.

Wireframes

Once you've completed a few rounds of paper-based testing, you might want to create a wireframe mock-up of your user interface. You can use a number of tools to this end, including the following:

- HTML
- PowerPoint
- Visio

Heck, you could probably just build the application with a framework like Rails (assuming of course you're building a web app). Testing an interactive smoke-and-mirrors version of your application can lead to further improvements, though, so you must manage expectations. If your wireframe looks too good, the customer might just think you're done. Though helpful, this step can easily be skipped.

15.5 Usability Heuristics

Usability testing is irreplaceable; however, it's not your only option when it comes to designing usable interfaces. Much like a desk check can discover flaws in code, examining an interface in the light of established user interface heuristics can uncover many flaws. Basic things to look for include the following:

- The interface should be consistent—users shouldn't have to guess where the Save button is from page to page.
- Prevent errors whenever possible.
- Don't make people remember too much—computers are good at remembering things, people aren't.
- Flexibility is key—judicious use of hotkeys can radically improve the experience for advanced users.
- When errors happen, make sure they are recoverable—don't destroy their work because they made a mistake.
- Let users explore—undo works wonders here.
- The system should match the users' world.

This list just scratches the surface; for more, see http://www.asktog.com/ basics/firstPrinciples.html and http://www.useit.com/papers/heuristic/heuristic_ list.html. Some companies will perform heuristic for a fee—this can be a reasonable way to improve an interface.

15.6 Summary

Whew! I've covered a lot of turf over the past few pages: I've defined usability, debunked a number of myths, and discussed a process for designing usable interfaces. Obviously, I could have covered a number of additional topics including accessibility, the use of color, and more arcane topics like Fitts' law. I hope this chapter has given you enough information to get started down the path to more usable applications.

15.7 Web Resources

useit.com: Jakob Nielsen's website . . . . http://www.useit.com/
The website of noted usability guru Jakob Nielsen contains the full archives of his must-read Alertbox columns.

Don Norman's jnd website . . . . http://jnd.org/index.html
The other *N* in the Nielsen Norman Group, this site holds a number of links and essays from one of the founding fathers of usability.

Ask TOG . . . . http://www.asktog.com/index.html
A principal in the Nielsen Norman Group, Bruce "Tog" Tognazzini's storied career includes stops at Sun Microsystems and WebMD, though he is best known for his work at Apple Computer where he founded the Apple Human Interface Group.

User Interface Engineering (UIE) . . . . http://www.uie.com/
Founded by Jared Spool, UIE is a leader in research and training in the usability space.

Cooper . . . . http://www.cooper.com/index.asp
The website of Alan Cooper, father of personas. Cooper newsletters are well worth the read.

Advanced Common Sense . . . . http://sensible.com/
The home of Steve Krug, Advanced Common Sense includes downloads of chapters from the first edition of his best-selling book *Don't Make Me Think*.

The Software Usability Research Laboratory . . .
. . . http://psychology.wichita.edu/surl/
A part of the Human-Computer Interaction (HCI) Laboratory at Wichita State University, SURL's Usability News is a must-read for the usability set.

## Chapter 16

Integrating Ruby with Your Legacy Code

by Jared Richardson

Jared Richardson is a consultant based in North Carolina who needs a better bio. He regularly speaks for a variety of groups, has written parts of three books, and has a lot of fun writing Ruby and Rails code, but he still has trouble writing a simple bio.

16.1 A Well-Stocked Toolbox

Ask five developers what the best tool is for a given job, and you'll probably get six answers. The truth is the development landscape is constantly shifting under our feet. You shouldn't chase after every shiny pebble, but you should also use the best tool for the job. There's a balancing act between using the technology you know well and shifting into a newer technology that offers other benefits. But today you're going to cheat. Rather than be forced entirely into a new technology, you'll look at ways to continue to leverage your existing investment while still using newer tools. In this case, the new tool is Ruby.

This chapter is a whirlwind tour of how to use Ruby even if the rest of your code is in another language. I'll specifically talk about Java and C integration, but similar projects exist for many other languages, and the basic principles are the same.

But why bother? Why mix different languages? There are many different reasons, but most boil down to economy and freedom. You have existing code that works fine. It's written, tested, and, most important, paid for. But for the problems you're solving today, Ruby is the better tool. Perhaps the language itself is the draw, or maybe there's a tool (such as Ruby on Rails) that requires this different language, but you've seen the advantages and want to keep using your new tool. You usually can't, and most likely shouldn't, start rewriting from scratch. Fortunately, you don't have to make an all-or-nothing choice. There are very viable, rock-solid options for accessing your existing code base from within Ruby.

We're not going to plumb the depths of these technologies. Instead, I'll dive in to each area, show how to get a "Hello, World"–style example working, and briefly mention the advantages and problems of each approach. I'll give you the basics, point you at some good resources, and then get out of your way. Rather than trying to map out an insanely large set of usage scenarios, I'll explain how each technology works, and then you'll be able to make your own commonsense choices on how to use each tool on your project. As Solomon once said, "Knowledge is easy to him who has understanding."[1] So, let's try to understand how the tech works, and then the knowledge will be there when you need it.

---

1. See Proverbs 14:6.

I'll start with the hottest Ruby integration project, JRuby, which actually runs your Ruby code from within your Java virtual machine. The second technology will be Java-Ruby bridges that pass messages seamlessly between language runtimes over sockets. Finally, we'll call C methods from within a Ruby program.

16.2 Your Ruby Got Into My Java!

JRuby[2] is a great option when you need Ruby to function alongside your existing Java code. In fact, JRuby is a great option when you have new development in both languages. Sun Microsystems, the company behind Java, recently hired Charles Nutter and Thomas Enebo, two core JRuby developers. The project had lots of success and momentum before this happened, but with both the funding and backing of Sun, the project can only get better.

JRuby is actually a rewrite of the Ruby language in Java.[3] Because of this intimate integration, JRuby has access to nearly everything in the Java world. Here's how it looks in the swing.rb file (from the samples folder in JRuby):

```ruby
require "java"
include_class "javax.swing.JFrame"
include_class "javax.swing.JLabel"

frame = JFrame.new("Hello Swing")
label = JLabel.new("Hello World")

frame.getContentPane().add(label)
frame.setDefaultCloseOperation(JFrame::EXIT_ON_CLOSE)
frame.pack()
frame.setVisible(true)
```

So, what do you see in this block? Once you've required the JRuby package (this is how Ruby does its includes), you include Java classes, and then use them. Yes, it's just that easy.

One important thing to note is how small this code snippet is. It still looks a bit like Java code, but we've really trimmed down the amount of code it takes to get productive. The more details that are handled automatically, the fewer chances we developers have to make mistakes.

---

2. JRuby is hosted at http://jruby.codehaus.org.
3. Ruby is written in C.

And besides, I'd rather solve the interesting problems, not worry about infrastructure details or variable declarations.

Installation

So how do you install JRuby and get started? You can either check it out of the Subversion repository directly[4] or download the binary release.[5] Then, when you want to use JRuby, just make sure the JRuby JAR is in your classpath. If you don't want to use the CLASSPATH environment variable, you can use the -jar flag:

```
java -jar jruby.jar my_ruby_code.rb
```

Now that you've gotten Ruby into your Java, what can you do?

Interesting Directions

My local copy of the JRuby JAR is 1MB. For bundling a language, that's a pretty small file. And that means you can use JRuby in ways you wouldn't expect. In fact, Charles Nutter has an applet in a blog entry[6] that downloads the JAR and runs irb in a Java applet. There's another project in which Ruby on Rails code deploys to a Java application server.[7]

There are many other more uses as well. Perhaps you need to access a JDBC driver for a database[8] with no Ruby support or some internal company libraries. The possibilities are vast because of the enormous investment that our industry has in the Java space.

Pros and Cons

So, JRuby is easy to install and trivial to use. . . let's look at the list of pros and cons.

These are the pros:

- Easy to get started and easy to use.
- Open source, so it can't just go away.

---

4. svn co svn://svn.codehaus.org/jruby/trunk/jruby

5. http://dist.codehaus.org/jruby/

6. See "JRuby in an Applet" at http://headius.blogspot.com/2006/11/ruby-for-web-check.html and "JRuby IRB Applet Revisited" at http://headius.blogspot.com/2006/12/jruby-irb-applet-revisited.html.

7. See "Deploying a Ruby on Rails Application in Glassfish" at http://blogs.sun.com/whacko/entry/deploying_a_ruby_on_rails.

8. See "Active Record-JDBC with JRuby" at http://ola-bini.blogspot.com/2006/09/activerecord-jdbc-020.html.

- The JRuby code runs inside your JVM, providing first-class access to the entire Java world.
- Backed by Sun.
- Active development community.

These are the cons:

- Performance. Traditionally speed has been JRuby's Achilles heel. However, the development community recognized this problem and has worked hard to address the issue. And it shows. Now that JRuby has official Sun backing, large gains have been made in this area. There are those who think in the long term that JRuby might be faster than traditional Ruby. Suffice it to say that although JRuby could have performance issues that could affect you today, it won't be a long-term problem.
- You can't use Ruby extensions written in C. It is surprisingly easy to add C code to a Ruby program, so it's not unexpected that many popular Ruby packages have key portions written in C. These libraries simply can't be used in JRuby.

16.3 A Bridge Over Troubled Waters...

Bridge technologies take a completely different approach. Rather than embed your runtime within the host language, they create proxy objects in Ruby that you can use, but any use of that proxy object sends the serialized message object sent over a socket to another proxy within the host language. The serializing of all data transfer, as well as the network overhead, introduces a significant performance penalty. When you use a Ruby-Java bridge, be aware that every access incurs this overhead and uses the technology intelligently.

That's not to say that bridges are too slow to use. In fact, I've found the opposite to be true...bridges can be effective tools. I recently wrote a database driver[9] that used a Ruby-Java bridge, and it worked great. But I was careful not to abuse the technology either. Just understand the technology, and use it sensibly. For instance:

- If you have code that needs to pass hundreds of messages a second, don't use a bridge.
- Don't access your bridge objects repeatedly within tight loops.

---

9. See http://rubyforge.org/projects/hypersonic/.

- Periodic or infrequent access works well. Do you need to access your Java libraries only from time to time? A bridge could be a perfect fit.
- Can you store up requests, send them in one burst, and get back a big answer (or a set of answers) at one time?

I've used two Ruby-Java bridge products. One is RJB (Ruby Java Bridge).[10] The other is YAJB (Yet Another Java Bridge).[11] I'll cover YAJB for this chapter. I've found it to be the easiest to install and get running.

Installation

Installing YAJB is trivial. Once you've downloaded the project, you'll need to compile it. You'll need Java,[12] Ant,[13] and JUnit[14] installed to compile, but if you're developing Java code, you probably already have these tools.

At that point, it's a one-line install:

```
ruby setup.rb
```

Getting Started

Now that you're installed and running, what does the code look like? Let's look at another Swing example:

```ruby
require 'yajb/jbridge'
include JavaBridge
jimport "javax.swing.*"

:JOptionPane.jclass.showMessageDialog( nil, "Hello World!")
```

Pros and Cons

Here are the pros:

- Open source, so it can't just go away.
- Very easy to get started and use.
- Separate from your JVM. This lets you do things like run your Ruby code on a different machine.

---

10. RJB is hosted at http://rjb.rubyforge.org/.
11. YAJB is hosted at http://www.cmt.phys.kyushu-u.ac.jp/~M.Sakurai/cgi-bin/fw/wiki.cgi?page= YAJB.
12. See http://java.sun.com.
13. See http://ant.apache.org/.
14. See http://junit.org.

Here are the cons:

- No active development. The last release was in 2005. On the other hand, does it need active development? Everything I tried to use worked.
- Performance can be an issue, and it's not likely to be resolved given the core technology and lack of active development.
- There's not much of a community around this project. Unlike JRuby, you won't find lots of other users you can ask for advice.

16.4 Access High-Performance C Code from Your Ruby

Finally, I'll cover the highest performance option, C code. If you've ever used (or tried to use) JNI,[15] you're in for a pleasant surprise. Integrating C and Ruby is fairly simple to use and very fast.

There are two main use cases for Ruby-C integration. You'll encounter the first when you have an existing library you need to access. Perhaps it's a vendor API to a hardware device[16] or existing high-performance calculation libraries.

The second use case is tuning up your Ruby application. Several years ago Andy Hunt told me that he and Dave Thomas were working on project for a client that had to be "high performance." They wrote the application in Ruby, knowing it might not be fast enough, but they wanted the productivity boost that Ruby provides. When they were done, they benchmarked the application, located the hotspots, and rewrote them in C. The client was quite impressed with the end result.

Installation

Here's where you see the first difference. There's nothing to install. Ruby can talk directly to C code because Ruby itself is written in C. However, one utility makes the task a great deal easier. There's a Makefile utility called mkmf[17]. It's a standard Ruby library now, but some earlier Linux Ruby versions don't seem to have it installed. If mkmf isn't

---

15. Java Native Interface is used to integrate C, C++, and Assembly code with Java. It's known for being a difficult technology to learn. See http://en.wikipedia.org/wiki/Java_Native_Interface.

16. *Programming Ruby: The Pragmatic Programmer's Guide* [TH01] is online and has a great example on interfacing with a hardware jukebox. See http://www.rubycentral.com/book/ext_ruby.html. It's also a great reference to the C interfaces.

17. mkmf docs are located at http://www.ruby-doc.org/stdlib/libdoc/mkmf/rdoc/index.html.

on your system (and you'll find out from the error messages in a few moments), install it via the gem.

Getting Started

You need three things to get started. You'll first need a C program, then you'll need a Ruby program, and finally you'll need a configuration file to tell mkmf how to build your Makefile for you.

Let's start with the C code:

```
#include "ruby.h"

static VALUE cSampleC;

static VALUE exec(VALUE self) {
        printf("\n\nExec, written in C, was run from within the Ruby code \n\n");
        return Qnil;
}

void Init_SampleC() {
        cSampleC = rb_define_class("SampleC", rb_cObject);

        rb_define_method(cSampleC, "exec", exec, 0);
        // continue to define more methods here...
}
```

Let's walk through this code. To begin with, you can see #include "ruby.h". This is a simple import of the Ruby header files.

Next you see a VALUE data type. The VALUE type is like a Ruby object. It's just a generic object. When you move between C and Ruby, you need a VALUE object to hold an object reference that can be passed around. In this code, that's cSampleC.

On the next line, static VALUE exec(VALUE self), you see the VALUE type used twice. The first is in the return statement. Your C routines that you'll call from Ruby must return a VALUE statement.

You also see VALUE as an argument. Any routine that is called from Ruby needs at least one argument, namely, VALUE self. Any other arguments must come after self. If you want to return void for your return type, use Qnil as the object you return.

The last block, Init_SampleC, declares your C objects so that Ruby can see them. This routine is the map that Ruby uses to find your C routine. If this block isn't set up properly, then Ruby won't be able to find your C routines.

rb_define_class creates an object your Ruby code can see. In my example, it's SampleC. This object must start with an uppercase letter, or Ruby won't see it.

Finally, create a mapping from your routine to your Ruby object. rb_define_method does this for you. The arguments? First, the static VALUE object again, then your Ruby object name, your C method name, and finally, the number of arguments you're passing in (don't count self).

That's enough C to get you started. Let's create that configuration file. The file you'll create is called extconf.rb. Because this example is so simple, we have a really short extconf.rb:

```
require 'mkmf' create_makefile("SampleC")
```

Now you use extconf.rb to build a Makefile:

```
ruby -r mkmf extconf.rb
```

If all goes well (and mkmf is installed), you'll see *creating Makefile*.

Now you need to compile and install your new C extension. Since this is a standard Makefile, you can type make and make install.

At this point, you created, compiled, and installed code that can be used from within Ruby. You could crank up IRB and type this:

```
require "SampleC"
i=SampleC.new
i.exec
```

And you'll see *Exec, written in C, was run from within the Ruby code.*

If you do pursue this path, I strongly encourage you to buy the famous Pickaxe book.[18] It has an entire chapter devoted to Ruby extensions in C and is a great resource.

Pros and Cons

Here are the pros:

- Ruby supports C extensions natively. You're not depending on any third-party projects or mapping layers.
- C code can be very fast.
- Easy to use.

---

18. *Programming Ruby: The Pragmatic Programmer's Guide* is known by the pickaxe on its front cover. See http://pragmaticprogrammer.com/titles/ruby.

- You get to write in C. When I recently had a C project, I was surprised by how much I enjoyed the C bits.

Here are the cons:

- You still have to write C code. There are so many things that we take for granted after a few years in Java, Ruby, or any higher-level language...like strings.

16.5 Wrapping Up

I've talked about Java and C code, but if you work in a Microsoft shop, Ruby also has dotNet bindings. Visit the Ruby section on the page at http://www.dotnetpowered.com/languages.aspx; there you'll find a few bridge projects and a few embedded projects.

So, no matter what your language you need to interface with, you can probably do it from Ruby. And it's not that hard for any of the technologies I've reviewed.

16.6 Web Resources

JRuby . . . . http://jruby.codehaus.org/
JRuby home page

YAJB. . .
. . . http://www.cmt.phys.kyushu-u.ac.jp/~M.Sakurai/cgi-bin/fw/wiki.cgi?page=YAJB
YAJB (Yet Another Java Bridge)

RJB . . . . http://rjb.rubyforge.org/
Rjb (Ruby Java Bridge)

IronRuby . . . . http://www.wilcob.com/Wilco/IronRuby.aspx
IronRuby (Ruby on the CLR)

C extensions I http://www.jaredrichardson.net/blog/2006/03/25/
C extensions

C extensions II . . . . http://www.rubycentral.com/book/ext_ruby.html
C extensions

Chapter 17

Executable Documentation with FIT and FitNesse

by David Hussman

David has spent many years creating software in a variety of domains: digital audio, digital biometrics, medical, financial, retail, and education—to name a few. For the past seven years, David has mentored and coached agile transitions of all sizes in the United States, Canada, Europe, Russia, and Ukraine. Along with presenting and leading workshops/tutorials at conferences in the United States and Europe, David has contributed to several books (Managing Agile Projects and Agile in the Large) and worked on agile curriculum for the University of Minnesota and Capella University. David is currently writing a book about agility for the Pragmatic Programmer series, and he is the assistant chairman of the Agile 2007 conference and the conference chairman for Agile 2008.

David co-owns SGF Software, a software development group based in Minneapolis, Minnesota. SGF Software is a software development company keenly focused on promoting agile development, both in practice and as mentors. SGF provides seasoned leaders who strive to pragmatically match technology, people, and solutions to create software that makes people happier and more productive. SGF provides agile services, product development services, and a host of quality software development consultants and contractors.

For more information, check out the SGF at http://www.sgfco.com.

Simply put, executable documentation (ED) is any project collateral that communicates something about a system or an application in a form that is runnable, most often in an automated test. Covering all of ED is too large a topic, so I am limiting this chapter to ED and story tests.

At best, you will read this chapter and head out to put some dead documents out of their misery and cut some ED of your own. At worst, you will learn a bit about the evolution of tests and learn that automated acceptance tests can replace the legacy documents of the future. I could rant for pages about numerous projects that produced reams of documents but failed to deliver anything or delivered something to a host of unsatisfied users. I could do that, but this is well-documented territory, if you will pardon the pun. It is simple: stop killing trees only to create documents destined to die a fast death, and start creating living documents in forms that are kept alive because of their quantifiable value, always communicating what a living system actually provides. But first, I'll start with a simple story....

17.1 Stumbling Toward Innovation

Some years ago, I helped create an automated testing framework. Our goal was not to re-create JUnit; we were trying to solve a problem outside of the JUnit sweet spot. The project's developers were fully test infected, and they had a wall of unit tests. Although the unit tests were adding value, telling the story of the code, the project—an agile project—was struggling with failing acceptance tests. Acceptance tests, also called *story tests*, are the tests that agile customers use to help define when a user story is "done." Not only were the acceptance tests sometimes failing during story sign-off, but acceptance tests for stories signed off in previous iterations, were failing in later iterations. Because of the high cost of maintaining automated scripts for regression testing, the regression testing was being done manually. Although the community was working well with user stories, it lacked a shared view of the product, and the developers were a bit lost in the love of technology over the needs of the customers. To address these problems, we created the automated testing framework (ATF), a tool for automating acceptance tests.

The ATF allowed us to create directories filled with input and output data sets that JUnit fixtures would run against the system under test (SUT), plugging in just under the presentation layer. Crude as it was, the ATF was starting to work just about the time I left the project. Automating a few acceptance tests raised awareness around failing tests and increased dialogue about the tests. In hindsight, the project community was stumbling toward a new way of working with stories and acceptance tests. Because the ATF was initially geek-driven development (GDD), it was a bit lacking in the usability department. As we engaged a variety of people, we realized the developer-centric nature of the tool was inhibiting its ability to clarify our shared definition of "done." Still, we had engaged customers and testers in a joint effort to automate acceptance tests. The very large test plan was shrinking, and the velocity was increasing as was customer satisfaction. We were, along with many other agile projects, stumbling toward a valuable form of executable documentation—automated acceptance tests.

17.2 Less Is More, Again!

After this experience, I started watching the evolution of stories and acceptance tests across various project communities. I also compared the use of user stories to other forms of requirements. In both cases, there was (and is) a tendency to add more words in the hopes of adding more clarity. The successful projects, agile or not, did not have the largest document pile, but they did have a shared understanding of product value. The struggling projects lacked a shared view of what was needed or why, and many tried in vain fix this by creating more and more detailed documentation.

So, why doesn't adding more detail produce better software products? Is it because stuffing more words into a requirements document, making them difficult or uninteresting to read, is not how people come to understand products and product value? History screams YES! Software products reflect the culture of their builders. Building cultures of excitement means looking for and promoting the ideas, conversation, incentives, and tools that connect people. It is clear to me that people rally around products they can experience and show off. When was the last time you were excited to show off a document?

The Origin of Value

I hesitate further abusing the word *value*. I fear that this word has been crushed under the grammar hammer of the IT community. This is sad because the origin of value is tied with the creation of story tests. If the user stories get the discussion started, the story tests help define the value. It is the creation of the stories where value is first manifest. Sadly, many product owners and sponsors know their product needs but struggle to translate these valuable ideas into specifications or requirements.

Thankfully, we now have user stories—a simpler and more powerful way to communicate product needs. Product owners are free to write less and say more. When we create a time and place for developers and product owners to discuss stories, smaller documents spawn more discussion and increased understanding and innovation. For this reason, and many more, stories are a great step forward. But stories do not solve all problems for the agile customer. The project community must continuously develop a common project/domain language that helps them define when a user story is "done." Defining "done" with story tests reduces the temptation to add more written words in the name of improved communication. The serious XP camper might argue that "this is fundamental to good user stories." This is true, but people still struggle with user stories and tend toward solving ambiguity with more words. Moving toward executable documentation, which quickly shows value by providing continuous feedback, promotes the habits of healthy and successful projects. A good smell for any project: people start talking in tests and creating testable contracts and executable documentation.

"Just the Tests Ma'am"
by Sam Clemens, champion for common sense

As customers, we had gathered to write stories for the next iteration. As we started selecting a collection of stories to present at the planning meeting, our coach asked us to write a few tests for each story, as a way to help us better define "done" for each story. As we added tests, we were changing the stories and increasing our understanding of each story. The more tests we added, the less detail we needed in the stories. Finally, I suggested we try to capture all details in the form of tests. Our stories were shorter and clearer, and the planning meeting was one of our best. The developers told us they had a much better understanding of the stories because the tests helped add clarity. We worked together to add and modify the tests during the planning game while we grew our shared domain knowledge and language.

Sam's story, a true story, is now a few years old. At the same point in time, many people were starting to use story tests as a way to keep stories small and communicative. The story still started the discussion, but the tests were now the developer's guide as they added tasks for the stories. We were evolving the nature and power of stories by simply doing more of a good thing, adding tests. We were also setting the stage for story test–driven development (SDD).

Evolving Tests

If better requirements come in the form of stories and story tests help promote clarity and define done, what's the problem? Well, one problem for many communities is the disconnect between the requirement's authors and the test plan creators. Another problem, until a few years ago, was the lack of tools for automating regression story test suites. Thankfully, the latter has changed, and we have FIT, FitLibrary, FitNesse, and many others. Now with these tools, we need to improve story and story test–writing skills. This cannot be deemed the sole responsibility of the customers or product owners. Being a customer is hard work, and a helping hand is most welcome.

The Life of a Story

At some point, someone has an idea for improving a product. The idea can flourish within an innovative space or suffocate under a heavyweight documentation process. If it survives, it enters the project queue and might be added to the development schedule. On its journey toward being clickable, people will poke and prod the idea, possibly adding to it or breaking it into several pieces. At some point in the process, someone will say, "How big is this thing?" This is the time to plant the seeds of executable documentation. One way to size a story is to work out a few tests. If you are helping a customer, try asking "When is this done?" The customer will most likely start talking in tests without calling them tests. This is the beginning of executable documentation. Instead of adding more words, which might quickly grow stale or out-of-date, capture their words in the form of simple tests that can be automated and kept alive. If you question this, jump in and write stories for a few iterations, which is a good experience for all developers!

As the stories progress toward the planning game, grow the tests and make them more concrete. One way to do this is to walk the day in the life of a persona. Personas, another large and interesting topic, are descriptions of people who will use the system. Each persona usually has a name, a short description, and a few statements of how the system is valuable in their work/life. Walking a day in their life will expose satisfying and/or frustrating experiences; both are valuable and testable.

Pairing Beyond Programming

It feels odd that I'm talking a great deal about testing, not the testers. For argument's sake, let's not worry about who does the testing or who should. Let's simply assume that someone will wear the testing hat at some point in the project. It might be a tester, a customer, an end user, or a developer. Testing is so very different from project to project. When there is a testing group, there tends to be less joy in tester land. As someone who spends a great deal of time working with testers, I hear their collective frustrations. Bad things tend to flow downhill, and the testers, too often connected too late in the process, feel the cumulative ills of the project wash over them like a wave nearing shore.

Often, in an effort to organize testing, someone creates "the test plan." This is yet another form of weighty documentation that quickly becomes obsolete. Furthermore, the test plan is often a manual script captured in a document. The costs to complete manual regression testing are huge and increase only with project success. You either hire an army of testers, who still struggle to keep up, or start to run up a regression deficit (a pile of testing not being addressed), which cuts into product value.

Maybe the reason we tend to talk about quality issues in the form of bugs is that we wait too long to engage testers in the product life cycle. Here's a simple solution: have the testers pair with customer to write story tests. After all, a tester who reads a story cannot help but think about when it is done; this is the testing mind-set. Testers have learned to see requirements in a form that is testable, reading past the words and into the way the application works (or is supposed to work). If they have this skill, the much needed support for the customer is readily available, and the story tests can be created by the defenders or definers of quality. This is one of many pairings that happen in successful project communities. Agile principles promote spontaneous collaboration, which FIT supports.

17.3 Tools of the Trade

So now we have all the players and the collateral we need to automate story tests and produce executable documentation. Continuing the pairing thread, testing and developers make a strong pairing. Again, this is not news or new to successful project communities. Once the stories are tasked, a developer and a tester sit together to discuss how to best automate the story tests. The story tests act as a simple API for tester and developer communication. The tester can suggest a test, and the developer can then create a fixture that mediates between the test and the system under test. Once again, this way of working is on the path of story test–driven development. Many tools are available to create automated story tests; in this chapter, you'll dive into FIT, but it is also possible to do simple automating with the xUnit frameworks.

Extending NUnit
by Joe Customer, chief story teller

As a customer, I was unsure when the developers told me that they were going to automate all my story tests. Stories were new to me, and I had learned to trust that I could write less in the stories and count on the story tests and the story sign-off process to ensure I was getting what I wanted. I knew the developers were automating their unit tests with NUnit, but I did not understand it well enough to see how this could help me. The developers made it simple. They created a special set of automated tests, each of which were named after the tests I provided for a user story, with each group of tests organized in an NUnit test named after the story I created. This level of automation became a contract I could count on as part of each story sign-off process. I now had more time for exploratory testing, because I could see the story tests run in an automated fashion. It took a while for me to realize that these new tests were run frequently, many times per day, and that I had my own set of functional regression tests. On previous projects, we were lucky to have regression testing more than once per month. I used these tests to support and reduce the amount of information I put into my other documentation for the project.

Getting FIT

Although it is possible to automate story tests with xUnit, or a home-grown solution such as the ATF, FIT is a better choice. Created by Ward Cunningham, FIT stands for the Framework for Integrated Testing and is available in multiple languages. It is a tool to automate functional tests and is a tool that fosters collaboration. FIT uses fixtures, created by developers, to exercise tests, created by customers and testers and written in HTML or Microsoft Excel. More than automating functional tests, FIT acts as a unifier, bonding communities around a common domain language and a quantifiable definition of quality. As FIT's popularity grew, it was enhanced by FitLibrary and FitNesse. Selecting from the FIT options, you have a strong vehicle for creating executable documentation. This chapter is not a full FIT primer. If you are looking for more information, you should read *FIT for Developing Software* by Rick Mugridge and Ward Cunningham.

Core FIT

So far, I have focused on how to combine people and process to create stories and story tests. Continuing on that path, let's assume you have a collection of people who have a set of acceptance tests ready for automation. FIT, like JUnit, is wonderfully simple. If you have created a JUnit test fixture or any other xUnit test fixture, you are ready to create FIT fixtures. The FIT fixtures plug in the same way as a JUnit test. The difference is that the FIT tests will now hold the data used by the fixture, and the fixture mediates between the test and the system under test.

The framework finds FIT tests, loads the FIT fixtures defined in the test, and then executes the rows in the test, using the fixture to mediate between the test and the system under test. For each test executed, the framework produces an HTML page that shows which rows passed and which rows failed. Like JUnit, the rows that passed are green, and the failed rows are red. Figure 17.1, on the next page shows two passing tests and one failing test. One of the passing tests expects an error and would have failed if no error/exception was produced.

Core FIT provides three basic ways to automate acceptance tests:

- Column fixtures: For testing calculations and constraints
- Action fixtures: For testing state
- Row fixtures: For testing lists

With story tests in hand, you need to determine which fixture will best serve your needs. You can use FIT and the fixtures in many ways. If you are new, you should start simple and evolve. Although you can use multiple fixtures in one test, select one type of fixture for your first test, and get it running and communicating. If you compare this to your TDD experience, you rough out a test, make it fail, create a fixture, and get one or two rows of the test to pass. You are now one step closer to SDD.

The fixtures are not hard to write. There is a learning curve, but the real work is in creating tests that communicate what the product should or should not do/provide. If the story is about a deep calculation, the column fixture is an obvious choice. Column fixtures provide strong input/output testing. I give you this; you give me this back. The frame-

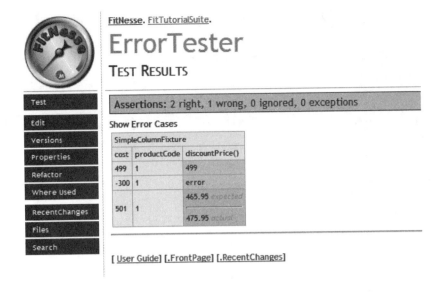

Figure 17.1: JUNIT-LIKE OUTPUT

work maps the names in the tests to the attributes and method names in the fixtures, executing the data row by row. For any tests, there can be multiple input and outputs. The first example of green and red test output is a column fixture.

Always keep in mind that creating executable documentation is about going past automated tests. You want to create tests that communicate how the system behaves. To add context to a FIT test, FIT allows for each test to have plain text within the test. Beware: adding plain text can help tests be helpful, but it should not replace choosing communicative names for tests and fixtures, and it can be a slippery slope away from executable documentation. If it is testable, put it in the test and not in the text.

The action fixture was created to test state, which provides a way to test business processes. For action fixtures, the framework starts the fixture and maintains state in the fixture as the tests are run. The action fixture provides testers with the ability to do the following:

- Enter: Entering data for testing
- Press: Executing an action (with the data entered)
- Check: Validating the state of the system under test

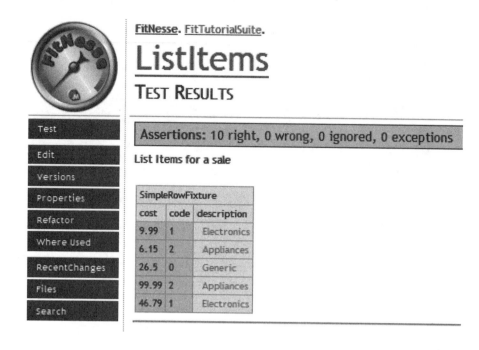

Figure 17.2: SIMPLE ROW FIXTURE

This simple set of actions provides much of what is needed to emulate many different process. Although this fixture is powerful, the tests are difficult to read and not self-documenting. Many customers do not find the semantics intuitive. As you read on, you will find that the DoFixture is the better choice for testing processes and many other types of testing. Action fixtures are often not flexible and can be costly to keep alive. Avoid them.

The last core FIT fixture is the row fixture as shown in Figure 17.2. The row fixture provides a way to validate lists. Of the many ways this is helpful, imagine using it to validate that search results are correct or the contents of an object to be displayed are as expected. The output can be formatted in many ways (that is, ordered), but the value of adding formatting complexity should be considered. Creating executable documentation is about tests that communicate what the system does. This can be done in simple ways, and this should be your (initial) mantra if you want ED to be a valued and sustainable practice.

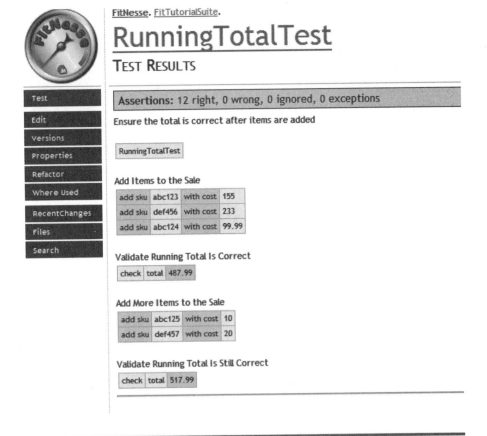

Figure 17.3: SIMPLE DoFIXTURE EXAMPLE

FitLibrary

Taking FIT to the next level, Rick Mugridge created FitLibrary, simplifying various aspects of FIT and introducing the idea of "flow style testing." The fixtures in FitLibrary allow for significantly more readable tests. Of the many fixtures FitLibrary provides, I'll focus only on DoFixture. Again, for more information, read the *FIT for Developing Software* book.

As I mentioned, if you want to test business processes, DoFixture is your friend. DoFixture, as shown in Figure 17.3, allows tests to be written in a more natural language. Gone are click, check, and validate. These are replaced with tests in the form of sentences that are much closer to the domain language for the project.

DoFixture increases our ability to craft tests in the customer's language or the domain language for the product. As communities move away from wordy requirements and toward readable tests, they start talking in tests and speaking a common language. As living things, the tests do not lay quiet when the system misbehaves, acting in an unexpected way. If FIT tests are part of your continuous integration, broken tests might start the build server screaming, indicating the project is not as healthy as it once was. Sometimes failing tests are due to new language created as the product evolves. For example, meaningless names can be found and refactored to reflect the current state/value of the product.

FitNesse

Where FIT and FitLibrary help promote executable documentation, they are not always highly accessible to the entire project community. FitNesse allows anyone to execute the tests with one click and simplifies navigating the results. Simply put, FitNesse is FIT running in a wiki. The HTML output from FIT is easy to read and easier to navigate. FitNesse provides many other features, such as a wiki-editing environment, basic refactoring functions, and the ability to convert tests in Excel by pasting in the spreadsheet and clicking Convert to FitNesse. Before rushing to FitNesse, you should consider your audience. If one of your goals is increased collaboration and your audience is not wiki savvy, FitNesse might not be a good selection. That said, nothing raises the ROI of executable documentation like empowering the big boss to run a set or regression tests on demand! This is a significant step in open and honest communication, and it raises the quality bar to a new level.

17.4 Where Do You Go from Here?

If this chapter speaks to you and you are looking to reduce or remove dead, dying, or wasteful documentation, you will need a convincing message to address the all-too-common fear of change. A simple selling point, previously mentioned, is the reduction in manual regression testing. Using FIT to create documentation reduces, but does not totally replace, the time needed to regression test your system and creates living documentation of what the system actually does. Being unambiguous, the tests either run or don't. Since they are easy and fast to run, you run them more often, and quality can be more frequently quantified, a goal of almost every project manager and a want of most product owners.

Getting Started

Start simple! Too many good tools are rejected or diminished because value was not shown early. FIT tests are similar but different from unit tests. The audience for FIT tests is wider, and the communicative nature of the tests is crucial. Adding a handful of FIT tests to your continuous integration process will go along way toward increasing domain discussions, clarifying and reducing detail in requirements, and improving quality and predictable deliveries.

If you want to take a huge step forward, investigate story test–driven development (SDD). This is too large a step for some project communities, but it is one of the most exciting things happening in agile development today. Building on TDD, SDD asks that developers do not start coding until a failing story test is in place. This challenges the project community to continuously collaborate around automated acceptance tests. Once a failing story test is in place, the developers can start the TDD cycle of red, green, clean—designing the code one test at a time and refactoring to reduce duplication and other velocity-inhibiting noise. Once the TDD produces a green story test, the developers have a new place to review refactoring opportunities. Now that the fixture mediates between the domain language of the customers and the system under test, large and complex fixtures are a smell worth considering. It might be that the code has strayed too far from the language of the customer, and the smell should be removed. When you find things that should be tested but can't be tested, bring on the FIT deodorizer!

17.5 Web Resources

NUnit . . . . http://www.nunit.org/
Testing framework for .NET, based on JUnit

FIT http://fit.c2.com/
The FIT testing framework

FitNesse . . . . http://fitnesse.org/
The FitNesse testing framework

Chapter 18

Introducing the iBATIS Persistence Framework

by Mark Richards

Mark Richards is a certified senior IT architect at IBM, where he is involved in the architecture and design of large-scale service-oriented architectures in J2EE and other technologies, primarily in the financial services industry. He has been involved in the software industry as a developer, designer, and architect since 1984, and he has significant experience and expertise in J2EE architecture and development, object-oriented design and development, and systems integration. Mark is the author of the book Java Transaction Design Strategies and contributing author of the book NFJS Anthology 2006. Mark served as president of the Boston Java Users' Group in 1997 and 1998 and as president of the New England Java Users' Group from 1999 through 2003, and he helped increase the group's membership from its original 30 members to more than 2,700, earning it the recognition as one of the top 25 Java Users' Groups in the world. Mark is an IBM Certified Application Architect, Open Group Certified Master IT Architect, Sun Certified J2EE Business Component Developer, Sun Certified J2EE Enterprise Architect, Sun Certified Java Programmer, BEA WebLogic Certified Developer, and Certified Java Instructor, and he has a master's degree in computer science from Boston University. He has spoken at several conferences around the country, including No Fluff Just Stuff, the ServerSide Java Symposium, Boston Java Users' Group, New England Java Users' Group, and other professional groups and conferences.

18.1   Introduction

Most developers are familiar with the popular object/relational mapping (ORM) framework Hibernate or the newly released Java Persistence API (JPA) persistence standard (JSR 220). Although these ORM solutions work well for some situations, they are not the answer for every persistence situation. The Holy Grail of Java persistence frameworks simply does not exist and probably never will. That is why it is important to know about and understand another type of Java persistence framework called iBATIS.

The iBATIS persistence framework is an open source project under Apache that was started by Clinton Begin in early 2002. iBATIS is a simple but powerful framework that can be used for small applications yet can scale to meet the demands of large-scale, enterprise-wide applications. The iBATIS framework has versions available for Java, .NET, and Ruby. iBATIS looks at the problem of Java persistence a little differently than the traditional ORM frameworks, and by doing so it differentiates itself quite nicely.

18.2   iBATIS vs. Traditional ORM Frameworks

One way to understand the iBATIS persistence framework is to understand how it differs from *traditional ORM frameworks*. The first major difference is that iBATIS does not generate SQL code. Instead, SQL statements and stored procedure calls are written in XML files called *SQLMaps*. The SQL statements are then referenced in Java code through the iBATIS *SqlMapClient Java interface*.

Next, unlike traditional ORM frameworks, iBATIS does not map Java objects to relational database *tables*. Instead, iBATIS maps Java objects to SQL *result sets*. In addition to mapping Java objects, you can also map HashMap and TreeMap data structures, as well as plain XML.

Object caching is another main difference between iBATIS and traditional ORM frameworks. iBATIS offers a caching model based on *query caching*. However, unlike traditional ORM frameworks, iBATIS does not act on a pool of objects to represent the database. This means there is no concepts in iBATIS of object cache synchronization, object reference lookup, and cache merging. Using the iBATIS Java API, applications interact directly with iBATIS SQLMap statements, which in turn execute SQL statements. I will be discussing iBATIS caching later in the chapter.

18.3 Why Use iBATIS?

As traditional ORM frameworks such as Hibernate become more widely adapted and used, the deficiencies of them begin to stand out. Traditional ORM frameworks are perfect for small and large CRUD-based applications where the data model closely matches the object model. However, when you start introducing features such as stored procedures and reporting-type queries, suddenly the traditional ORM solutions don't seem like such a great idea.

Although you can certainly map and execute stored procedures in traditional ORM frameworks, it is not always an easy task. This effort usually requires defining a named native query in the XML configuration file and then either defining a result mapping or manually mapping the result set in your Java code. Furthermore, you cannot usually leverage the caching model in the traditional ORM frameworks when using stored procedures, which makes you start wondering what benefits you are really getting from the Java persistence framework. The same problems hold true for reporting-type queries as well. Consider a simple reporting-type query that returns a list of all the stocks that have been traded, grouped by symbol and side (buy or sell):

```
SELECT SYMBOL, SIDE, SUM(SHARES) AS TOTAL_SHARES
  FROM TRADE
GROUP BY SYMBOL, SIDE
```

This query produces a result set containing the total number of shares bought or sold for each stock in the TRADE table. Because this query does not return a key, it would require defining a *named native query* in the XML configuration file and then either defining a result mapping or manually mapping the result set in your Java code. Depending on the ORM framework you are using, you may be able to use the provider query language to execute this query against the cache, but this solution also requires additional coding in the application layer. iBATIS handles stored procedures and reporting-type queries in the same way it handles standard SQL statements, so with iBATIS no additional coding or configuration is required.

Another situation where the traditional ORM frameworks don't work well is when the data model (schema) does not closely match the object model. Although you can certainly use traditional ORM solutions in this case, the coding effort required to fix this problem usually requires the use of complex table relationship code. Since iBATIS uses SQL statements rather than generated SQL and maps result sets rather than the tables, this problem is removed from the scope of the application and persistence framework when using iBATIS.

A final situation where iBATIS would be a better persistence choice than the traditional ORM frameworks is when you have existing SQL you need to use or when you need to tune *SQL* rather than *application code* to get the maximum performance out of the database layer. It is hard to tune SQL when it is being generated by the application layer. In this case, you would need to use the ORM provider API to perform specialized *SQL tuning* within your Java code, something that complicates your Java code and is usually beyond the knowledge of your average Java developer.

18.4 Setting Up Data Sources and Transactions

Being a persistence framework, iBATIS requires a connection to a *data source* and must also manage *database transactions*. Typically this would be configured and managed in a container or framework like Spring or EJB. However, there may be cases where you want iBATIS to manage these resources, particularly for smaller web-based applications. To do this you can specify the data sources and transaction manager through the *SQLMap config XML file*. This file allows you to specify data sources, transactions, and global settings (such as namespaces) and also allows you to specify the SQLMaps that should be loaded and managed by iBATIS.

The following code illustrates how to set up a data source using iBATIS and how to load the SQLMaps that contain the SQL statements and mapping elements. I used DB2 in this example. I will call this file SqlMapConfig.xml:

```
<sqlMapConfig>
   <transactionManager type="JDBC" >
      <dataSource type="SIMPLE">
         <property name="JDBC.Driver"
                   value="com.ibm.db2.jcc.DB2Driver"/>
         <property name="JDBC.ConnectionURL"
                   value="jdbc:db2://server:60000/dbname"/>
         <property name="JDBC.Username" value="dbuser"/>
         <property name="JDBC.Password" value="dbpwd"/>
         <property name="JDBC.DefaultAutoCommit" value="false" />
      </dataSource>
   </transactionManager>
```

```
    <sqlMap resource="TradeOrderSQLMap.xml"/>
    <sqlMap resource="CustomerSQLMap.xml"/>
    <sqlMap resource="SettlementSQLMap.xml"/>
</sqlMapConfig>
```

You can specify many other iBATIS settings in the SQLMap config file to manage the database connection, such as *transaction timeouts* and *connection pool properties*. You can find a complete list of these settings in the iBATIS documentation.

18.5 Mapping SQL Statements

SQL statements and stored procedure calls are written in XML files called *SQLMaps*. You can have as many SQLMap XML files in an application as you want. Generally, these SQLMap files are organized by functional areas within the application (that is, trade order processing, customer management, trade settlement, and so on). SQLMaps contain a collection of SQL statements and corresponding *parameter maps* (input) and *result maps* (output). You can also specify *aliases* for classes you want to map to parameters or result sets. For example, suppose you are using a class called TradeData for input or output mapping. You could specify an alias to that class in the SQLMap XML file as follows:

```
<typeAlias alias="tradeData" type="com.trading.TradeData"/>
```

You can now use the alias reference in parameter maps and result maps without having to specify the fully qualified class name. Using the alias element facilitates refactoring and can also act as a reference catalog for the entities used in the SQLMap (assuming the aliases are all defined at the beginning of the SQLMap).

You can specify SQL statements through one of six statement elements:

- <statement>
- <procedure>
- <select>
- <insert>
- <update>
- <delete>

The <statement> element is a generic catchall statement element that can be used for any type of SQL statement, but it does not contain statement-type specific capabilities (such as retrieving the key after an insert). Therefore, it is recommended that you use the specific SQL type element rather than the <statement> element since the type of SQL is generally known and unlikely to change. The <procedure> element is used to specify a stored procedure call, whereas the other statement elements are used to specify specific CRUD operations containing SQL statements.

To illustrate how to use iBATIS to specify and map a simple SQL statement, consider the example of selecting a list of stock trades for a particular action (buy or sell) where the number of shares traded is greater than a certain amount. For instance, to retrieve a list of trades where the number of shares purchased was greater than 10,000, you could use the following SQL:

```
SELECT TRADE_ID, SIDE, SYMBOL, SHARES, PRICE
  FROM TRADE
 WHERE SIDE = 'BUY' AND SHARES > 10000
```

To map this SQL statement in iBATIS, you will need to map the SQL statement, input parameters, and output results.

Mapping the SQL Statement

Using the previous example, you can map the SQL statement using the <select> element. An example of this is as follows:

```
<select id="getTrades" parameterMap="tradeQueryMap"
       resultMap="tradeResult">
       SELECT TRADE_ID, SIDE, SYMBOL, SHARES, PRICE
         FROM TRADE
        WHERE SIDE = ? AND SHARES > ?
</select>
```

Notice here that the getTrades SQL statement is using a tradeQueryMap parameter map to map the input parameters and a tradeResult map to map the result set coming back from the query (you will see how to map these in the next two sections).

Mapping the Input Parameters

You can map input parameters using the <parameterMap> element in the SQLMap XML file or implicitly using the <parameterClass> property. Using the previous example, you can map the input parameters to the SQL statement using a simple HashMap as follows:

```
<parameterMap id="tradeQueryMap" class="map">
   <parameter property="p_action" jdbcType="VARCHAR" mode="IN"/>
   <parameter property="p_shares" jdbcType="INTEGER" mode="IN"/>
</parameterMap>
```

Notice how the HashMap contains two entries, one with a key value of *p_action* and the other with a key value of *p_shares*. You will see how this map is populated in Java in a moment. The *jdbcType* property is optional and can usually be derived; however, because of differences in various database drivers, it is recommended that it be added to the parameter map.

An alternative approach to using parameter maps is to use *implicit mapping*. This is typically a preferred approach over using parameter maps mainly because unlike result maps, parameter maps are not highly reusable. To use implicit mapping in an iBATIS SQL statement, you would specify a parameterClass property rather than the parameterMap property:

```
<select id="getTrades" parameterClass="map"
      resultMap="tradeResult">
    SELECT TRADE_ID, SIDE, SYMBOL, SHARES, PRICE
      FROM TRADE
      WHERE SIDE = #p_action# AND SHARES > #p_shares#
</select>
```

Notice in the previous example how the positional markers (question marks) from the prior example are replaced by #p_action# and #p_shares#, which are the same key values as in the previous parameter map example. Implicit mapping is more intrusive to the SQL statement but reduces the amount of XML you have to write.

Mapping the Output Parameters

Now that the input parameters are mapped, the next step is to define the results mappings that come back from the SQL query. Using the previous example, assume you have a standard Java transfer object called TradeData you want to map that contains the following attributes (we will call this file TradeData.java):

```
public class TradeData implements java.io.Serializable
{
    private long tradeId;
    private String action;
    private String symbol;
    private long shares;
    private double price;

    //getters and setters defined here
    ...
}
```

To define the mappings from the results of the SQL query to the Trade-Data object, you would use the <resultMap> element in the SQLMap XML file as follows:

```
<resultMap id="tradeResult" class="tradeData">
    <result property="tradeId" column="TRADE_ID"/>
    <result property="action" column="SIDE"/>
    <result property="symbol" column="SYMBOL"/>
    <result property="shares" column="SHARES"/>
    <result property="price" column="PRICE"/>
</resultMap>
```

Notice that the alias tradeData defined earlier is used to reference the TradeData transfer object used by this result map. The result map simply maps the columns from the result set to the attributes in the transfer object by invoking the corresponding setter methods in the mapped object.

The complete SQLMap file for the example looks like this (we will call this file TradingSqlMap.xml):

```
<?xml version="1.0" encoding="UTF-8"?>
<!DOCTYPE sqlMap PUBLIC "-//iBATIS.com//DTD SQL MAP 2.0//EN"
    "http://www.ibatis.com/dtd/sql-map-2.dtd">
<sqlMap>
   <typeAlias alias="tradeData" type="com.trading.TradeData"/>

   <resultMap id="tradeResult" class="tradeData">
       <result property="tradeId" column="TRADE_ID"/>
       <result property="action" column="SIDE"/>
       <result property="symbol" column="SYMBOL"/>
       <result property="shares" column="SHARES"/>
       <result property="price" column="PRICE"/>
   </resultMap>

   <select id="getTrades" parameterClass="map"
           resultMap="tradeResult">
         SELECT TRADE_ID, SIDE, SYMBOL, SHARES, PRICE
           FROM TRADE
           WHERE SIDE = #p_action# AND SHARES > #p_shares#
   </select>
</sqlMap>
```

Within the SQLMap XML files, parameter maps (if you use them) and result maps can be grouped with the statements using them, or they can be grouped by element type within the SQLMap (that is, declare all parameter maps, then declare all result maps, and then declare all of the statements). One advantage to keeping the parameter maps, result maps, and statements together is for quick referencing. However, grouping them by element type is also good if the parameter maps and result maps are shared by other statements. Regardless of which method you choose, just be sure to be consistent throughout all your SQLMaps.

18.6 Invoking iBATIS SQL Statements in Java

To invoke the iBATIS SQL statements contained in the SQLMap XML files, you use the *SqlMapClient Java interface*. The SqlMapClient interface is a straightforward Java interface that contains some core methods you can use to perform the basic CRUD operations. The following is a list of the core methods that are defined in the SqlMapClient interface:

- queryForList()
- queryForObject()
- insert()
- update()
- delete()

Each of these CRUD methods takes two arguments; the first is a String value containing the ID of the iBATIS statement (in our case the *get-Trades* ID property value from the <select> statement), and the second is an object containing the input parameters that are used by the SQL statement. For example:

```
sqlMapClient.queryForList("getTrades", map);
```

The queryForList() method will return a list of objects specified in the <resultMap> element as a java.util.List, whereas the queryForObject() will return a single object type specified in the class property of the <resultMap> element.

Typically the SqlMapClient interface is injected into the Java class (that is, the business object) through a framework such as Spring. An example of this is as follows (we will call this file beans.xml):

```
<bean id="sqlMap"
     class="org.springframework.orm.ibatis.SqlMapClientFactoryBean">
   <property name="configLocation">
      <value>classpath:SqlMapConfig.xml</value></property>
   <property name="dataSource" ref="dataSource"/>
</bean>

<bean id="tradingService" class="com.trading.TradingService">
   <property name="sqlMapClient" ref="sqlMap"/>
</bean>
```

If you are not using Spring, you can load the SqlMapClient interface in Java using the iBATIS SqlMapClientBuilder factory object. Assuming the SqlMapConfig.xml file is in the classpath (which it should be), you could use the following Java code to load the SqlMapClient object:

```
Reader reader = Resources.getResourceAsReader(''SqlMapConfig.xml");
SqlMapClient  sqlMapClient = SqlMapClientBuilder.buildSqlMapClient(reader);
```

To invoke the getTrades statement to return a list of stock trades with a specific action and number of shares, you could use the following Java code:

```
HashMap map = new Hashmap();
map.put("p_action", "BUY");
map.put("p_shares", new Integer(10000));
List trades = sqlMapClient.queryForList("getTrades", map);
```

Notice the link between the string values specified as the HashMap keys in the put() methods and the property values specified in the corresponding parameter map. iBATIS will execute the query, map the results to the object, and return the list of objects.

The complete listing for the TradingService.java file is as follows:

```
import com.ibatis.sqlmap.client.SqlMapClient;
import java.util.*;

public class TradingService {
    private SqlMapClient sqlmapClient = null;

    public void loadSqlMap() {
        Reader reader = Resources.getResourceAsReader(''SqlMapConfig.xml");
        SqlMapClient = SqlMapClientBuilder.buildSqlMapClient(reader);
    }

    public List getTrades(String action, long shares) throws Exception {
        HashMap map = new Hashmap();
        map.put("p_action", action);
        map.put("p_shares", shares);
        return sqlMapClient.queryForList("getTrades", map);
    }
}
```

18.7   Using HashMaps vs. Java Transfer Objects

In the preceding example I showed a simple parameter map that used a HashMap to pass values from the Java method into iBATIS:

```
<parameterMap id="tradeQueryMap" class="map">
    <parameter property="p_action" jdbcType="VARCHAR" mode="IN"/>
    <parameter property="p_shares" jdbcType="INTEGER" mode="IN"/>
</parameterMap>
```

An alternative approach is to use a Java *transfer object* instead of the HashMap object:

```
<typeAlias alias="tradeInputData" type="com.trading.TradeInputData"/>
<parameterMap id="tradeQueryMap" class="tradeInputData">
    <parameter property="action" jdbcType="VARCHAR" mode="IN"/>
    <parameter property="shares" jdbcType="INTEGER" mode="IN"/>
</parameterMap>
```

In the previous example, the corresponding tradeInputObject Java transfer object might look as follows (we will call this file TradeInputData.java):

```
public class TradeInputData implements java.io.Serializable
{
    private String action;
    private long shares;

    //getters and setters defined here
    ...
}
```

Using a HashMap to pass input parameters to the parameter map has one major drawback in that it creates a *tight coupling* between the iBATIS parameter map and the Java code invoking the iBATIS statement. This is because of the HashMap key/property name binding between Java and the iBATIS parameter map. Using a Java transfer object reduces this tight coupling but creates more objects to manage. Although both options are viable solutions, I have found the latter (using transfer objects) to be a better choice because errors in the mappings are caught at compile time rather than runtime. Also, keep in mind that the parameter class does not need to be a separate object; in the previous example, you could just as easily have used the existing TradeData class instead of creating a new one.

18.8 Caching in iBATIS

iBATIS offers *query caching* as its cache model, but it is not the same concept as the cache model used in traditional ORM frameworks such as JPA, Hibernate, and Toplink. In traditional ORM frameworks, the cache is used as an object representation of the database. CRUD operations from the application act upon the object cache rather than the database directly. Traditional ORM frameworks also have the concept of synchronizing the object cache with the database. Once you are done inserting, updating, deleting, or querying the objects, the ORM will detect what has changed and generate the necessary SQL statements to apply the changes to the database. With iBATIS, the cache is solely used as a traditional query cache so that repeated queries to nonmodified data are retrieved from the cache rather than from the database.

iBATIS offers four types of *caching models*: LRU, FIFO, Memory, and OSCACHE. The LRU model specifies that when the cache becomes full, iBATIS will remove the items that are least used to make room for the new ones. The FIFO model specifies that when the cache becomes full, iBATIS will remove the oldest objects from the cache. The Memory model relies on the garbage collector to manage the cache size, and the OSCACHE model uses the *Open Symphony* OSCache 2.0 caching engine.

Cache models in iBATIS are specified in the SQLMap XML file using the <cacheModel> element. You can specify as many caching models as you want or need. The cache model is associated with <select> or <statement> elements within the SQLMap XML file. The following is an example of an LRU cache model containing 1,000 objects:

```
<cacheModel id="tradeCache" type="LRU"
        readOnly="true" serialize="false">
    <flushInterval hours="24"/>
    <flushOnExecute statement="trading.updateTrade"/>
    <property name="cache-size" value="1000"/>
</cacheModel>
```

The readOnly property of the <cacheModel> element works in conjunction with the serialize property to determine how objects from the cache should be returned. The following values are the ones that make sense for these properties:

- readOnly="true", serialize="false": With these settings it is assumed that the objects from the cache will not be modified, so the object reference is returned from the cache rather than a copy of the object.

- readOnly="false", serialize="true": These settings will return a deep copy of an object in the cache rather than a reference.

There are several ways of flushing the cache. The <flushInterval> element, as shown earlier, specifies the time interval when the cache should expire and be flushed. The <flushOnExecute> element indicates what iBATIS statements will cause the cache to become invalid and therefore be reset when that statement is executed. In the earlier example, when the updateTrade statement executes, iBATIS will flush the cache. You can also programmatically flush the cache by invoking the SqlMapClient.flushDataCache(cacheModelId) method from within your Java code.

Depending on which model you specify, you can also set properties on the cache through the <property> element. In the earlier example, the LRU cache has a cache-size property that specifies how many objects can occupy the cache (in this case 1,000).

You can add a cache model to statement elements by using the cacheModel property. Note that cache models can be used by any number of statements. In the earlier example, you can modify the getTrades statement to use the tradeCache cache model by adding the cacheModel property to the <select> element as follows:

```
<select id="getTrades" parameterClass="map"
        resultMap="tradeResult" cacheModel="tradeCache">
    SELECT TRADE_ID, SIDE, SYMBOL, SHARES, PRICE
      FROM TRADE
     WHERE SIDE = #p_action# AND SHARES > #p_shares#
</select>
```

When this statement executes, it will populate the tradeCache cache model with the results from the query. When you subsequently invoke the getTrades statement with the same parameters, iBATIS will pull the results from the cache rather than from the database.

18.9 Namespaces

Perhaps the best piece of advice for using iBATIS in the real world is to use namespaces from the very start. *Namespaces* allow you to add a scoping qualifier to your iBATIS SQLMaps, which not only makes it easy to find the statement in the SQLMaps but also helps avoid nasty *naming conflicts*.

To specify that you want to use namespaces, set the useStatementNamespaces settings property to true in the SqlMapConfig.xml file:

```
<sqlMapConfig>
        <settings useStatementNamespaces="true"/>
    ...
</sqlMapConfig>
```

Next, in each SQLMap file, specify the name of the namespace you want for that particular SQLMap in the namespace property of the <sqlMap> element:

```
<sqlMap namespace="trading">
   ...
</sqlMap>
```

Finally, to reference the iBATIS statement in your Java code, you would add the namespace qualifier to the iBATIS statement ID name as follows:

```
public List getTrades(String action, long shares) throws Exception {
   ...
   return sqlMapClient.queryForList("trading.getTrades", map);
}
```

18.10 Conclusion

iBATIS is a simple but powerful framework that allows you to easily map existing SQL statements and stored procedure calls to Java objects but without the complexities associated with the traditional ORM frameworks. The iBATIS framework differentiates itself from the traditional ORM frameworks in several ways: ease of use, result set–to–object mapping rather than table-to-object mapping, and the lack of SQL code generation. iBATIS is well suited for those situations where you are faced with having to use stored procedures, existing SQL statements, or reporting-type queries that do not return table keys or direct table mappings. It is also well suited for situations where you need to tune SQL (rather than Java code) to get optimal performance out of your database persistence layer.

There are many features of iBATIS that I did not cover in this chapter, such as retrieving the key from insert statements and stored procedure calls, using XML for statement input and output (think *Ajax* here), managing multiple data sources, and using the iBATIS *dynamic query language*. To find out more about iBATIS, I encourage you to attend the many iBATIS sessions at the NFJS Java Symposium conferences, read Clinton's new book *iBATIS in Action*, consult the documentation that comes with iBATIS, or, better yet, just download the iBATIS Java persistence framework and start using it.

18.11   Web Resources

iBATIS website . . . . http://www.ibatis.org
Project website for iBATIS where you can download the framework and supporting documentation.

Introducing the iBATIS Persistence Framework. . .
. . . http://www.nofluffjuststuff.com/speaker_topic_view.jsp?topicId=382
NFJS Java Symposium Series conference session by Mark Richards that covers how to use iBATIS through lecture, slides, and interactive coding.

iBATIS and the Enterprise Database. . .
. . . http://www.nofluffjuststuff.com/speaker_topic_view.jsp?topicId=180
NFJS Java Symposium session by Clinton Begin that covers how to use iBATIS, with a great discussion about relational database mapping concepts. This session also covers some great tricks for using iBATIS with Ajax.

iBATIS in Action . . . . http://www.manning.com/begin/
New book by Clinton Begin, Brandon Goodin, and Larry Meadors that covers the iBATIS framework in detail.

## Chapter 19

Data Access Using Spring, Hibernate, and JDBC

by Scott Leberknight

Scott is chief architect at Near Infinity Corporation, an enterprise software development and consulting services company in Reston, Virginia. He has been developing enterprise and web applications for almost twelve years professionally and has been developing web applications using Java and related technologies since 2000. His main areas of interest include object-oriented design, system architecture, testing, and frameworks of all types including Spring, Hibernate, and most recently Ruby on Rails. Scott has a bachelor's of science degree in engineering science and mechanics from Virginia Tech and a master's of engineering in systems engineering from the University of Maryland. Scott has spoken at several conferences including No Fluff Just Stuff and the Spring Experience.

In his (nonexistent) spare time, Scott enjoys spending time with his wife, two daughters, and two cats. He also tries to find time to go snowboarding and mountain biking whenever he can.

19.1 Introduction

Data access is a difficult problem faced by developers on almost every project, whether it be in the form of files, relational databases, LDAP directories, content management systems, or any number of other data sources. To be sure, data access is not what most developers consider cutting edge, sexy, or even sometimes fun. How many times have you ever gotten really excited when pulling some records from a database or inserting a couple of new records? But it is a necessary and critical part of almost all software development projects.

Most enterprise and web applications use a relational database for data persistence, and most developers know how to use SQL to interact with a database. But there are many different persistence options available that allow interaction between programming languages such as Java and relational databases, ranging from low-level JDBC through sophisticated *object/relational mapping* (ORM) frameworks such as Hibernate. Selecting a persistence strategy when designing an application depends on many factors, and it can be a very difficult choice. Frequently teams choose to employ a combination of ORM and JDBC in order to get the "best of both worlds."

The Spring framework simplifies data access code significantly by handling or simplifying many of the tedious, repetitive, and error-prone tasks you need to perform when implementing a persistence solution such as managing database connections and transactions, exception handling, and testing. Spring provides support for Hibernate as the ORM solution and allows you to easily combine this ORM choice with plain JDBC code when and where necessary. I'll show exactly how this all works by first comparing ORM to JDBC and then walking through setting up the Spring integrations for using Hibernate and JDBC in your applications and by pointing out best practices and issues you might encounter along the way.

19.2 ORM vs. JDBC

One of the most fundamental differences between ORM and JDBC is the abstraction of relational databases provided by ORM products. ORM solutions generally abstract the underlying persistent storage mechanism so developers can work with objects and traditional object-oriented constructs such as inheritance and polymorphism, rather than database tables. ORM products such as Hibernate usually define their own object query language and generate SQL at runtime based on the object mappings to database tables and by translating the object query language into database-specific SQL. JDBC, on the other hand, does not abstract the database and leverages SQL as the language for interaction with the database. Application code is responsible for the translation between tables and objects, and data interaction is result set–oriented and statement-oriented rather than object-oriented.

Another fundamental difference between ORM and traditional JDBC code is that ORM products implement *transparent persistence*. Transparent persistence means that the ORM product provides *automatic change detection* to persistence objects and some form of *persistence by reachability*. Automatic change detection means the ORM product tracks changes made to objects; Hibernate, for example, uses CGLIB to bytecode enhance domain objects and marks objects as "dirty" when a property changes. Persistence by reachability, a form of *transitive persistence*, means that the ORM solution will persist any object that is "reachable" from a persistent object *automatically*. Consider the following code:

```
User user = getPersistentUser();
Address address = new Address("123 Main St", "Reston", "VA", "20194");
user.getAddresses().add(address);
address.setUser(user);
```

When this code executes within a transaction, ORM products that implement transitive persistence will automatically persist the address when the transaction commits. Hibernate implements a form of transitive persistence using *cascading*, whereby the developer is responsible for telling Hibernate exactly how to cascade the persistence to child objects. With Hibernate, you do not need to explicitly save the new address in the previous example, which can be confusing for people reading code who are not familiar with the transitive persistence mechanism. Straight JDBC code provides no analog to transparent persistence. The developer is solely responsible for determining when objects must be persisted, creating the necessary SQL, tracking changes to objects, and handling object graphs.

One last major feature provided by ORM frameworks is *lazy loading* of domain objects, which prevents the resolution of an entire object graph when a single object is fetched from the database. For example, if a User object contains collections of Address, Preference, and Account objects, which of those collections, if any, should be fetched from the database when a query returns a User object? Fetching all those collections using an *eager fetching* strategy would result in SQL containing three left outer joins. If those collections are never used in a specific use case in application code, then those extra joins were useless and added unnecessary additional overhead to the backend database. Lazy loading in ORM products fetches the required data only when accessed. So if none of the collections attached to the User object was accessed in a specific use case, then no additional queries are performed. Although lazy loading can be very convenient to application developers, it can result in an explosion of additional database queries (which will not please your DBAs at all). For these cases, it is usually necessary to tune the lazy loading behavior when using ORM tools. Plain JDBC code, on the other hand, must explicitly define all the data it needs in SQL; there is no notion of lazy loading.

19.3   When to Use ORM vs. JDBC

There are no hard and fast rules for choosing which parts of an application should use ORM and which should employ JDBC, but you can follow certain guidelines. The following situations indicate that ORM is a good fit for an application:

- There is a natural mapping between objects and tables. This might be the case if the development team can influence the database design, the database design can be changed relatively easily, or the problem domain naturally lends itself toward database tables that map directly to objects.

- The application generally persists individual objects rather than large sets of objects. In other words, application code generally retrieves an object, makes changes to its properties, and then updates the object. Note that ORM has no problems performing read operations that return many objects that are then displayed in the presentation layer.

- Domain objects can be cached, such as when an application uses lots of relatively static reference data or when objects are immutable once initially created. Most ORM products provide significant performance benefits when objects are cacheable, since no database queries are required to retrieved the cached objects.

On the other hand, the following are some situations when ORM is probably not a good fit and where JDBC might be a better solution, either for the entire application or for just one specific instance:

- The application needs to work with a legacy or extremely normalized database schema. In the former case, the database generally cannot be changed, which might make mapping between objects and tables very difficult. In the latter case, perhaps many database joins are required to form each logical entity, making object/relational mapping much more difficult.
- Data access performed by the application is predominantly via batch operations dealing with large data sets, aggregation, or bulk updates and deletes. In this case, ORM probably does not add value since the mode of interaction is via sets, which plain SQL is designed to handle very efficiently.
- The application calls stored procedures to create, find, update, and delete data. The main benefits of ORM tools are generally lost in this situation since the developer would need to manually code the mapping between object and stored procedure.
- SQL queries must be tunable by hand because of performance considerations or a complicated schema. An ORM product that generates SQL from the mappings or its custom query language is probably not a good fit in this scenario.
- Significant use of native database features by the application may obviate benefits provided by ORM tools.
- The application performs write-only data access, for example to audit tables. In this case, you might not want to map domain objects for write-only operations and would prefer just to persist the information and be done with it!

19.4 Why Use Spring?

You might be asking why you should use Spring when you already know how to use Hibernate and straight JDBC just fine. There are many reasons why you should add Spring into the mix. First, you get all the benefits of *inversion of control* (IoC) and *dependency injection* that Spring normally provides. These benefits include the ability to easily design to interfaces rather than concrete classes, resulting in loose coupling between components; configuration of object dependencies, thereby eliminating factory-based lookups such as required when using JNDI; and code that is vastly easier to unit test since *mock objects* can be used to simulate dependencies. In addition, Spring itself relies on a layered architecture and makes it much easier to implement a layered architecture with the proper separation of concerns between layers.

Second, Spring brings additional benefits specific to data access code. For example, Spring's transaction management abstraction defines a unified API via the PlatformTransactionManager interface; this means transactions are managed consistently and transparently, whether data access is performed using Hibernate, JDBC, iBATIS, or another technology. In addition, transactions can be specified in a declarative fashion that makes it easy to configure how transactions should be applied when certain operations execute. In addition, Spring handles database connections and Hibernate sessions transparently; no explicit code is required to open or close connections and sessions.

Spring also defines its own data access exception hierarchy to ensure consistency regardless of which persistence framework(s) are in use. For example, an application using both Hibernate and JDBC would throw Spring data access exceptions, rather than SQLException and HibernateException. Further, all Spring's data access exceptions are *unchecked exceptions*. Without getting too deep into the checked vs. unchecked exception debate, the Spring philosophy is that data access exceptions are usually unrecoverable, so why should application code be forced to handle checked exceptions? In addition, data access code becomes much cleaner without all the try/catch blocks. All these benefits combine to provide a consistent data access strategy within an application.

Last but not least, Spring makes both unit and integration testing data access code much easier. Because classes are simple POJOs that conform to an *interface*, unit testing becomes greatly simplified because mock objects can simulate data access objects. For example, you can unit test a service layer class using mock *data access objects* (DAO) rather than real ones. This also makes tests faster since there is no actual database involved. But testing the DAOs themselves still requires interaction with a live database, and here Spring provides several base test classes that simplify integration testing.

Now, let's jump in and start coding.

19.5 Setting Up Hibernate in Spring

To use Hibernate in an application, you have to manage four major things:

- Configuring Hibernate (that is, persistent object mappings, database dialect, and so on)

- Creating the Hibernate SessionFactory
- Opening and closing Hibernate sessions
- Applying transactions to sessions

Using Spring, you configure Hibernate and create a SessionFactory in the Spring application context. You then create DAOs with *only* data access logic, service layer classes, and transaction policies for those services. You then wire up all these classes in the usual Spring fashion. First, let's configure the SessionFactory in the Spring application context. Assume you have two domain objects, User and Preference, annotated using Java Persistence API (JPA) annotations:

```xml
<bean id="propertyConfigurer"
      class="org.springframework.beans.factory.config.PropertyPlaceholderConfigurer">
  <property name="location" value="classpath:jdbc.properties" />
</bean>

<bean id="dataSource"
      class="org.springframework.jdbc.datasource.DriverManagerDataSource">
  <property name="driverClassName" value="${jdbc.driverClassName}" />
  <property name="url" value="${jdbc.url}" />
  <property name="username" value="${jdbc.username}" />
  <property name="password" value="${jdbc.password}" />
</bean>

<bean id="sessionFactory"
      class="org.springframework.orm.hibernate3.annotation.AnnotationSessionFactoryBean">
  <property name="dataSource" ref="dataSource" />
  <property name="annotatedClasses">
    <list>
      <value>com.nearinfinity.model.User</value>
      <value>com.nearinfinity.model.Preference</value>
    </list>
  </property>
  <property name="hibernateProperties">
    <props>
      <prop key="hibernate.dialect">org.hibernate.dialect.MySQL5Dialect</prop>
      <prop key="hibernate.query.substitutions">true 'Y', false 'N'</prop>
      <prop key="hibernate.show_sql">true</prop>
      <prop key="hibernate.format_sql">true</prop>
    </props>
  </property>
  <property name="namingStrategy">
    <util:constant
      static-field="org.hibernate.cfg.ImprovedNamingStrategy.INSTANCE" />
  </property>
</bean>
```

In the previous code, you first create a JDBC *data source*, which you then inject into the SessionFactory. The propertyConfigurer bean pulls in properties from the jdbc.properties file so you don't need to hard-code them. This is useful when you have multiple environments with different properties, such as development, test, and production environments. Since this example used JPA annotations, you use the Spring AnnotationSessionFactoryBean instead of the LocalSessionFactoryBean. SessionFactory configuration is relatively straightforward. You specify the data source, define the annotated domain objects, and specify one or more Hibernate properties. Specifying the Hibernate properties here means there is no need for separate hibernate.cfg.xml or hibernate.properties files and that you can keep the Hibernate configuration in one place in your application. If these properties vary across different environments, you can use the same property placeholder mechanism that you used for the JDBC properties.

Next, you'll configure the DAOs:

```
<bean id="baseHibernateDao" abstract="true">
  <property name="sessionFactory" ref="sessionFactory" />
</bean>

<bean id="userDao"
      class="com.nearinfinity.dao.impl.UserDaoHibernate"
      parent="baseHibernateDao" />
```

The first step is to create an abstract bean, baseHibernateDao, which defines common properties for all the Hibernate-based DAOs. To create Hibernate-based DAOs, you need to specify the SessionFactory from which the DAO can obtain Hibernate sessions. You then create the userDao and inherit from baseHibernateDao. In this case there is only one DAO, userDao, so the extra code to define the abstract parent bean doesn't add much value. But since most real-world applications have more than just one DAO, using the bean inheritance adds value since the SessionFactory property is defined in only one place.

Next you define the transaction manager. Spring abstracts transaction management via the PlatformTransactionManager interface and permits either declarative or programmatic transaction handling via this interface. For a Hibernate application, you can use a Hibernate transaction manager as follows:

```
<bean id="transactionManager"
      class="org.springframework.orm.hibernate3.HibernateTransactionManager">
  <property name="sessionFactory" ref="sessionFactory" />
</bean>
```

At this point, you have two things left to configure: service classes and the transaction policy. *Service* has no extra connotation such as with web services; it is typical in Spring applications to define an explicit service layer to which you apply transactions. This leaves the DAOs to perform only data access and also means one service can call multiple DAOs in a single transaction. In addition to transactions, the service layer will typically contain some business logic (though recently the trend toward domain-driven design puts as much business logic in domain objects as possible). By layering your application this way, it becomes trivial to expose the transactional service layer to different client types. For example, you can just as easily use the services in web services as you use those from a typical web application controller layer. Here is the configuration of the transaction policy and the services:

```xml
<tx:advice id="txAdvice" transaction-manager="transactionManager">
  <tx:attributes>
    <tx:method name="find*" read-only="true" />
    <tx:method name="*" />
  </tx:attributes>
</tx:advice>

<aop:config>
  <aop:pointcut id="serviceMethods"
        expression="execution(public * com.nearinfinity.service.*.*(..))" />
  <aop:advisor advice-ref="txAdvice" pointcut-ref="serviceMethods" />
</aop:config>

<bean id="userService" class="com.nearinfinity.service.impl.UserServiceImpl">
  <property name="userDao" ref="userDao" />
</bean>
```

This code looks more complicated than it really is. The <tx:advice/> and <aop:config/> code uses the new Spring 2.0 schemas designed specifically for transaction management and *aspect-oriented programming* (AOP). The <tx:advice/> first defines the AOP advice that should be applied whenever certain methods are called. In this example, anytime a method whose name *starts with* "find" is called, Spring executes the method within a read-only transaction, as defined by the read-only attribute. All other methods (defined by the * catchall) will be executed within a regular read/write transaction.

Next, the <aop:config/> code defines a *pointcut* named serviceMethods as the execution of any public method, taking any parameters, in any class in the com.nearinfinity.service package, returning any value. This pointcut defines the entire service layer. The <aop:advisor/> specifies that the txAdvice advice should be applied to the serviceMethods point-

@Transactional vs.

You can apply transactions using AOP as shown earlier, or you could use the Spring @Transactional annotation directly in your services' classes. For example, you could create a base Service interface like this:

```
@Transactional
public interface Service {}
```

If all your other service interfaces then extend the Service interface, all of them inherit the @Transactional behavior. You then need to specify only the following line of XML in your Spring application context. (This line replaces the <tx:advice/> and <aop:config/> configuration elements, so the application context configuration is much simpler.)

```
<tx:annotation-driven />
```

The only other thing to remember is that if one or more methods need transactional behavior different from the defaults, you'll need to specify a @Transactional annotation on those methods. For example, suppose you want the findUser() method to execute within a read-only transaction and support but not require propagation of a transaction. You could override the default behavior like this:

```
@Transactional(readOnly = true, propagation=Propagation.SUPPORTS)
public User findUser(Long id) {
  // actual code...
}
```

cut. Finally, you create the service, userService, as a regular Spring bean, injecting the previously configured userDao, which is required by the service. Transactions will be applied to this service automatically by the AOP advice you've defined.

At this point you have configured Hibernate, defined all the DAOs, specified the transaction policy, and configured the service classes. Now all that's left is to actually code the DAOs and services—and of course test them!

19.6 Implementing Hibernate-Based DAOs

To provide an idea of how Hibernate DAOs look when you use Spring, let's start with an example. As with all Spring applications, you start by defining a business interface, which is independent of the implementation technology:

```
public interface UserDao {

  List<User> findAllUsers();

  User findUser(Long id);

  void saveUser(User user);

  User deleteUser(Long id);

}
```

Now let's look at the implementation using Spring support classes:

```
public class UserDaoHibernate extends HibernateDaoSupport implements UserDao {

  @SuppressWarnings("unchecked")
  public List<User> findAllUsers() {
    return getHibernateTemplate().find("from User u order by u.lastName");
  }

  public User findUser(Long id) {
    return (User) getHibernateTemplate().load(User.class, id);
  }

  public void saveUser(User user) {
    getHibernateTemplate().saveOrUpdate(user);
  }

  public User deleteUser(Long id) {
    User deleted = (User) getHibernateTemplate().get(User.class, id);
    getHibernateTemplate().delete(deleted);
    return deleted;
  }

}
```

Even if you have never used Spring or Hibernate, you can probably read this code and understand exactly what it does; the code is very clean and simple. However, the most interesting part of this code is actually what's *not* there. The "missing" elements are as follows:

- Opening and closing Hibernate sessions
- Transaction management
- Exception handling (that is, no try/catch/finally blocks!)

What magic is going on here that you don't need to obtain sessions, manage transactions, or handle exceptions? The implementation class

UserDaoHibernate implements the UserDao business interface as expected. But it extends HibernateDaoSupport, which is a Spring class designed to be used as a base class for Hibernate-based DAOs. HibernateDaoSupport exposes another Spring class named HibernateTemplate. You use HibernateTemplate to perform Hibernate operations.

HibernateDaoSupport requires a Hibernate SessionFactory in order to perform its work. If you remember, you configured your Hibernate-based DAOs by setting the sessionFactory property. Since UserDao-Hibernate extends HibernateDaoSupport, it inherits the setSessionFactory method. HibernateDaoSupport uses the SessionFactory to create a HibernateTemplate, which encapsulates all the session, transaction, and exception handling that is "missing" from your Hibernate DAO. I definitely recommend that you look at the Spring source code to get a better idea of all the work being done by this class.

HibernateTemplate follows the common Spring "template" idiom that is used throughout Spring to encapsulate repetitive, boilerplate, and error-prone code. Spring templates use a *callback*-based approach, and HibernateTemplate is no different. It exposes many convenience methods for common Hibernate operations such as get() and saveOrUpdate(). You can also use the execute() methods to work directly with the native Hibernate Session API via HibernateCallback, like this:

```
@SuppressWarnings("unchecked")
public List<User> findUsersByExample(final User example) {
  return (List<User>) getHibernateTemplate().execute(new HibernateCallback() {
    public Object doInHibernate(Session session)
      throws HibernateException, SQLException {
      Criteria criteria = session.createCriteria(User.class);
      Example ex = Example.create(example);
      criteria.add(ex);
      return criteria.list();
    }
  });
}
```

To use HibernateCallback, you create an anonymous inner class and implement the doInHibernate() method. This method accepts a Hibernate Session and throws HibernateException and SQLException. When this code runs, Spring passes the Hibernate Session to the callback and catches and handles any exceptions.

Another HibernateTemplate feature is the conversion of Hibernate exceptions to Spring's own data access exception hierarchy, which has the unchecked DataAccessException as the root exception class. The main benefit is consistency in data access exceptions across any persistence technology, whether Hibernate or other ORM product, straight JDBC, or even nonrelational data sources. Having a consistent set of unchecked, data access exceptions becomes more compelling when you are using multiple persistence technologies in the same project, as you'll see later.

Lazy Loading

Hibernate 3 lazily initializes domain objects, deferring execution of SQL statements as long as possible. For example, the following line of code will not cause any database queries to be executed:

```
User user = (User) session.load(User.class, id);
```

This code causes Hibernate to return an uninitialized *proxy* for the actual domain object. Only when a property of the user object is accessed will Hibernate execute the database query and populate the object. Although this seems simple on the surface, beneath the surface lurks a host of new problems to solve.

First, the Hibernate Session that loaded an object *must* be open to lazily initialize that same object. If the Session was closed after the object (proxy) was retrieved but before the object was accessed, a LazyInitializationException is thrown. This means it is possible and likely that an object retrieved in the service and data access layers could throw a LazyInitializationException in another application tier, for example a JSP displaying the object in the web tier.

You can ensure Hibernate is able to lazily initialize objects in two primary ways:

- Data assembly while the Session is open
- The Open Session in View pattern

With data assembly, you explicitly initialize all data required for a specific view in the service layer while the Hibernate Session is still open. As you might expect, this can potentially result in an explosion of service layer code whose sole purpose is data assembly for specific views. This violates the separation of concerns since services now need to know what specific data to assemble. For these reasons I generally avoid performing data assembly in the service layer and instead rely on the Open Session in View pattern. The Open Session in View (OSIV) pattern holds the Hibernate Session open until the view has rendered, thereby permitting lazy loading in the presentation layer. Spring provides the OpenS-

"Plain-Hibernate" DAOs

Hibernate 3 introduced contextual sessions to make it easy to obtain a session from multiple resources in the same logical transaction. For example, service class methods often call several different DAOs. The problem is how to provide each DAO access to the same session, for example a thread-bound Session. Spring solved this problem by exposing a thread-bound session and provides classes like HibernateTemplate to hide the underlying infrastructure code that retrieves the existing session or creates a new one if necessary.

With Hibernate 3 contextual sessions, it is possible to write Hibernate DAOs in "plain-Hibernate" style without needing the Spring HibernateDaoSupport machinery. You simply inject the Session-Factory directly into your DAO and then use the getCurrrentSession() method. Here is an example:

```java
public class UserDaoPlainHibernate implements UserDao {

  private SessionFactory sessionFactory;

  public void setSessionFactory(SessionFactory sessionFactory) {
    this.sessionFactory = sessionFactory;
  }

  public User findUser(Long id) {
    return (User)
      sessionFactory.getCurrentSession().load(User.class, id);
  }

  // additional methods...
}
```

Note the example doesn't use any Spring support classes and works with the native Hibernate APIs. Spring provides an implementation of the Hibernate CurrentSessionContext interface, which works with the existing Spring session and transaction handling. The other thing to note is that with this strategy, native Hibernate exceptions are thrown and are not converted to the Spring DataAccessException hierarchy. You could use Spring's AOP capabilities to catch Hibernate exceptions and rethrow them as Spring data access exceptions, which would allow you to develop "plain-Hibernate" DAOs and still get consistency across data access exceptions.

If you choose to go this "plain-Hibernate" route for your DAOs, be consistent and ensure that all your DAOs use this strategy, and consider whether you need to convert native Hibernate exceptions to Spring DataAccessExceptions.

essionInViewFilter servlet filter that opens a Session for a web request and keeps it open throughout the web request to allow lazy loading in the web tier, for example in a JSP. (Spring also provides the OpenSessionIn-ViewInterceptor web request interceptor for use in Spring MVC or portlet environments.) You could argue whether lazy loading in a view violates separation of concerns, but that is beyond the scope of this chapter.

The second major issue with lazy loading is the *N + 1 selects* problem. The N + 1 selects problem occurs when a list of top-level domain objects is retrieved and a collection of dependent objects contained within each top-level object is fetched lazily, usually in the presentation tier. The reason this is a problem is because literally N + 1 select statements are executed, where N is the number of top-level domain objects returned by the original query. If that didn't make sense, let's look at an example of some code that would cause this behavior, along with the notional SQL that would be executed:

```java
// select * from users;
List<User> users = getHibernateTemplate().loadAll(User.class);

for (User u : users) {
  // select * from user_preferences p where p.user_id = ?
  int numPrefs = u.getPreferences().size();
  System.out.println(u.getFullName() + ": " + numPrefs);
}
```

In the previous code, the first query finds all Users and results in one select statement that returns rows from the users table. Then it loops through all User objects and prints the number of preferences that each one contains. Each time through the loop results in a select statement that lazily fetches the collection of preferences for the user. So although the Java code looks simple and clean, behind the scenes there is a potential performance problem since with each additional lazy load comes an additional database query!

The most efficient way to solve the N + 1 selects problem is eagerly fetching all required data in a single shot. You could take the code from the previous example and rework it to eagerly fetch the preferences collections of all users, like this:

```java
List<User> users = getHibernateTemplate().find(
  "select distinct u from User u left join fetch u.preferences");
```

Here you've joined preferences and added the **fetch** keyword to the HQL. This tells Hibernate to fetch all the user and preference information in a single database query using a left outer join. Most of the time, you'll want to combine the OSIV pattern with eager fetching in select cases to balance ease of development that the OSIV pattern provides with the potential for improved performance using eager fetching.

19.7 Implementing Spring JDBC-Based DAOs

Implementing DAOs using Spring JDBC is similar to implementing Hibernate DAOs. The main difference is that you work with the normal JDBC API instead of the Hibernate session. Like we saw with Hibernate-based DAOs, the same elements are "missing" from a DAO leveraging Spring JDBC. Specifically, you do not need to open or close Connections, manage transactions, or handle SQLExceptions. Here is a snippet of a Spring JDBC DAO:

```
public class AuditDaoSpringJdbc extends SimpleJdbcDaoSupport
    implements AuditDao {

  public int getNumberOfUsersCreatedToday() {
    return getSimpleJdbcTemplate().queryForInt(
      "select count(*) from user_audit" +
      " where audit_action = ?" +
      " and audit_date >= current_date()", "INSERT");
  }

  // additional methods...
}
```

Spring JDBC provides several support classes to help you implement DAOs. First there are the base classes JdbcDaoSupport and its Java 5–enabled cousin SimpleJdbcDaoSupport. Like HibernateDaoSupport, both of these base classes provide subclasses with a "template" that handles connections, transactions, and exceptions. JdbcDaoSupport provides a JdbcTemplate, while SimpleJdbcDaoSupport provides a Java 5–aware SimpleJdbcTemplate. Both the original and "simple" version essentially provide the same capabilities, except that the "simple" variety makes good use of Java 5 features like varargs. All you need to do is supply the DAO with a data source via normal Spring setter injection.

The Spring JDBC support classes manage database connections and transactions automatically. In addition, the Spring JDBC template classes convert checked SQLExceptions to unchecked Spring DataAccessExceptions. The only thing left is to actually configure the DAOs for use in your application. Assuming you already have set up the data source and transaction manager as you did when setting up the Hibernate-based DAOs, all you need to do is configure the Spring JDBC-based DAOs. They will use the same data source and transaction manager as the Hibernate DAOs. HibernateTransactionManager manages transactions for both Spring JDBC and Hibernate DAOs and in fact is the recommended transaction manager when using Hibernate and Spring JDBC together in the same application.

So all that's left now is to configure the Spring JDBC DAOs. As with the Hibernate DAOs, I'll show how to create an abstract parent bean from which Spring JDBC-based DAOs can inherit the data source property:

```
<bean id="baseJdbcDao" abstract="true">
    <property name="dataSource" ref="dataSource" />
</bean>

<bean id="auditDao"
      class="com.nearinfinity.dao.impl.AuditDaoSpringJdbc"
      parent="baseJdbcDao" />
```

19.8 Mixing DAO Implementations

With Spring, it is easy to mix and match Hibernate (or another ORM tool) with Spring JDBC code. Hibernate and JDBC data access code shares the same underlying data source and transaction manager, and DAOs are implemented similarly. Spring performs resource management and exception handling automatically. In fact, Hibernate and Spring JDBC DAOs can execute in the same transaction. There are, however, a few potential issues when combining Hibernate and Spring JDBC code.

First, because the Hibernate session caches objects, JDBC code will not see changes made to dirty Hibernate objects unless the session is explicitly flushed. This is because Hibernate tries to batch operations and defer execution of database queries until necessary. Because Hibernate is not aware of JDBC code executing within the same transaction, changes won't necessarily be written to the database in time for the Spring JDBC code to see them. A second issue is order of operations. Depending on how you partition the work between Hibernate and Spring JDBC, you might need to ensure database operations execute in the correct order, for example to ensure a parent record is created before a child record so that referential integrity is not violated.

Third, objects in the Hibernate *second-level cache* will become invalid if Spring JDBC code makes updates to the underlying tables. In other words, with the second-level cache applied to domain objects, Hibernate assumes it is the only source of updates to those domain objects and thus the underlying tables. Should updates be made to those tables

Do I Need JTA?

Most applications work with a single database and do not require distributed transactions. In these cases, using a native transaction manager such as HibernateTransactionManager works great, and there is no need to introduce the added complexity of JTA-driven transactions. In fact, HibernateTransactionManager is recommended when combining Hibernate and Spring JDBC data access code in the same application.

If you do have transactions that span multiple resources, then JTA is your only choice. Fortunately, with Spring it is simply a matter of configuration to use JTA transactions. This is how you would configure a JTA transaction manager:

```
<bean id="transactionManager"
    class="org.springframework.transaction.jta.
    JtaTransactionManager"/>
```

With JTA transactions and Hibernate data access code, you might want to switch the Hibernate *connection release mode* to after_statement by setting the useTransactionAwareDataSource property of the LocalSessionFactoryBean to true. This is extensively documented in the LocalSessionFactoryBean Javadocs.

via Spring JDBC code, Hibernate will not know about those updates, and some cache objects will become invalid. The best strategy in this situation is to ensure Spring JDBC code does not manipulate data in tables shared with objects in the Hibernate second-level cache. Fourth, although Hibernate and other ORM tools provide direct support for *optimistic locking*, Spring JDBC code must handle this manually.

A final consideration when mixing ORM and Spring JDBC in the same application is the nature of objects returned from DAOs. Objects returned by ORM products are typically "live" objects, whereas objects coming from JDBC code are "dead." Objects returned by ORM frameworks are "live" in the sense that the transparent persistence features of ORM means that changes are automatically detected and persisted in the scope of a transaction and also that these objects have additional behavior such as lazy loading. By comparison, objects returned by JDBC code are "dead" because there is none of the ORM magic like transparent or transitive persistence.

The best way to avoid these integration issues is to avoid combining Hibernate data access in the same transaction with Spring JDBC code. For most applications, this is not overly difficult. Hibernate tends to be the primary data access tool for most applications, with Spring JDBC stepping in when Hibernate is not the best fit, for example when calling a stored procedure. However, it is certainly possible to have Hibernate and Spring JDBC code interacting in the same transaction; in those cases, developers need to understand which objects might have side effects and which will not. This is arguably a leakage of the persistence concern into other application tiers, but in practical use, the pros usually outweigh the cons.

With Hibernate and Spring JDBC code mixed into the same application, the benefits of Spring's consistent data access exception hierarchy become much more apparent. Rather than have separate exception types for each data access technology, the Spring DataAccessException hierarchy provides a common set of exceptions independent of persistence technology. In addition, since the Spring exceptions are unchecked exceptions, there is no need to declare them in method signatures, though you can certainly do that if you want. In addition, if you swapped one data access technology for another, you would not need to change anything related to data access exceptions since the new technology would use the Spring exceptions, assuming there is a Spring integration like with JPA or iBATIS.

19.9 DAO Design Considerations

There are two primary considerations when designing DAOs:

- Interface granularity
- Interface genericity

The first consideration, *interface granularity*, deals with the number of DAO methods needed to effectively work with the application's domain objects. Because ORM tools such as Hibernate implement transparent persistence, DAO interfaces can be designed in a coarse-grained manner with fewer methods that deal only with top-level domain objects. So, Hibernate-based DAOs typically will not have separate methods to persist every type of domain object. In contrast, JDBC-based DAOs must have fine-grained interfaces since there is no transparent persistence; essentially, you need a separate method to handle each type of domain object.

Interface genericity defines whether the DAO interface is strongly or weakly typed. ORM-based DAOs tend to lend themselves easily to using weakly typed objects in persistence operations, which significantly reduces the number of methods required. For example, the Hibernate session can persist any object that it knows about using the same save() method call. It then becomes easy to define a generic DAO containing methods that can persist any type of entity in the application.

```
@SuppressWarnings("unchecked")
public <T> T get(Class type, Long id) {
  return (T) getHibernateTemplate().get(type, id);
}

public <T> void saveOrUpdate(T entity) {
  getHibernateTemplate().saveOrUpdate(entity);
}
```

The previous code is completely generic since any entity type can be persisted. The main problem with this approach is that no special handling can be defined for specific entities. One alternative that could alleviate this concern is AOP; special handling such as security or logging could be performed by aspects. In contrast, JDBC-based DAOs by necessity work with strongly typed domain objects, since there is no generic mechanism in JDBC to persist any object type; you must define how an object is persisted explicitly using the JDBC API classes such as PreparedStatement. Interestingly, an AOP solution might even be preferable for handling special requirements.

19.10 Testing

Testing is an integral part of any development project and should be used constantly and consistently throughout development. Since testing should be done continuously, tests should execute as fast as possible, ideally being on the order of seconds instead of minutes, or even worse hours. The core dependency injection and IoC features that Spring is based on and the interface-based programming model it encourages and facilitates combine to make testing much easier and faster.

First, because in Spring you program to interfaces instead of concrete classes, you can easily use mock objects in unit tests. For example, Spring MVC controller tests can easily use mock service objects, and service tests can use mock DAOs. In both these cases, mocks are used to remove the need to run certain tests in a web container or against a real database. Mocking also isolates the *unit* under test, for example a Spring MVC controller. Using mock objects has the additional benefit that tests run extremely fast, because there is no latency from real-world resources.

As an example, I'll show how to write a unit test for a service using mock DAOs. The service interface is UserService, which requires a UserDao to perform data access. UserDao is an interface, so the service has no clue about the actual implementation class. The UserService implementation exposes, in Spring fashion, a setter method to set the actual UserDao object it will use to perform data access. For this test you'll use the *EasyMock* framework. EasyMock is a "record-and-replay" framework; you tell the object how to behave and then replay the behavior during the test. In this example, you'll create a mock UserDao, record the behavior you need, and replay. You'll also inject the mock DAO into the service implementation using the setter method.

```
@Test
public void testFindUser() throws Exception {
  UserServiceImpl service = new UserServiceImpl();
  UserDao mockUserDao = createMock(UserDao.class);
  service.setUserDao(mockUserDao);
  User user = createSampleUser();

  expect(mockUserDao.findUser(user.getId())).andReturn(user);
  replay(mockUserDao);
  User foundUser = service.findUser(user.getId());
  assertSame(user, foundUser);
  verify(mockUserDao);
}
```

First, you instantiate the service implementation class; it is just a POJO, so this is nothing special. Next you create the mock DAO using the static EasyMock createMock method that was statically imported. To create the mock, you need to supply the type of mock, in this case the interface UserDao. Then you inject the mock into the service, and finally you create a test User object; creating the User is also nothing special because User is a plain Java class. Next, you use the EasyMock methods expect() and andReturn() to define the expected behavior of the mock DAO. Finally, you put the mock in replay mode using EasyMock's replay() method. After that you call the service method, make a normal JUnit assertion, and verify the expected behavior using EasyMock's verify() method. That's it. You can get a lot more complicated with Easy-Mock, and I encourage you to take a look at EasyMock.

Testing web controllers and services with mocks makes sense, since you want to test their behavior in isolation. But when testing data access code, you must test against a real database. This form of testing is not really unit testing; rather, it is *integration testing*. Spring provides several integration test base classes you can extend to perform integration tests. The one you'll want to use when testing data access code is AbstractTransactionalDataSourceSpringContextTests. This class provides several key benefits:

- Dependency injection into tests
- Caching the Spring application context
- Transaction rollback after each test executes

Dependency injection into tests means you simply declare any test dependencies via setter methods, and Spring automatically finds and injects the required resource. Caching the Spring application context across tests means the contexts are loaded only once, not before every single test, and improves test speed.

Finally, the key benefit is that tests execute in a transaction that is automatically rolled back after the test completes. This feature makes integration tests significantly faster since no data is ever committed to the database. It has the added benefit that you can run unit tests against a shared development database since the transaction rollback ensures no changes are actually made in the database! Let's look at some key parts of a typical integration test:

```java
public class UserDaoHibernateIntegrationTest
  extends AbstractTransactionalDataSourceSpringContextTests {

  private List<User> users;
  private UserDao userDao;
  private SessionFactory sessionFactory;

  public void setSessionFactory(SessionFactory sessionFactory) {
    this.sessionFactory = sessionFactory;
  }

  public void setUserDao(UserDao userDao) {
    this.userDao = userDao;
  }

  @Override
  protected String[] getConfigLocations() {
    return new String[] { "/WEB-INF/applicationContext.xml" };
  }
```

```
  @Override
  protected void onSetUpInTransaction() throws Exception {
    super.onSetUpInTransaction();
    deleteFromTables(new String[] {"user_preference", "user"});
    Session session = sessionFactory.getCurrentSession();
    users = new ArrayList
    users.add(TestHelper.createUser("Draco", "Malfoy"));
    users.add(TestHelper.createUser("Lucius", "Malfoy"));
    users.add(TestHelper.createUser("Albus", "Dumbledore"));
    for (User user : users) {
      session.save(user);
    }
    session.flush();
    session.clear();
  }

  public void testFindAllUsers() throws Exception {
    List<User> results = userDao.findAllUsers();
    assertNotNull(results);
    assertEquals(3, results.size());
  }

  // additional tests...
}
```

In this code, you first extend the Spring integration test class. Then you define setter methods for the required dependencies. When the test is run, Spring retrieves the required beans from the application context and injects them into the test. In order to do this, you need to override getConfigLocations() to tell Spring which context(s) to use.

Next, you perform test setup within the transaction using the onSetUpIn-Transaction() method. You first call the deleteFromTables() convenience method to delete all data from the user_preference and user tables; since this occurs within a transaction that will be rolled back upon test completion, the data is not really deleted! After that, you create some users in the database. I've actually used Hibernate to create the User objects, so I need to explicitly flush and clear the session to ensure the data is available to tests. Rather than use Hibernate to create the test data, you could also have used the JdbcTemplate supplied by AbstractTransaction-alDataSourceSpringContextTests. Now all your tests can test the DAO. For example, the testFindAllUsers() method tests that you find all the users you created during setup. Once again, no changes whatsoever to the database are made since the transaction is rolled back upon completion of each test method.

There are several useful methods in the Spring test classes worth mentioning. endTransaction() makes it simple to test lazy loading behavior in

ORM tools; it ends the active transaction prematurely (and rolls it back so no changes are actually made). startNewTransaction(), new in Spring 2.0, enables testing ORM object detachment and subsequent reattachment in a different session.

19.11 Summary

When you are using Hibernate and/or JDBC technologies, Spring makes your life easier. Spring provides powerful integration with both Hibernate and Spring JDBC and allows easy integration between these two technologies. It manages Hibernate sessions and JDBC connections transparently to application code, enables you to define transactional semantics in a declarative fashion and without any actual transaction management code, makes DAO implementation much simpler via the use of the Spring template idiom, and finally provides a useful set of base classes to aid integration testing. I recommend finding more out about Spring using any or all of the resources listed next and encourage you to attend the Spring and Hibernate sessions at your local No Fluff Just Stuff Software Symposium Series.

19.12 Web Resources

Spring website . . . . http://www.springframework.org
The Spring project website, which contains tons of information and documentation on Spring including the reference guide and APIs.

Hibernate website . . . . http://www.hibernate.org
Hibernate's website, containing all things Hibernate including APIs, the reference guide, and more.

Professional Java Development with the Spring Framework. . .
. . . http://www.amazon.com/dp/0764574833
A great book covering Spring, written by the Spring developers.

Pro Spring http://www.amazon.com/dp/1590594614
An excellent resource for using the Spring framework.

Hibernate in Action http://www.amazon.com/dp/193239415X
Great book covering basic ORM concepts and Hibernate best practices. The book covers the 2.x version of Hibernate.

Java Persistence with Hibernate. . . http://www.amazon.com/dp/1932394885
Sequel to *Hibernate in Action*, updated for Hibernate 3.x and the EJB 3.0 Java Persistence specification.

Appendix A

The Authors Speak!

A.1 Glenn Vanderburg

Favorite Books

Most of the cool books I've been reading lately have been theology books, but I'll be nice and spare you those. Two technical books stand out. The first is *Dream Machines: J.C.R. Licklider and the Revolution That Made Computing Personal* [Wal02] by M. Mitchell Waldrop. If you know anything about the history of computers, you've probably heard of Alan Kay and his group at Xerox PARC that developed Smalltalk; Marvin Minsky and MIT's Project MAC; Doug Engelbart's research at RAND; and Vint Cerf, Bob Kahn, and the early days of ARPANET. But you might not have heard of J.C.R. Licklider. In a way, though, he made all of that other great work happen. As the man who controlled the purse strings at ARPA, he believed in a vision of what computers could do and made those crucial projects happen. Waldrop's book is a terrific look at that formative period; Licklider's story makes a great vantage point from which to view several parallel developments that together turned computers from giant number crunchers to personal creativity and communication tools.

The other technical book I've really enjoyed recently is by Eric Evans, *Domain-Driven Design* [Eva03]. I've known about this book for years and for some reason wasn't very interested in it. But I finally picked it up this year, and it's brilliant. Evans has found many great ways of explaining a very difficult topic: the process of good object-oriented software design.

Favorite Technical Tool

There's no question that my favorite tool discovery of the year is Capistrano. I learned about it last year, but this year I rapidly came to depend on it for more than just deploying Rails applications, and I can't count the hours it has saved me this year. I'm glad David Bock chose to write about it for this anthology; I only wish I had thought of that topic first!

A.2 Venkat Subramaniam

Favorite Books

I'm going to start with a couple of nontechnical books. Life has shown us that it is not the question of if but the question of when (and in what form) challenges arise. Dealing with change is so critical in all aspects of life—from developing software to coping with professional and social changes. One book I have read, reread, and given as gift is Spencer Johnson's *Who Moved My Cheese?* [Joh98].

I value productivity. I multitask quite a bit, and I think I have a good handle on dealing with the day-to-day tasks. That does not stop me from finding ways in which I can improve or sometime read something that might simply reaffirm some ideas. Finally, I got around to reading *Getting Things Done: The Art of Stress-Free Productivity* [All02] by David Allen.

My recent favorite technical book is *Rails for Java Developers* [SH07] by Stuart Halloway and Justin Gehtland. I learned quite a few things about Java and Ruby/Rails while reviewing this book, and it was also a fun read (it kept me company for a long flight to Europe).

Last year I attended Neal Ford's Productive Programmer talk and came away with many tricks that have substantially improved my productivity. By far some of the things I learned from his talk are what I use constantly as I navigate my computer. So, one of my favorite books that I have not read yet is the book he's working on with David Bock. I can't wait not only to read it but also to give a copy of it to some of my dearest programmer friends. So, my dear authors, there it is...you have no excuse not to complete it now!

Favorite Technical Tool

I was going to mention TiddlyWiki, but my friend Mr. Richards has also mentioned it!

Again, going back to productivity, I try to minimize the usage of the mouse as much as possible. I spend time learning keyboard shortcuts. I try to create macros and use them. One tool that I have found useful on Windows is AutoHotKey (http://www.autohotkey.com). It lets me create macros for some long commands and machine names I have to frequently type. Check it out.

Another favorite tool (and a great substitute to Notepad) on Windows is Notepad2 (yes, you might have seen me use this quite extensively in my presentations last year). One feature I really like is that you can write Ruby or Groovy code and, in one keystroke, execute it. It even has syntax highlighting for Ruby. Get your copy from http://www.flos-freeware.ch/notepad2.html.

Talking about reducing mouse usage, for most of us, frequent mouse use comes in the form of hyperlink clicks. For mouseless browsing, I use the Firefox plug-in NumberFox (https://addons.mozilla.org/firefox/2317). You can activate it using a keyboard shortcut (Alt+W on Windows, Cmd+E on Mac). It numbers all the links and keys in the number (or you can cycle through the links as well) to navigate to the numbered link. This worked great for Firefox 1.*x*. However, when I upgraded to Firefox 2.0, this quit working because of a conflict with a keyboard shortcut. I recently found Hit-a-Hint (https://addons.mozilla.org/firefox/1341) that works similarly to NumberFox. You hit the spacebar (that's configurable), and you will see that the links are numbered. Enter the number you desire, and off you go to that site.

I've started using a Mac recently (I couldn't stand the peer pressure from the crowd I hang around with), and I have found QuickSilver to be awesome. If you're a Mac user and are not using QuickSilver, you must give it a try. Visit http://quicksilver.blacktree.com to download it.

A.3 Brian Sletten

Favorite Books

I read too many books to pick meaningful favorites, so here are some of my recent favorites:

- *The God Delusion* [Daw06] by Richard Dawkins
- *Data and Reality* [Ken84] by William Kent
- *Thinking on the Web : Berners-Lee, Gödel, and Turing* [AS06a] by Alesso and Smith

- *Semantic Management of Middleware* [Obe07] by Daniel Oberle
- *Adaptive Information: Improving Business Through Semantic Interoperability, Grid Computing, and Enterprise Integration* [Pol04] by Pollock and Hodgson
- *A Long Way Down* [Hor05] by Nick Hornby
- *The 101 Most Influential People Who Never Lived: How Characters of Fiction, Myth, Legends, Television, and Movies Have Shaped Our Society, Changed Our Behavior, and Set the Course of History* [Kar06] by Karlan, Lazar, and Salter (Note: This is brain candy, but as a fan of pop culture, I enjoyed reading it.)
- *Against the Day* [Pyn06] by Thomas Pynchon
- *Consider the Lobster* [Wal05] by David Foster Wallace

Favorite Technical Tool

I have picked up a bunch of cool little apps on my Mac recently. iAlertU[1] allows you to secure your notebook, car alarm style. You can use the new remote that ships with MacBooks and MacBook Pros to activate the alarm. Not only does your computer spaz out and make car alarm noises when it is picked up (it uses the accelerometer in the new machines to detect movement), but it also uses the built-in camera to snap a photo of the potential evildoer. Jared Richardson turned me on to Robbie Hanson's Alarm Clock 2,[2] which will now wake my computer from sleep to wake me from sleep. It is much nicer to stir to the gentle tones of *Divided Sky* than a buzzer!

For non-Mac-specific tools, the Simile Project[3] from MIT has some of my favorite new tools. Timeline, Exhibit, Solvent, Piggy Bank, and so on, give you a taste of what is coming from the Semantic Web in today's browsers (Firefox).

A.4 Howard Lewis Ship

Favorite Books

Emergence: The Connected Lives of Ants, Brains, Cities, and Software [Joh02b]. Lately, I've been enjoying books that try to integrate a bunch of ideas, and this is a good one for stretching your brain.

---

1. See http://www.slappingturtle.com/home/.
2. See http://www.robbiehanson.com.
3. See http://simile.mit.edu.

Favorite Technical Tool

Inform7[4] is a great, integrated tool for building the Zork-style interactive text adventures some of us remember from the 80s. It's a fabulous tool, built on an incredible domain-specific language that looks surprisingly like simple English. It's a tool for creative people who lack programming experience to build worlds within the computer. I appreciate Mr. Nelson's laser focus on his domain, which shows up in the language and in the specialized IDE for the language. I've been trying to adopt the same attitude—that the environment should bend over backward to accommodate the developer, not the other way around.

In terms of day-to-day work, I have a love-hate relationship with Javassist.[5] Javassist is a very powerful, poorly documented, completely indispensable tool for performing runtime creation and modification of classes. The metaprogramming that comes so easily in the Ruby world comes at great effort in the Java space, but Javassist makes the impossible merely difficult and, at times, completely manageable.

Beyond that, there's a host of technologies that are indispensible: Subversion for source code control, JIRA (http://www.atlassian.com/software/jira/) for issue management, Eclipse as an IDE, and the various Java tools I describe in my chapter. I'm also very dependent on VMware (http://www.vmware.com/) for my training (and thus my income). I use VMware as a way to provide clients with a complete, working development environment for use in my Tapestry workshop. It used to take most of a day to get everyone up and running with all the necessary labs, plug-ins, and JDKs. Now it takes ten minutes.

A.5 Nathaniel T. Schutta

Favorite Books

- *A Whole New Mind* [Pin05] by Daniel Pink
- *How to Win Friends & Influence People* [Car90] by Dale Carnegie
- *The Blind Side: Evolution of a Game* [Lew06] by Michael Lewis

Favorite Technical Tool

- TextMate (http://macromates.com/)

---

4. http://inform-fiction.org/I7/Welcome.html
5. http://www.jboss.com/products/javassist

A.6 Jared Richardson

Favorite Books

I've spent a good portion of this year in either the Pickaxe book (*Programming Ruby: The Pragmatic Programmer's Guide, Second Edition* [TH01] by Andy Hunt and Dave Thomas;[6] as well as *The Ruby Way* [Ful06] by Hal Fulton,[7] so I'll call them a tie. The Pickaxe book is better for Ruby basics, and *The Ruby Way* is much better when I have a question on how to do something specific. I haven't seen the latest version of *The Ruby Way*, but I hear it's even better.

Favorite Technical Tool

I'm going to have to pick two again: my MacBook Pro combined with Parallels.

The MacBook is my first Apple purchase. Between the dual-core processor and OS X (all the power of Linux, but the Bluetooth works!), it has been a great tool to learn. Sometimes it has been frustrating, but I'm glad I invested the time.

Parallels (http://www.parallels.com/) is a tool that lets me run other operating systems on my Mac at native speeds. I've developed code in both Fedora Core/Red Hat Linux and Windows XP on my Mac using Parallels. It turns my single laptop into as many different laptops as I need. It's one of those tools that frees you up so you can work the way you want to work.

A.7 Mark Richards

Favorite Books

My favorite recent book is *My American Journey* [Pow95] by Colin Powell. What an inspirational book. It is a great success story, full of interesting stories and pragmatic leadership tips. I would recommend this book to anyone without hesitation.

Favorite Technical Tool

My favorite recent tool is still TiddlyWiki (http://www.tiddlywiki.com)—can't live without it! I have also grown quite fond of the simple hammer,

---

6. http://pragmaticprogrammer.com/titles/ruby
7. http://rubyhacker.com/coralbook/

particularly for those times when you are in middle of a presentation and your laptop decides to reboot because of the latest Microsoft Windows XP fix install. It's funny how fast I go through laptops. . . .

A.8 Rebecca J. Parsons

Favorite Books

Freakonomics: A Rogue Economist Explores the Hidden Side of Everything [LD05] by Steven D Levitt and Stephen J Dubner. This is a fascinating book applying rigorous data analysis to other activities to uncover hidden biases and activities, including such diverse topics as whether real estate agents really work hard for their clients and whether sumo wrestlers cheat.

Favorite Technical Tool

When all else fails—Emacs. Like many general-purpose tools, it is quite flexible, and so often one wants to create or find and use a more specialized tool. I suspect eventually the Eclipse platform will get there, but, to me, extending Emacs to suit my needs has always been quite easy.

A.9 Ted Neward

Favorite Books

The 33 Strategies of War by Green; *The Campaigns of Napoleon* by Chandler; the classic GOF *Design Patterns* by Gamma, Helm, Johnson, and Vlissides; and the ongoing volume set of *The Wheel of Time* by Jordan.

Favorite Technical Tool

People close by who are smarter than me.

A.10 Scott Leberknight

Favorite Books

The Pragmatic Programmer [HT00] remains one of my favorites, because it is a book you can read over and over again and continue to get valuable information that will be relevant no matter what technologies you are using. I'd also have to say *Agile Web Development with Rails* [TH06], since it encapsulates a ton of knowledge and real-world experience for people developing with Rails. *Expert One-on-One J2EE Design and Development* [Joh02a] also remains one of my favorites, since it exposes the ideas behind Spring and gives developers insight into Spring's origins and design philosophy—even though it is now perhaps a bit dated, this book will definitely help any developer using Spring.

As for nontechnical books, one of my recent favorites is *Snow Crash* [Ste00] by Neal Stephenson, which Stu Halloway recommended to me and which is just a really fun read (thanks Stu!). On the more serious side, *Collapse: How Societies Choose to Fail or Succeed* [Dia05] and *The World is Flat: A Brief History of the Twenty-first Century* [Fri06] are two books I've read and enjoyed in the past few months.

Favorite Technical Tool

For web development, the Firebug Firefox plug-in has become pretty much indispensable—it is just amazing. Clover is also a great tool for determining test coverage within your IDE. And last but not least, IntelliJ is still my favorite IDE even though I use Eclipse most of the time since my customers use it—that, and the fact that IntelliJ isn't allowed because of some silly restrictions!

A.11 David Hussman

Favorite Books

This is a large list for me, so I will narrow it to those books that help me create better software. *Zen and the Art of Motorcycle Maintenance* breathed new life into old words for me. The author, Robert Pirsig, takes the word *quality* to a new level and provides humorous definitions for underused words such as *gumption*. Although *gumption* is not commonly heard in software circles, the spirit of gumption, sometimes defined as "the ability to see what needs to be done (common sense) and then to do it (courage)," is alive within successful software projects. Differing from gumption, you cannot escape the word *quality* in software circles. Pirsig was a technical writer for Control Data Corporation (CDC) in the 70s, when CDC was a rising star. Living within CDC, he too was unable to avoid discussions about quality. Unlike many IT folks then and now, Pirsig challenges us to define quality before bandying the term. I hear many people use the word *quality* in a way that makes me want to quote the Spaniard from the *Princess Bride*—"You keep saying that word. I do not think it means what you think it means."

More directly applicable, and approachable (*Zen* is a tough but rewarding read), I think *Freakonomics* and *The Tipping Point* are both well written and offer a great deal of insight into why we do what we do. Directly to technology, and in the spirit of redefining quality, *FIT for Developing Software* is a great introduction to FIT. It is filled with practical and well-organized information about bringing FIT and acceptance testing into a company or project.

Favorite Technical Tool

Though there are many great software tools, my favorite tool is still a small digital camera. With camera in hand, I never run out of white board space or fear losing those important drawings—drawings that also capture the meaningful discussion that inspired the picture. Taking this one step further, I also have a tablet PC that provides the same power as the camera but also allows people in different locations to quickly and collaboratively create a shared view of their systems. The resulting image can be emailed to all and/or checked in to source control on the spot. If only my favorite operating system would run on a tablet! Feel free to pass this request along to any influential friends you might have working for Apple.

A.12 David Geary

Favorite Books

As some of you might know, I love French. In general, I find real languages (computer languages are a horrible misnomer) fascinating, and in particular, I love to listen to French; it is such a beautiful, lyrical language (for those of you familiar with Gomez of the Addams family, I'm a lot like him). I'm intensely interested in how humans acquire language skills, how they use them, and how languages differ from one another. Did you know that the female brain has 11% more neurons for hearing and language processing than men? I'm jealous.

So, my favorite recent book, which is really recent because I'm only a few chapters into it at the moment, is *Suite Francaise* [Nem06]. It's not about French per se but is a fictional account of the Nazi occupation of France in 1940, written by Irene Nemirovsky, a Jew of Russian descent who lived in France at the time and was ultimately murdered at Auschwitz. So, it has fictional characters but is steeped in a real-life account of the occupation. This is a poignant, beautifully written book by an author who was fluent in seven spoken languages. Evidently, she put those extra 11% of her neurons to good use! What a shame that the world lost such a prolific writer.

The twist for me is that I'm reading both the English translation and the original French version in parallel. I read one chapter in English and then slough through the same chapter in French before returning to the English version.

Since I spend a lot of time on airplanes, a good deal of it traveling to see you folks, I also grabbed a few more books for next year's flights: *The Female Brain* [Bri06], *Small Is the New Big*, and *The Perfect Thing* [Lev06]. I'm looking forward to reading all of them next year. For *NFJS Anthology 2008*, perhaps I'll tell you about one of them....

Favorite Technical Tool

Without a doubt, the coolest tool I've run across lately is the Google Web Toolkit (GWT). A Java framework that ultimately compiles Java into JavaScript, the GWT makes developing Ajaxified, rich-client UIs very accessible to Java developers. The GWT is a well-thought-out framework, and the more I use it, the more impressed I am with its implementation and the capabilities it offers.

I am writing a GWT book with my good friend Rob Gordon. We're constantly uncovering cool stuff in the GWT and finding ways to extend the framework in (what we consider, at least) cool and useful ways.

Recently, Rob and I figured out how to debug GWT applications in an external server (Tomcat) and, not only that, but how to debug an application with both JSP and GWT views. We've been able to debug both kinds of views in the same application, which is really cool for folks who might want to switch from JSP to GWT for their display technology. At the moment, I'm looking into using a GWT front end with a JavaServer Faces (JSF) back end, which is another exciting possibility, especially for me and I hope for our readers.

I consider myself lucky to be alive at this point in history, when the Internet is in the process of radically changing our lives in so many respects. I love exploring new technologies such as Rails, the GWT, and Seam, and even though I was on the JSF Expert Group, I try not to get emotionally attached to any one technology so that I can enjoy them all. If I had been born 100 years ago, I don't know what I would've done.

A.13 Neal Ford

Last year, we were going to put the favorite books and technical tools on the authors' introduction pages to give everyone a better feel for the author. To that end, we asked each author to submit *one* favorite book and *one* technical tool. Well, if you've ever been to a No Fluff Just Stuff show, you know that you just can't shut these guys up, and, true to form, everyone sent a handful of each. We finally decided to isolate them all into an appendix so that they could spread out as much as possible.

I bring this up now because, like a good editor, I submitted only one of each last year, which made me look like some kind of slacker. This year I get my revenge, submitting as many as I want. So there!

Favorite Books

Last year was a good one for books. One of the best out was (and still is) *Practices of an Agile Developer* [Sub06] by Andy Hunt and Venkat Subramaniam. It is told in an engaging style, pitting common sense against what we know works better in software development. I found myself nodding vigorously the whole time I was reading the book.

As far as important books go, two came out last year. *Refactoring Databases: Evolutionary Database Design* [AS06b] by Scott Ambler and Pramodkumar J. Sadalage debunks the notion that you can't do agile development with databases. The other eye-opening book of the year was *Java Concurrency in Practice* [Goe06] by Brian Goetz, Tim Peierls, Joshua Bloch, Joseph Bowbeer, David Holmes, and Doug Lea. This is the book that made everyone realize that they don't really understand threading in Java after all.

Another good book I read last year was *The Perfect Thing* [Lev06] by Steven Levy about the creation and history of the iPod. Traveling as much as I do and being such a music addict, I find the iPod to be an important piece of equipment (along with noise-canceling headphone). But even if you don't care about the iPod, this book has important lessons about technology and software. The iPod beat its competitors despite that it was more expensive and (at the time of its release) for Mac only because the folks at Apple understand *design* and elegance. You still see companies come out every day with their "iPod killer" (Zune, anyone?), and they just can't understand why the world prefers the iPod. A great companion book to this one is *Revolution in the Val-*

ley [Her04] by Andy Hertzfeld, which a great book about the development of the original Apple Macintosh.

Finally, I want to recommend a nontechnical book. As software developers, we spend too much time reading technical material at the expense of other forms of reading. So, put down that technical book (but not this anthology!), and pick up a great classic. In fact, most of you have probably read *1984* [Orw50] by George Orwell, but have you *really* read it? Here's a question and a hint: is 1984 a tragedy? Does the book end on a hopeless note? Hint: what if the last chapter isn't actually the last chapter? What if the *appendix* is the last chapter?

Favorite Technical Tool

This is an expensive no-brainer: my 17-inch MacBook Pro. For most of my career, I've used Microsoft operating systems: first DOS and then Windows from 3.0 through 3.1, NT 3.1, Windows 95, NT 4, Win 2K, and finally XP. About a year ago, I bought a Mac PowerBook G4 and fell in love with it. You're tired of hearing it, but Everything Just Works. For about a year, I traveled with two laptops: my company-issued Dell Latitude 610 and my G4. Then, when the Intel MacBook Pro's came out, I waited long enough to verify that Parallels is all it claimed to be and then went out and bought my current laptop and gave the company laptop back. I now do Java, Ruby on Rails, and .NET development all on my very own Mac. A lot of attendees at No Fluff Just Stuff ask the speakers why so many of them have Macs. It's simple: because we can. The Mac is simply a better machine + operating system combination. I get paid for interacting with a computer, and if I can make that interaction smoother and less frustrating for myself, it's a no-brainer to do just that.

On a slightly cheaper note (but only in price), I've been making heavy use of mind-mapping software lately to help organize things. You know the Pensieve from the *Harry Potter* books? It's kind of a software version of that. I've been using MindManager from MindJet, a commercial offering for all the major operating systems. Before that, I used a nice open source Java mind mapper called FreeMind (available at http://freemind. sourceforge.net/wiki/index.php/Main_Page). These mind mappers make it easier to gather disparate thoughts and organize them in a less rigid hierarchy than an outline. I find myself using this tool when brainstorming, with excellent results.

A.14 Paul M. Duvall

Favorite Books

- *Brave New World* by Aldous Huxley
- *Freakonomics* by Steven Levitt and Stephen J. Dubner
- *Refactoring* by Martin Fowler
- *Code Complete* by Steve McConnell
- *The World Is Flat* by Thomas Friedman

Favorite Technical Tool

- EditPlus, my ubiquitous editor
- CCTray, which monitors my CruiseControl builds in Windows
- FreeMind, free mind-mapping software
- Cygwin, Unix on Windows
- ViewletBuilder, easy-to-create Flash movies
- CutePDF, a free PDF creation tool
- SourceMonitor, static analysis for multiple programming environments
- BlogDesk, blog from your desktop

A.15 Scott Davis

Favorite Books

Subjectively, it feels like I've enjoyed more of the books that I read in 2006 than in years past. This is probably because I was busier by an order of magnitude in 2006 than in previous years—any time spent reading was a guilty pleasure, given that it was a conscious choice over doing actual work. . . .

I reread a couple of classics after name checking them in my Real-World Web Services talk: *Loosely Coupled: The Missing Pieces of Web Services* [Kay03] by Doug Kaye and *Small Pieces Loosely Joined: A Unified Theory of the Web* [Wei02] by David Weinberger. Neither book has a lick of code in it. Instead, both reinforce the "big thoughts" behind web services and the Web, respectively. Doug Kaye has a great podcast series in which he spends an hour talking to an impressively wide array of thought leaders in our industry. David Weinberger was one of the coauthors of *The Cluetrain Manifesto* and occasionally pops up on NPR saying wise things.

In terms of more tactical books, I read *Ruby on Rails: Up and Running* [Tat06] by Bruce Tate and Curt Hibbs cover to cover several times. That's less impressive than it might sound: it's a quick read but quite content-rich. It walks you through setting up a Ruby on Rails application step by step. For a book with an August 2006 copyright, it is disproportionately dog-eared compared to other books on my shelf. For a short "get-to-the-point" book about Ruby on Rails, this is the book I recommend.

If a PDF could get dog-eared, that honor would go to *The Definitive Guide to Grails* by Graeme Rocher. (I read it in prerelease; the dead-tree edition is now available.) Similar in spirit to Bruce's book, Graeme's book covers a Grails application end to end. Although Rails has a few more rings around its trunk than Grails, Grails takes most of the good things about Rails and moves it to a solidly Java-friendly environment. If I could recommend only one book to professional Java developers for 2007, this book would be it. I promise it will make you excited about Java again.

A.16 David Bock

Favorite Books

Book is such a broad category that I need to throw out a few answers to that question. Depending on my mood, I have different answers for that question:

- *Harrington on Hold'em* [Har04] by Dan Harrington and Bill Robertie: For the past few years, I have been swept up in the popularity of Texas hold 'em, playing regularly with a group of friends. This book isn't a book that will teach you Texas hold 'em, but if you already know how to play, it will teach you some of the things a pro considers situationally while playing hands.

- *A Whack on the Side of the Head* [vO98] by Roger van Oech: This book came up on a mailing list in a discussion about Malcom Gladwell's *Blink* and is a much better book for actually teaching you how to think creatively. Actually, a better description might be that it's a book that teaches you how to *not* think *noncreatively*, because part of the premise of the book is to unlock your natural creativity by challenging the kinds of assumptions you have when trying to come up with answers.

I also have to mention the *Harry Potter* audiobooks read by Jim Dale. My wife and I have listened to those while driving to and from Maine, New Jersey, and Virginia. As a voice artist, Jim Dale is incredible—he plays dozens of separate characters and manages to give each one a distinct and recognizable voice.

Favorite Technical Tool

The first tool that comes to mind is Capistrano, but since that is the chapter I contributed, I'll rave about my MacBook Pro. After close to ten years on Windows, it is nice to be using a Mac as my primary platform again. I switched from a Mac years ago because I was doing more and more Java work, and Java was really lagging on the Mac back then. I remember the day my boss told me I had to give up my Mac; I was moving my email over to the PC and thinking, "This won't be for long." I was gone for too long, but I sure came back to some nice hardware!

Appendix B

Bibliography

[All02]   David Allen. *Getting Things Done: The Art of Stress-Free Pro-
           ductivity*. Penguin, New York, NY, 2002.

[AS06a]   H. Peter Alesso and Craig F. Smith. *Thinking on the Web :
           Berners-Lee, Gãŭdel and Turing*. John Wiley and Sons, Inc.,
           Hoboken, NJ, 2006.

[AS06b]   Scott W. Ambler and Pramodkumar J. Sadalage. *Refactoring
           Databases: Evolutionary Database Design*. Addison-Wesley,
           Reading, MA, 2006.

[Bec00]   Kent Beck.   *Extreme Programming Explained: Embrace
           Change*. Addison-Wesley, Reading, MA, 2000.

[Bec02]   Kent Beck. *Test Driven Development: By Example*. Addison-
           Wesley, Reading, MA, 2002.

[Bri06]   Louann Md Brizendine. *The Female Brain*. Morgan Read,
           New York, 2006.

[Car90]   Dale Carnegie. *How to Win Friends and Influence People*.
           Pocket, New York, 1990.

[Cla04]   Mike Clark. *Pragmatic Project Automation. How to Build,
           Deploy, and Monitor Java Applications*. The Pragmatic Pro-
           grammers, LLC, Raleigh, NC, and Dallas, TX, 2004.

[Dav06]   Scott Davis. *Pragmatic GIS*. The Pragmatic Programmers,
           LLC, Raleigh, NC, and Dallas, TX, 2006.

[Daw06]   Richard Dawkins. *The God Delusion*. Houghton Mifflin, New York, NY, 2006.

[DB07]   Neal Ford David Bock. *The Productive Programmer*. The Pragmatic Programmers, LLC, Raleigh, NC, and Dallas, TX, 2007.

[Dia05]   Jared Diamond. *Collapse: How Societies Choose to Fail or Succeed*. Penguin, New York, 2005.

[Eva03]   Eric Evans. *Domain-Driven Design: Tackling Complexity in the Heart of Software*. Addison-Wesley Professional, Reading, MA, first edition, 2003.

[FBB+99] Martin Fowler, Kent Beck, John Brant, William Opdyke, and Don Roberts. *Refactoring: Improving the Design of Existing Code*. Addison Wesley Longman, Reading, MA, 1999.

[For03]   Neal Ford. *Art of Java Web Development: Struts, Tapestry, Commons, Velocity, JUnit, Axis, Cocoon, InternetBeans, Web-Work*. Manning Publications Co., Greenwich, CT, 2003.

[Fri06]   Thomas L. Friedman. *The World is Flat: A Brief History of the Twenty-first Century*. Farrar, Straus and Giroux, New York, 2006.

[Ful06]   Hal Fulton. *The Ruby Way, 2nd Edition*. Addison-Wesley, Reading, MA, 2006.

[FWA+99] Neal Ford, Ed Weber, Talal Azzouka, Terry Dietzler, and Casey Williams. *JBuilder 3 Unleashed*. Sams Publishing, Indianapolis, IN, 1999.

[Goe06]   Brian Goetz. *Java Concurrency in Practice*. Addison-Wesley, Reading, MA, 2006.

[Har04]   Dan Harrington. *Harrington on Hold'Em*. Two Plus Two, New York, 2004.

[Her04]   Andy Hertzfeld. *Revolution in the Valley*. O'Reilly & Associates, Inc, Sebastopol, CA, 2004.

[Hor05]   Nick Hornby. *A Long Way Down*. Riverhead, New York, 2005.

[HT00]   Andrew Hunt and David Thomas. *The Pragmatic Programmer: From Journeyman to Master*. Addison-Wesley, Reading, MA, 2000.

[HT03]   Andrew Hunt and David Thomas. *Pragmatic Unit Testing In Java with JUnit*. The Pragmatic Programmers, LLC, Raleigh, NC, and Dallas, TX, 2003.

[Joh98]   Spencer Johnson. *Who Moved My Cheese? An Amazing Way to Deal with Change in Your Work and in Your Life*. Putnam Adult, New York, NY, 1998.

[Joh02a]   Rod Johnson. *Expert One-on-One J2EE Design and Development*. Wrox, 2002.

[Joh02b]   Steven Johnson. *Emergence: The Connected Lives of Ants, Brains, Cities, and Software*. Scribner, New York, 2002.

[Kar06]   Dan Karlan. *The 101 Most Influential People Who Never Lived: How Characters of Fiction, Myth, Legends, Television, and Movies Have Shaped Our Society, Changed Our Behavior, and Set the Course of History*. Harper, New York, 2006.

[Kay03]   Doug Kaye. *Loosely Coupled: The Missing Pieces of Web Services*. RDS Press, 2003.

[Ken84]   William Kent. *Data and Reality*. North-Holland, Netherlands, 1990 edition, 1984.

[Lar04]   Craig Larman. *Agile and Iterative Development: A Manager's Guide*. Addison-Wesley, Reading, MA, 2004.

[LD05]   Steven D. Levitt and Stephen J. Dubner. *Freakonomics: A Rogue Economist Explores the Hidden Side of Everything*. William Morrow, 2005.

[Lev06]   Steven Levy. *The Perfect Thing*. Simon and Schuster, New York, 2006.

[Lew06]   Michael Lewis. *The Blind Side: Evolution of a Game*. W. W. Norton, New York, 2006.

[Mar02]   Robert C. Martin. *Agile Software Development, Principles, Patterns, and Practices*. Prentice Hall, Englewood Cliffs, NJ, 2002.

[MC05]   Rick Mugridge and Ward Cunningham. *Fit for Developing Software: Framework for Integrated Tests*. Prentice Hall PTR, Englewood Cliffs, NJ, 2005.

[MD05]   Tom Marrs and Scott Davis. *JBoss at Work: A Practical Guide*. O'Reilly & Associates, Inc, Sebastopol, CA, 2005.

[Nem06]   Irene Nemirovsky. *Suite Française.* Knopf, New York, 2006.

[Obe07]   Daniel Oberle.   *Semantic Management of Middleware.* Springer, New York, NY, 2007.

[Orw50]   George Orwell. *1984.* Signet Classics, New York, 1950.

[Pin05]   Daniel H. Pink. *A Whole New Mind: Moving from the Information Age to the Conceptual Age.* Penguin Group, New York, 2005.

[Pol04]   Jeffrey T. Pollock.   *Adaptive Information: Improving Business Through Semantic Interoperability, Grid Computing, and Enterprise Integration.* John Wiley & Sons, San Francisco, 2004.

[Pow95]   Colin L. Powell. *My American Journey.* Random House, New York, 1995.

[Pyn06]   Thomas Pynchon. *Against the Day.* Penguin, New York, 2006.

[Sch04]   Ken Schwaber.   *Agile Project Management with Scrum.* Microsoft Press, Redmond, WA, 2004.

[SH07]   Justin Gehtland Stuart Halloway. *Rails for Java Developers.* The Pragmatic Programmers, LLC, Raleigh, NC, and Dallas, TX, 2007.

[Ste00]   Neal Stephenson. *Snow Crash.* Spectra, 2000.

[Sub06]   Venkat Subramaniam. *Practices of an Agile Developer: Working in the Real World.* The Pragmatic Programmers, LLC, Raleigh, NC, and Dallas, TX, 2006.

[Tat06]   Bruce Tate.   *Ruby on Rails: Up and Running.*   O'Reilly & Associates, Inc, Sebastopol, CA, 2006.

[TH01]   David Thomas and Andrew Hunt. *Programming Ruby: The Pragmatic Programmer's Guide.* Addison-Wesley, Reading, MA, 2001.

[TH06]   David Thomas and David Heinemeier Hansson. *Agile Web Development with Rails.* The Pragmatic Programmers, LLC, Raleigh, NC, and Dallas, TX, second edition, 2006.

[vO98]   Roger von Oech. *A Whack on the Side of the Head.* Warner Business Books, New York, 1998.

[Wal02] M. Mitchell Waldrop. *The Dream Machine: J.C.R. Licklider and the Revolution that made Computing Personal.* Penguin Putnam Inc, New York, N.Y., reprint edition, 2002.

[Wal05] David Foster Wallace. *Consider the Lobster.* Little, Brown and Company, New York, NY, 2005.

[Wei02] David Weinberger. *Small Pieces Loosely Joined: A Unified Theory of the Web.* Perseus Books Group, Cambridge, MA, 2002.

[WFW95] Edward C. Weber, J. Neal Ford, and Christopher R. Weber. *Developing with Delphi: Object-Oriented Techniques.* Prentice Hall, Englewood Cliffs, NJ, 1995.

Index

Symbols

Pragmatic Methodology

Welcome to the Pragmatic Community. We hope you've enjoyed this title.

Do you need to get software out the door? Then you want to see how to *Ship It!* with less fuss and more features.

And if you want to improve your approach to programming, take a look at the pragmatic, effective, *Practices of an Agile Developer*.

Ship It!

Page after page of solid advice, all tried and tested in the real world. This book offers a collection of tips that show you what tools a successful team has to use, and how to use them well. You'll get quick, easy-to-follow advice on modern techniques and when they should be applied. **You need this book if:** • You're frustrated at lack of progress on your project. • You want to make yourself and your team more valuable. • You've looked at methodologies such as Extreme Programming (XP) and felt they were too, well, extreme. • You've looked at the Rational Unified Process (RUP) or CMM/I methods and cringed at the learning curve and costs. • **You need to get software out the door without excuses**

Ship It! A Practical Guide to Successful Software Projects
Jared Richardson and Will Gwaltney
(200 pages) ISBN: 0-9745140-4-7. $29.95
http://pragmaticprogrammer.com/titles/prj

Practices of an Agile Developer

Agility is all about using feedback to respond to change. Learn how to apply the principles of agility throughout the software development process • Establish and maintain an agile working environment • Deliver what users really want • Use personal agile techniques for better coding and debugging • Use effective collaborative techniques for better teamwork • Move to an agile approach

Practices of an Agile Developer: Working in the Real World
Venkat Subramaniam and Andy Hunt
(189 pages) ISBN: 0-9745140-8-X. $29.95
http://pragmaticprogrammer.com/titles/pad

Pragmatic Tools

Interested in learning Ruby on Rails, but want a shortcut? If you already know Java, you can learn Rails easily using *Rails For Java Developers*.

In Rails or any Web 2.0 adventure, you need to know Ajax. What better way to start than with *Pragmatic Ajax*?

Rails for Java Developers

Enterprise Java developers already have most of the skills needed to create Rails applications. They just need a guide which shows how their Java knowledge maps to the Rails world. That's what this book does. It covers: • The Ruby language • Building MVC Applications • Unit and Functional Testing • Security • Project Automation • Configuration • Web Services This book is the fast track for Java programmers who are learning or evaluating Ruby on Rails.

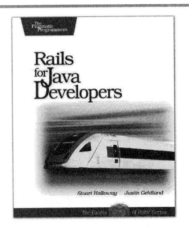

Rails for Java Developers
Stuart Halloway and Justin Gehtland
(300 pages) ISBN: 0-9776166-9-X. $34.95
http://pragmaticprogrammer.com/titles/fr_r4j

Pragmatic Ajax

AJAX redefines the user experience for web applications, providing compelling user interfaces. Now you can dig deeper into AJAX itself as this book shows you how to make AJAX magic. Explore both the fundamental technologies and the emerging frameworks that make it easy.

From Google Maps to Ajaxified Java, .NET, and Ruby on Rails applications, this Pragmatic guide strips away the mystery and shows you the easy way to make Ajax work for you.

Pragmatic Ajax: A Web 2.0 Primer
Justin Gehtland, Ben Galbraith, Dion Almaer
(296 pages) ISBN: 0-9766940-8-5. $29.95
http://pragmaticprogrammer.com/titles/ajax

The Pragmatic Bookshelf

The Pragmatic Bookshelf features books written by developers for developers. The titles continue the well-known Pragmatic Programmer style, and continue to garner awards and rave reviews. As development gets more and more difficult, the Pragmatic Programmers will be there with more titles and products to help you stay on top of your game.

Visit Us Online

No Fluff, Just Stuff 2007's Home Page
http://pragmaticprogrammer.com/titles/nfjs07
Source code from this book, errata, and other resources. Come give us feedback, too!

Register for Updates
http://pragmaticprogrammer.com/updates
Be notified when updates and new books become available.

Join the Community
http://pragmaticprogrammer.com/community
Read our weblogs, join our online discussions, participate in our mailing list, interact with our wiki, and benefit from the experience of other Pragmatic Programmers.

New and Noteworthy
http://pragmaticprogrammer.com/news
Check out the latest pragmatic developments in the news.

Save on the PDF

Save PDF version of this book. Owning the paper version of this book entitles you to purchase the PDF version at a terrific discount. The PDF is great for carrying around on your laptop. It's hyperlinked, has color, and is fully searchable.

Buy it now at pragmaticprogrammer.com/coupon.

Contact Us

Phone Orders:	1-800-699-PROG (+1 919 847 3884)
Online Orders:	www.pragmaticprogrammer.com/catalog
Customer Service:	orders@pragmaticprogrammer.com
Non-English Versions:	translations@pragmaticprogrammer.com
Pragmatic Teaching:	academic@pragmaticprogrammer.com
Author Proposals:	proposals@pragmaticprogrammer.com